1st Workshop on Linking Models of Lexical, Sentential and Discourse-level Semantics (LSDSem 2015)

Held at EMNLP 2015

Lisbon, Portugal
18 September 2015

ISBN: 978-1-5108-1402-8

Printed from e-media with permission by:

Curran Associates, Inc.
57 Morehouse Lane
Red Hook, NY 12571

Some format issues inherent in the e-media version may also appear in this print version.

Printed by Curran Associates, Inc. (2015)

For permission requests, please contact the Association for Computational Linguistics at the address below.

Association for Computational Linguistics
209 N. Eighth Street
Stroudsburg, Pennsylvania 18360

Phone: 1-570-476-8006
Fax: 1-570-476-0860

acl@aclweb.org

Additional copies of this publication are available from:

Curran Associates, Inc.
57 Morehouse Lane
Red Hook, NY 12571 USA
Phone: 845-758-0400
Fax: 845-758-2634
Email: curran@proceedings.com
Web: www.proceedings.com

EMNLP 2015

Workshop on Linking Models of Lexical, Sentential and Discourse-level Semantics (LSDSem)

Workshop Proceedings

18 September 2015
Lisbon, Portugal

Introduction

Welcome to the EMNLP 2015 Workshop on Linking Models of Lexical, Sentential and Discourse-level Semantics.

This workshop takes place for the first time, with the goal of gathering and showcasing theoretical and computational approaches to joint models of semantics, and applications that incorporate multi-level semantics. Improved computational models of semantics hold great promise for applications in language technology, be it semantics at the lexical level, sentence level or discourse level. Large-scale corpora with corresponding annotations (word senses, propositions, attributions and discourse relations) are making it possible to develop statistical models for many tasks and applications. However, developments in lexical and sentence-level semantics remain largely distinct from those in discourse semantics.

This workshop aims to bridge this gap. Our goal is to gather and showcase theoretical and computational approaches to joint models of semantics, and applications that incorporate multi-level semantics. This workshop will serve as a venue for dialog between researchers from various areas: linguists and cognitive scientists working on aspects of representing text with multiple levels of semantics, machine learning researchers interested in joint inference over different types of semantic cues, and also researchers who are interested in applications which require multi-level semantics.

We received 24 papers in total, out of which we accepted 12. These papers are presented as talks at the workshop as well as in a poster session. In addition, the workshop program features talks from three invited speakers who work on different aspects of computational semantics. The day will end with a panel session where invited speakers and workshop participants further discuss the insights gained during the workshop.

Our program committee consisted of 32 researchers who provided constructive and thoughtful reviews. This workshop would not have been possible without their hard work. Many thanks to you all. Finally, a huge thank you to all the authors who submitted papers to this workshop and made it a big success.

Michael, Annie, Bonnie and Tim

Organizers:

Michael Roth, University of Edinburgh
Annie Louis, University of Edinburgh
Bonnie Webber, University of Edinburgh
Tim Baldwin, University of Melbourne

Program Committee:

Regina Barzilay, Massachusetts Institute of Technology
Johan Bos, University of Groningen
Jill Burstein, Educational Testing Service
Asli Celikyilmaz, Microsoft Research
Nate Chambers, United States Naval Academy
Martin Chodorow, City University of New York
Ido Dagan, Bar Ilan University
Hal Daumé III, University of Maryland
Vera Demberg, Saarland University
Micha Elsner, Ohio State University
Katrin Erk, University of Texas at Austin
Anette Frank, Heidelberg University
Yoav Goldberg, Bar-Ilan University
Dan Jurafsky, Stanford University
Min-Yen Kan, National University of Singapore
Beata Beigman Klebanov, Educational Testing Service
Ruli Manurung, University of Indonesia
Daniel Marcu, Information Sciences Institute, USC
Katja Markert, Leeds University
Marie-Catherine de Marneffe, Ohio State University
Ani Nenkova, University of Pennsylvania
Hwee Tou Ng, National Univcrsity of Singapore
Martha Palmer, University of Colorado at Boulder
Manfred Pinkal, Saarland University
Dan Roth, University of Illinois at Urbana-Champaign
Jan Šnajder, University of Zagreb
Swapna Somasundaran, Educational Testing Service
Caroline Sporleder, Trier University
Manfred Stede, University of Potsdam
Joel Tetreault, Yahoo! Labs
Marilyn Walker, University of California Santa Cruz
Luke Zettlemoyer, University of Washington

Invited Speakers:

Michael Strube, Heidelberg Institute for Theoretical Studies
Jacob Eisenstein, Georgia Institute of Technology
Rada Mihalcea, University of Michigan

Table of Contents

An Exploration of Discourse-Based Sentence Spaces for Compositional Distributional Semantics
Tamara Polajnar, Laura Rimell and Stephen Clark 1

Linking discourse modes and situation entity types in a cross-linguistic corpus study
Kleio-Isidora Mavridou, Annemarie Friedrich, Melissa Peate Sørensen, Alexis Palmer and Manfred Pinkal 12

Recovering discourse relations: Varying influence of discourse adverbials
Hannah Rohde, Anna Dickinson, Chris Clark, Annie Louis and Bonnie Webber 22

Semantics and Discourse Processing for Expressive TTS
Rodolfo Delmonte and Rocco Tripodi 32

Semantically Enriched Models for Modal Sense Classification
Mengfei Zhou, Anette Frank, Annemarie Friedrich and Alexis Palmer 44

Identification and Disambiguation of Lexical Cues of Rhetorical Relations across Different Text Genres
Taraneh Khazaei, Lu Xiao and Robert Mercer 54

Bridging Sentential and Discourse-level Semantics through Clausal Adjuncts
Rashmi Prasad, Bonnie Webber, Alan Lee, Sameer Pradhan and Aravind Joshi 64

Lexical Level Distribution of Metadiscourse in Spoken Language
Rui Correia, Maxine Eskenazi and Nuno Mamede 70

Idiom Paraphrases: Seventh Heaven vs Cloud Nine
Maria Pershina, Yifan He and Ralph Grishman 76

Where Was Alexander the Great in 325 BC? Toward Understanding History Text with a World Model
Yuki Murakami and Yoshimasa Tsuruoka 83

Predicting word sense annotation agreement
Héctor Martínez Alonso, Anders Johannsen, Oier Lopez de Lacalle and Eneko Agirre 89

Distributional Semantics in Use
Raffaella Bernardi, Gemma Boleda, Raquel Fernandez and Denis Paperno 95

Conference Program

Friday, September 18, 2015

09:00–10:30 Morning Session

09:00–09:05 *Introduction*
Michael Roth

09:05–09:50 *Invited Talk: From Distributed Semantics to Discourse, and Back*
Jacob Eisenstein

09:50–10:05 *An Exploration of Discourse-Based Sentence Spaces for Compositional Distributional Semantics*
Tamara Polajnar, Laura Rimell and Stephen Clark

10:05–10:20 *Linking discourse modes and situation entity types in a cross-linguistic corpus study*
Kleio-Isidora Mavridou, Annemarie Friedrich, Melissa Peate Sørensen, Alexis Palmer and Manfred Pinkal

10:20–10:30 *Recovering discourse relations: Varying influence of discourse adverbials*
Hannah Rohde, Anna Dickinson, Chris Clark, Annie Louis and Bonnie Webber

10:30–11:00 *Coffee Break*

11:00–12:30 Pre-Lunch Session

11:00–11:15 *Semantics and Discourse Processing for Expressive TTS*
Rodolfo Delmonte and Rocco Tripodi

11:15–11:30 *Semantically Enriched Models for Modal Sense Classification*
Mengfei Zhou, Anette Frank, Annemarie Friedrich and Alexis Palmer

11:30–11:45 *Identification and Disambiguation of Lexical Cues of Rhetorical Relations across Different Text Genres*
Taraneh Khazaei, Lu Xiao and Robert Mercer

11:45–11:55 *Bridging Sentential and Discourse-level Semantics through Clausal Adjuncts*
Rashmi Prasad, Bonnie Webber, Alan Lee, Sameer Pradhan and Aravind Joshi

11:55–12:05 *Lexical Level Distribution of Metadiscourse in Spoken Language*
Rui Correia, Maxine Eskenazi and Nuno Mamede

Friday, September 18, 2015 (continued)

12:05–12:15 *Idiom Paraphrases: Seventh Heaven vs Cloud Nine*
Maria Pershina, Yifan He and Ralph Grishman

12:15–12:25 *Where Was Alexander the Great in 325 BC? Toward Understanding History Text with a World Model*
Yuki Murakami and Yoshimasa Tsuruoka

12:30–14:00 ***Lunch Break***

14:00–15:30 **Post-Lunch Session**

14:00–14:05 *TextLink: EU COST action on Structuring Discourse in a Multi-Lingual Europe*
Bonnie Webber

14:05–14:50 *Invited Talk: What Men Say, What Women Hear: Using Semantics To Make Better Sense of Gender Differences in Social Media*
Rada Mihalcea

14:50–15:00 *Predicting word sense annotation agreement*
Héctor Martínez Alonso, Anders Johannsen, Oier Lopez de Lacalle and Eneko Agirre

15:00–15:10 *Distributional Semantics in Use*
Raffaella Bernardi, Gemma Boleda, Raquel Fernandez and Denis Paperno

15:10–16:00 **Poster Session (Including Coffee Break)**

15:30–16:00 ***Coffee Break***

Friday, September 18, 2015 (continued)

16:00–17:30 Afternoon Session

16:00–16:45 *Invited Talk: The (Non)Utility of Semantics for Coreference Resolution*
Michael Strube

16:45–17:30 *Panel Discussion*
Various speakers

An Exploration of Discourse-Based Sentence Spaces for Compositional Distributional Semantics

Tamara Polajnar, Laura Rimell, and Stephen Clark
Computer Laboratory
University of Cambridge
Cambridge, UK
{tamara.polajnar,laura.rimell,stephen.clark}@cl.cam.ac.uk

Abstract

This paper investigates whether the wider context in which a sentence is located can contribute to a distributional representation of sentence meaning. We compare a vector space for sentences in which the features are words occurring within the sentence, with two new vector spaces that only make use of surrounding context. Experiments on simple subject-verb-object similarity tasks show that all sentence spaces produce results that are comparable with previous work. However, qualitative analysis and user experiments indicate that extra-sentential contexts capture more diverse, yet topically coherent information.

1 Introduction

Distributional word representations (Turney and Pantel, 2010) have proven useful for a wide variety of tasks, including lexical similarity, sentiment analysis, and machine translation. By far the most typical method of building distributional word vectors is based on co-occurrences in a small context window around the word. In contrast, there has been little investigation of different distributional representations for sentences, though the current hypothesis is that the wider discourse in which the sentence is situated may provide relevant information (Baroni et al., 2014; Clark, 2013, 2015). If word representations could be composed into sentence vectors that reflect typical discourse contexts, this might be of great use in sentence-level tasks such as sentence similarity, automatic summarisation, and textual entailment.

Previous work in compositional distributional semantics largely defines the sentence vector space to be the same as the noun space (Kartsaklis et al., 2012; Socher et al., 2011b, 2012), and produces sentence vectors in that space by a sequence of operations on word representations. However, embedding a sentence into a vector space whose dimensions are based on lexical semantics may fail to capture important aspects of sentential meaning. We believe there are two reasons behind the rather surprising lack of attention to sentence spaces. The first is doubt as to whether the distributional hypothesis applies to sentences, i.e. whether sentence meaning is contextual. The second is a question of data sparsity in obtaining contextual sentence representations.

In this paper we explore the idea that contextual sentence representations are viable, and that the surrounding discourse, in the form of adjacent sentences, provides useful information for modelling sentence meaning. We introduce two sentence spaces based on extra-sentential context, one consisting of a variety of context words and the other only of the surrounding verbs, and compare them with an intra-sentential contextual sentence space similar to that proposed in Grefenstette et al. (2013).

We situate our work within the Categorial framework (Coecke et al., 2010; Baroni et al., 2014; Clark, 2013, 2015) where nouns and sentences are considered atomic types, represented as vectors, and other words as functions, represented as tensors. This framework provides a natural setting in which the sentence space can differ from the spaces of sentence constituents, since argument-taking words such as verbs are maps from argument space into sentence space. Following Grefenstette and Sadrzadeh (2011a,b) and Kartsaklis et al. (2012) we focus on simplified sentences consisting of a subject, transitive verb, and object (SVO). We train transitive verb tensors using a single-step multilinear regression algorithm.

We evaluate our composed representations on two standard SVO sentence similarity tasks. The results show that the discourse-based sentence spaces perform competitively, both with the intra-

Proceedings of the EMNLP 2015 Workshop on Linking Models of Lexical, Sentential and Discourse-level Semantics, pages 1–11,
Lisboa, Portugal, 18 September 2015.

sentential contextual space and with previous work on SVO composition, although not beating the state of the art on these tasks. We then provide a qualitative analysis of the topics resulting from Singular Value Decomposition in each sentence space, showing that both intra- and extra-sentential spaces contain highly coherent topics, but that the extra-sentential spaces are able to group together SVO triples with greater lexical diversity. We evaluate topic coherence with a novel SVO triple intrusion task.

2 Background and Related Work

The majority of previous work producing vector representations for sentences uses the same space for sentences as for words. Within the Categorial framework, several previous experiments (Grefenstette and Sadrzadeh, 2011a,b; Kartsaklis et al., 2012; Kartsaklis and Sadrzadeh, 2014) have defined the sentence space to be the same as the noun space. The noun space is based on co-occurrences with frequent words in the corpus in a small window, which may not be the ideal space to represent sentences, which have distinct semantics involving propositional meaning and links to surrounding discourse (see Section 2.1 for more detail).

Neural language modelling approaches such as Socher et al. (2011a, 2013) recursively build sentence representations from constituent word vectors, which themselves are embeddings based on local context, such that the phrase space after each composition step remains the same, including the space for sentences at the root of a derivation. In these models the features are less interpretable, but since the original word embeddings are based on local co-occurrences, sentences are effectively being represented in a lexical semantic space.

Grefenstette et al. (2013) use a dedicated sentence space for SVO sentences, in which the features are intra-sentential co-occurrences of VO pairs and SVO triples with the 10,000 most frequent words in the corpus. They learn tensors for transitive verbs by multi-stage linear regression, incorporating objects and subjects in two separate steps. Fried et al. (2015) also use an intra-sentential sentence space when learning low-rank approximations for verb tensors (see Section 2.1). We experiment with a similar intra-sentential space alongside our extra-sentential spaces. Another intra-sentential sentence space is described in Le and Mikolov (2014), who learn embeddings for larger text segments, including sentences, based on n-grams internal to the text segments. A variant of this approach was also adopted by Fried et al. (2015) to learn verb tensors mapping to an intra-sentential sentence space for the Categorial framework using single-step linear regression.

Sentence spaces need not be contextual, but may also represent other aspects of meaning relevant to propositions, such as plausibility or feature norms (McRae et al., 1997). A non-contextual option that has been previously implemented is a two-dimensional "plausibility space", in which the sentence vector represents a plausibility judgement. This type of space was explored in theory in Clark (2013, 2015) and implemented with multilinear regression training for verb tensors by Polajnar et al. (2014a).

Contemporaneously with our work, Kiros et al. (2015) have used an encoder-decoder recurrent neural network architecture to encode a sentence vector conditioned on the previous and following sentences, providing further support for the utility of extra-sentential context for sentence meaning.

2.1 Categorial Framework Background

In the Categorial framework, nouns are represented as vectors, while argument-taking words such as verbs and adjectives are represented as functions. Specifically, they are tensors that perform multilinear transformations of lower-dimensional tensors, e.g. noun vectors. The Categorial Grammar derivation of a sentence guides the combination of vector and tensor objects representing the words in the sentence to ultimately produce a single sentence vector.

For example, a transitive verb in Combinatory Categorial Grammar (CCG) has the syntactic type $(S\backslash NP)/NP$, which defines it as a function that takes a noun phrase as an input from the right, and then another noun phrase from the left, to produce a sentence. Interpreting such categories under the Categorial framework is straightforward. First, for each atomic category there is a corresponding vector space; in this case the sentence space $\mathbf{S}$ and the noun space $\mathbf{N}$.[1] Hence the meaning of a noun or noun phrase, for example *people*, will be a vector in the noun space: $\overrightarrow{people} \in \mathbf{N}$. In order to obtain the meaning of a transitive verb, each slash is re-

[1] In practice, for example using the CCG parser of Clark and Curran (2007), there will be additional atomic categories, such as PP, but not many more.

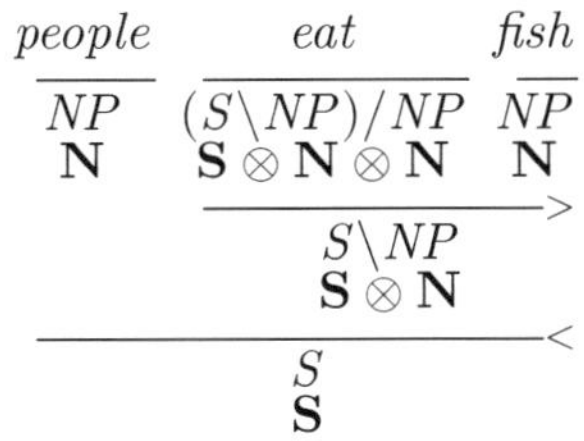

Figure 1: Syntactic reduction and tensor-based semantic types for a transitive verb sentence.

placed with a tensor product operator, so that the meaning of *eat*, for example, is a 3rd-order tensor: $\overline{eat} \in \mathbf{S} \otimes \mathbf{N} \otimes \mathbf{N}$. Just as in the syntactic case, the meaning of a transitive verb is a function (a multi-linear map) which takes two noun vectors as arguments and returns a sentence vector.

Meanings combine using *tensor contraction*, which can be thought of as a multi-linear generalisation of matrix multiplication (Grefenstette, 2013). Consider first the adjective-noun case, for example *black cat*. The syntactic type of *black* is N/N; hence its meaning is a 2nd-order tensor (matrix): $\overline{black} \in \mathbf{N} \otimes \mathbf{N}$. In the syntax, N/N combines with N using the rule of forward application ($N/N \ N \Rightarrow N$), which is an instance of function application. Function application is also used in the tensor-based semantics, which, for a matrix and vector argument, corresponds to matrix multiplication.

Figure 1 shows how the syntactic types combine with a transitive verb, and the corresponding tensor-based semantic types. Note that, after the verb has combined with its object NP, the type of the verb phrase is $S\backslash NP$, with a corresponding meaning tensor (matrix) in $S \otimes N$. This matrix then combines with the subject vector, through matrix multiplication, to give a sentence vector.

Some previous work in the Categorial framework has taken the sentence space to be the same as the noun space (Grefenstette and Sadrzadeh, 2011a,b; Kartsaklis et al., 2012; Kartsaklis and Sadrzadeh, 2014). The verb is defined, not as an $\mathbf{S} \otimes \mathbf{N} \otimes \mathbf{N}$ tensor, but an $\mathbf{N} \otimes \mathbf{N}$ matrix summing the outer products of its observed subjects and objects. Because this results in a type mismatch when presented with two noun vector arguments, tensor contraction cannot be used directly to produce a sentence vector. Instead, various combinations of matrix multiplication, pointwise multiplication, and addition are employed. As a result, the sentence representation is a purely compositional function of the context vectors of its component words; the observed contexts of SVO triples are not part of the representation.

One effect of reducing a verb tensor to a matrix is to reduce the number of parameters required to learn the verb. However, recent work in the Categorial framework offers other ways to reduce the number of parameters while retaining the higher type of the tensor. Fried et al. (2015) introduce low-rank approximations for verb tensors, which provide a large reduction in the number of parameters while increasing the speed of training, without substantial loss in accuracy on standard SVO tasks.

3 Sentence Spaces

We focus on SVO triples, which we also refer to as transitive sentences or simply sentences. Although real-world sentences are more complex, SVO is currently the standard grammatical construction for sentence composition within the Categorial framework, because it is manageable for current learning methods.

This section describes our three contextual sentence spaces. The first follows Grefenstette et al. (2013) and Fried et al. (2015) in using intra-sentential word co-occurrenes with SVO triples. The others use extra-sentential co-occurrences. We consider the extra-sentential spaces to be a primitive way of incorporating the surrounding discourse into distributional representations. We know that individual sentences are linked to their neighbours in a coherent discourse, and investigate whether that linkage can be leveraged for natural language understanding. We make the assumption that Wikipedia articles, the source of our vectors, are a good source of coherent sequences of sentences.

3.1 Intra-Sentential Context

Following previous work, our first sentence space is the intra-sentential context of the SVO triple. We call this the Internal Distributional (IDist) space. We first select the top $N = 10,000$ most frequent words from the corpus (excluding stopwords) as contexts. Any of these words appearing inside the same sentence as the SVO triple are counted as features for that triple. Figure 2 shows an example of IDist.

When the V, S, or O itself is frequent enough

$\mathbf{S}_{t-2}$**:** M. Atget captured the old Paris in his pictures. $\mathbf{S}_{t-1}$**:** His photographs show the city in its various facets. $\mathbf{S}_{t}$**:** He photographed stairwells and architectural details. $\mathbf{S}_{t+1}$**:** His interests also extended to the environs of Paris. $\mathbf{S}_{t+2}$**:** He also photographed street-hawkers and small tradesmen, as well as popular amusements.
IDist: stairwell, architectural, detail
DDist: capture, old, paris, picture, photograph, show, city, various, interest, extend, popular, amusement
DVerb: capture, show, extend, photograph

Figure 2: Example features in sentence spaces for a target sentence $\mathbf{S}_t$.

to be one of the context words, we had to decide whether to retain or discard it as context for the triple. We chose to discard the verb, because it is the verb tensor itself that is being learned. On the other hand, if either the S or O is one of the context words, we retained it as context for the triple. The reasoning is related to a somewhat strange aspect of using intra-sentential context for a sentence: as composition methods become more sophisticated, and more of the sentence is included in the composition, there would eventually be no intra-sentential context left to use if all composed words were removed.

3.2 Extra-Sentential Contexts

Our other sentence spaces use the surrounding discourse as context for a sentence. There are many ways one could create a discourse context for an SVO triple, with the size of the context ranging from the surrounding sentences to the full document, and the context features ranging from the same words as in IDist, to specific parts of speech, phrase types, or discourse markers deemed more representative of sentence meaning.

We define two extra-sentential sentence spaces. Both use a window of two sentences on either side of the target sentence $\mathbf{S}_t$. The first space is the Discourse Distributional (DDist) space, which takes as context features any of the top 10,000 words from the corpus occurring in the two sentences either side of $\mathbf{S}_t$ (but not in $\mathbf{S}_t$ itself). This sentence space is analogous to IDist, but using an extra- rather than intra-sentential window.

The second space is the Discourse Verb (DVerb) space, which takes as context features any verbs occurring in the two sentences either side of $\mathbf{S}_t$. This space was loosely inspired by work on unsupervised learning of narrative event chains (Chambers and Jurafsky, 2008, 2009), in which sequences of events such as *accuse – claim – argue – dismiss* or *appoint – work – oversee – retire* are extracted from text. That work links event types which share a protagonist in a connected discourse; in contrast, we do not check whether neighbouring verbs share arguments, but simply hypothesise that verbs near the target verb represent related events and are therefore particularly suited to be context features. Figure 2 shows examples of DVerb and DDist.

We expect DVerb to suffer from a certain amount of data sparsity since the number of verbs in a window of two sentences on either side of the target can be expected to be low, despite the fact that we do not restrict the context features to the main verbs of those sentences. DVerb is therefore the most speculative of our sentence spaces.

3.3 Combined Spaces

In order to examine the interaction between the intra- and extra-sentential contexts, we also create two combined spaces: ID.DD, a concatenation of IDist and DDist, and ID.DV, a concatenation of IDist and DVerb. To create the combined spaces, we use the vector spaces as defined above which are created separately and reduced to 20-dimensions (Section 4). Then for each triple we concatenate the vector from each of the spaces we are combining to create a 40-dimensional vector.

4 Training

To train the noun vectors and verb tensors we used an October 2013 download of Wikipedia articles, which was tokenised using the Stanford NLP tools,[2] lemmatised with the Morpha lemmatiser (Minnen et al., 2001), and parsed with the C&C parser (Clark and Curran, 2007).

We selected a total of 345 verbs, which include the verbs in our test datasets, along with some additional high-frequency verbs included to produce more representative sentence spaces. To train the verbs, we required high-quality SVO triples that occurred enough times in the corpus to provide us with distributional representations of their contexts. For each verb we therefore selected up to

[2]http://nlp.stanford.edu/software/index.shtml

600 triples which occurred more than once and contained subject and object nouns that occurred at least 100 times. This resulted in $M \approx 150,000$ triples overall.

We first generated distributional vectors for all the nouns contained in the training triples and the test datasets. We used Wikipedia as the source corpus, with sentences as the context window and the top $N = 10,000$ most frequent words (excluding stopwords) as the context words. Following the procedure outlined in Polajnar and Clark (2014), we employed t-test weighting (Curran, 2004) and context selection, and reduced our noun vectors ($\mathbf{n}$) to $K = 100$ dimensions using Singular Value Decomposition (SVD).

For each verb V we have a set of M_V training instances, where each instance $i \in M_V$ consists of subject and object noun vectors $\mathbf{n}^{(s)}{}_i$, $\mathbf{n}^{(o)}{}_i$ and a true sentence space representation vector $\mathbf{t}_i$. The vector $\mathbf{t}_i$ is the SVD-reduced version of the Wikipedia context vector for the triple $\mathbf{n}^{(s)}{}_i\ \mathbf{V}\ \mathbf{n}^{(o)}{}_i$.

The true IDist and DDist vectors were generated using the same $N = 10,000$ context words as for the nouns, weighted by t-test. The entire $M \times N$ matrix was reduced to $S = 20$ or $S = 40$ dimensions.[3]

The DVerb context words consist of $N = 2,641$ verbs that occurred at least 10 times within the two sentences surrounding our triples. DVerb was also weighted using t-test and the matrix encoding the co-occurrence of triples with verb contexts was reduced with SVD to produce an $M \times S$ matrix.

Regression (reg) We learn the values of the $S \times K \times K$ tensor representing the verb as parameters ($\mathbf{V}$) of a regression algorithm. To train the tensor we minimise the sum of the mean squared errors ($MSQE$) between each of the training sentence space vectors $\mathbf{t}_i$ and classifier predictions $\mathbf{s}_i$ using the following regularised objective:

$$O(\mathbf{V}) = -\frac{1}{M_V}\left[\sum_{i=1}^{M_v} MSQE(\mathbf{t}_i, \mathbf{s}_i) + \frac{\lambda}{2}||\mathbf{V}||\right]$$

where the l-th index of the predicted sentence vector is produced by tensor contraction

$$s_l = \sum_{jk} V_{ljk} n_j^{(s)} n_k^{(o)} \quad (1)$$

between the tensor and the subject and object noun vectors $\mathbf{n}^{(s)}$ and $\mathbf{n}^{(o)}$. The training was performed through gradient descent with ADADELTA (Zeiler, 2012), with minibatches, and with 10% of the training triples reserved as a validation set for early stopping. The regularisation parameter was set to $\lambda = 0.05$ without tuning.

Distributional Tensors (dist) As an alternative to learning the verb function, we produce a verb tensor using a procedure inspired by Grefenstette and Sadrzadeh (2011a). The intuition behind this method is that the tensor should encode higher values for topics that frequently co-occur within the subject, object, and sentence vectors in the triples used to train a particular verb. Specifically, we generate an $S \times K \times K$ tensor $\mathbf{V}$ for each verb as the average of the tensor products ($\otimes$) of K-dimensional subject and object vectors and the S-dimensional sentence space vector ($\mathbf{s}$) from the training triples:

$$\mathbf{V} = \frac{1}{M_V}\left[\sum_{i=1}^{M_V} \mathbf{s}_i \otimes \mathbf{n}^{(s)}{}_i \otimes \mathbf{n}^{(o)}{}_i\right]$$

where M_V is the number of training triples for the verb V. Our procedure differs from Grefenstette and Sadrzadeh (2011a) because it generates a tensor, while they treated verbs as matrices and effectively disregarded the sentence space.

5 Quantitative Experiments

We perform two experiments using composed sentence vectors. The first involves disambiguation of a polysemous verb in the context of its subject and object, and the second involves measurement of sentence similarity, without disambiguation. We make use of two existing SVO datasets.

5.1 Datasets

GS11 The first dataset is from Grefenstette and Sadrzadeh (2011a) (GS11), and consists of 200 sentence pairs (400 sentences total). Each sentence pair shares a subject and an object. The first member of the pair has an ambiguous verb, while the second has a 'landmark' disambiguating verb. Gold standard annotation provides similarity ratings for each pair on a scale of 1 (low) to 7 (high). For example, *people try door* and *people test door* have high similarity ratings, while *people try door* and *people judge door* have low ratings.

[3]We examined other configurations of noun and sentence space dimensions. Larger tensors learned by regression or distributionally did not consistently lead to increased scores. Although the dimensionality of the sentence space is small, the $K \times K \times S$ tensors are sufficiently large that we believe they are already capturing a significant amount of information from the interaction of the noun and sentence spaces.

GS11	Distributional		Regression	
	S=20	S=40	S=20	S=40
IDist	0.18	0.15	0.31	**0.33**
DDist	0.18	0.20	0.26	0.27
DVerb	**0.21**	**0.21**	**0.32**	0.32
ID.DV	-	**0.22**	-	**0.33**
ID.DD	-	0.19	-	0.29

KS14	Distributional		Regression	
	S=20	S=40	S=20	S=40
IDist	0.15	0.07	**0.42**	**0.43**
DDist	0.17	**0.17**	0.34	0.37
DVerb	**0.18**	0.14	0.33	0.37
ID.DV	-	**0.22**	-	**0.40**
ID.DD	-	0.16	-	0.38

Table 1: Spearman-ρ results for the GS11 dataset (left) and KS14 dataset (right).

KS14 The second dataset (Kartsaklis and Sadrzadeh, 2014) (KS14), consists of 72 sentences arranged into 108 sentence pairs. The sentences in each pair do not share verbs, subjects, or objects. Gold standard annotation provides similarity ratings for each pair on a scale of 1 (low) to 7 (high). For example, *medication achieve result* and *drug produce effect* have high similarity ratings, while *author write book* and *delegate buy land* have low ratings. Sentence pairs with mid-similarity ratings tend to have high relatedness but are not mutually substitutable, e.g. *team win match* and *people play game*.

Both tasks are formulated as ranking tasks. Each SVO triple is composed as in Equation 1 and the resulting vectors are compared using cosine to give a similarity value. Sentence pairs are ordered according to similarity and Spearman's ρ is used to compare the automatically-obtained similarity ranking with that obtained from the gold standard judgements.

5.2 Results

Table 1 shows the results for the two tasks. Each task is evaluated with both the distributionally-built tensors and regression trained tensors and with 20 and 40 dimensional sentence spaces. This led to eight separate experiments. Overall, different conditions favour different sentence spaces. DVerb achieves the highest or near-highest score for all the GS11 experiments, which is interesting given that DVerb is the sparsest sentence space of the three. Although it is well known that the arguments of an ambiguous verb are important for disambiguation, this result suggests that extra-sentential verb co-occurrences may also reflect different verb senses. On the other hand, IDist achieves some of the highest overall scores with regression training, on both GS11 and KS14. DDist and DVerb lag somewhat behind IDist on KS14. We also note that the results on all experiments are higher with regression-trained tensors.

In the combined space experiments, we find that IDist and DVerb provide mutually complementary information and high scores that are close to or outperform single space models.

To put these results in context, our regression results for IDist, DVerb, and ID.DV are comparable with the highest distributional results in Fried et al. (2015) ($\rho = 0.34$ on GS11 and $\rho = 0.42$ on KS14), which were obtained with a sentence-internal space with 100-dimensional vectors, much higher dimensionality than ours. Kartsaklis and Sadrzadeh (2014) obtain $\rho = 0.42$ on GS11, using a distributional matrix with a composition method which effectively disregards the sentence space, and a 300-dimensional noun space. The state-of-the art for KS14 is $\rho = 0.58$ with vector addition and 100- or 300-dimensional vectors (Polajnar et al., 2014b; Kartsaklis and Sadrzadeh, 2014), demonstrating that so far, no sophisticated composition method has been able to beat vector addition on this dataset.[4] Although our contextual sentence spaces do not reach the state of the art, their performance is good enough to show that the method is viable and merits continued development.

6 Qualitative Analysis

In this section we provide a qualitative analysis of how the sentence spaces represent meaning. We contrast the space that has been used in previous literature (IDist) with the extra-sentential spaces (DDist, DVerb) to highlight the differences encoded by different contextual information.

6.1 Topic Comparison

In a word-context matrix, it is common to perform qualitative analyses of dimensionally reduced spaces by looking at the top-weighted words per topic, where the topics are induced by a dimensionality reduction technique. In our case,

[4]The results of Milajevs et al. (2014) and Hashimoto and Tsuruoka (2015) are not comparable, as they average across annotators for each SVO pair. The standard treatment of these datasets considers each annotator judgement as a separate test point, which leads to lower results overall.

	IDist	DDist	DVerb
	Topic 5	**Topic 9**	**Topic 2**
1	fire **destroy** building - *fire building downtown rebuild disastrous main*	man **start** business - *business company businessman work shop*	wind **cause** damage - *damage flood cause dissipate report total destroy*
2	fire **damage** building - *building fire severely rebuild badly disastrous*	man **become** partner - *firm partner law solicitor company business*	tornado **cause** damage - *touch damage destroy dissipate cause rate*
3	building **suffer** fire - *fire building rebuild restore severe porch remodel*	man **join** business - *business father businessman firm educate company*	tornado **destroy** home - *damage touch injure destroy spawn cause*
4	Fire **destroy** building - *fire building great salem rebuilt displacement*	company **change** name - *company product inc. acquire subsidiary*	tornado **kill** people - *strike confirm touch destroy damage kill dissipate*
5	building **replace** building - *building consulate construct current*	man **become** owner - *owner business purchase businessman serve*	storm **kill** people - *dissipate cause flood strike estimate destroy*
20	fire **destroy** Building - *building fire disastrous syndicate richardson*	man **marry** widow - *daughter firstly marry die son widow sir marriage*	tornado **strike** town - *touch strike damage injure destroy rate sweep*
21	building **replace** one - *building brick wooden one demolish*	company **offer** product - *product insurance products customer company*	storm **destroy** house - *flood damage destroy neighbor dissipate affect*
22	building **cover** area - *building area meter floor square storey*	company **announce** plan - *company million announce merger*	flooding **damage** home - *cause impact amount isolate collapse*
23	man **enter** building - *building petrol thor suspected printing randall*	man **marry** Elizabeth - *son daughter elizabeth die tudor eldest bury*	wind **destroy** house - *weaken dissipate damage estimate evacuate*
24	people **destroy** building - *building machinery explosive withdrawal*	man **join** firm - *firm law counsel attorney partner practice serve clerk*	storm **drop** rainfall - *dissipate weaken cause flood total damage*

Table 2: Top triples (in roman type, with verb in bold) for two sample topics per space with S=20. The top distributional terms for each triple are listed in italics.

the sentence space was trained by using, not the co-occurrences of *words* and contexts, but of *SVO triples* and contexts. Therefore, we can look at the highest-weighted triples from the training data for each topic.

Table 2 shows sample topics from IDist, DDist, and DVerb. Every triple has a weighting in every dimension; here we show the five top-weighted triples from the chosen topics, as well as five triples at ranks 20-24. We also show the top-weighted context words for that triple from the original unreduced space.

All three spaces show strong topical coherence; however, lexical coherence seems a greater factor in the clustering of triples for IDist. The IDist topic seems to rely heavily on the word *building*, which occurs as either subject or object (or both) in all of the triples shown here, and in fact in 23 of the top 30 triples. It can also be seen as a top context for many of the triples. Although the overall topic appears to be mostly about damaged buildings, there are several instances of triples that have to do with buildings, but not with damage, for example *building replace one* and *man enter building*.[5] Since the arguments can serve as contexts, it is very likely that triples containing similar arguments will be clustered together.

The DDist topic exhibits moderate coherence, but also more lexical variety in the argument slots than IDist. This topic is also an example of the interleaving that occurs when there are over 150,000 triples grouped into only 20 topics, with marriage triples interspersed with business-related ones. The top highest ranked context words for DDist triples often contain the subject or the object from the triple. Since the subject and object were not counted as co-occurrences for DDist (as they are intra-sentential, and DDist contexts are explicitly extra-sentential), this would seem to indicate that DDist does indeed incorporate some discourse continuity, as the entities are mentioned in surrounding sentences.

The DVerb topic appears quite coherent, and also exhibits more lexical diversity in the subject and object slots than IDist. Some top triples include light verbs such as *cause*, with the subjects and objects making it clear that they are relevant to the topic: *wind cause damage, tornado cause damage*. This is particularly exciting because the subjects and objects were not encoded in the feature space that was used to produce the topics. This space only contains the surrounding verbs, so the topical grouping of *wind* and *tornado* with *storm* and *flooding* is produced by their co-occurrence with the highly-frequent context verbs such as *destroy, damage*, and *injure*.

[5]To avoid sparsity, all instances of masculine pronouns were replaced with "man" and feminine pronouns with "woman" during preprocessing.

6.2 Coherence Analysis

To further explore the coherence of the topics in each sentence space, we introduce a *triple intrusion task*. This task is based on the word intrusion task for evaluation of topic models (Chang et al., 2009). In the word intrusion task, the top five words from a topic are grouped together with a sixth word which ranks low in that topic, but high in other topics. Human annotators must pick the "intruder" from a randomly-ordered list of these six words. The more coherent the topic, the easier it is for humans to identify the intruder.

Analogously, we ask human annotators to identify an intruding SVO triple. In the first version of this experiment (top5), we carry the word intrusion method over directly to triples. The top five SVO triples from each topic are chosen. The intruder is chosen as the lowest-ranking SVO triple from a topic that is also ranked in the top 1% of triples in at least one other topic. This ensures that the intruder is semantically plausible in its own right.

In the second version of the triple intrusion task (lexdiv), we explore the interaction of topic coherence with lexical coherence, by choosing from each topic the five highest-ranked SVO triples having no lexical overlap with one another. In this way we seek to test the intuition that arose from direct examination of the topics, namely that some sentence spaces have topics exhibiting semantic coherence along with greater lexical diversity.

To obtain the lexdiv triples for a topic, we begin with the top-ranked triple. We then add the next highest ranked triple which shares no lexical items (subject, verb, or object) with the first triple. We proceed to add triples in this way until we have a set of five triples. In some cases it is necessary to go fairly far down the topic rankings to find such a set; the average rank of the lowest-ranked triple for IDist is 186.5, 64.3 for DDist, and 63.9 for DVerb. These rankings themselves indicate that IDist is less lexically diverse than DDist and DVerb. The intruder is obtained as in the top5 setting, except that we also require it not to have any lexical overlap with any of the five high-ranked triples, to ensure that it blends in. Sample triple sets are shown in Figure 3. The triples were randomised and the rank was not displayed to the annotators.

We created sets of six triples for all topics from our three sentence spaces and two experiment settings, yielding 120 sets in all. We randomised the order of sets and distributed them among four annotators such that each set of triples was annotated by two annotators. The annotators were PhD students and postdoctoral researchers in computer science or linguistics. They were given no background on the source of the triples, and were instructed to pick the odd one out from each set.

IDist (top5)	**DDist (lexdiv)**
man join force	man play character
people kill man	woman join cast
force take part	station air program
man send force	executive produce series
force cross river	show win award
program provide student	region become part

Figure 3: Intrusion examples before randomisation. The intruder is shown as the last item in each set.

We report model accuracy and Fleiss' kappa (κ) for each sentence space and setting. Model accuracy is the proportion of examples for which the annotator chose the correct intruder. For model accuracy, we report the average accuracy over two annotators. Since no single annotator saw all the sets of triples, we arbitrarily assigned annotators to be the first or second annotator on a given division of the data. Higher model accuracy corresponds to greater topic coherence.

Higher human accuracy on the lexdiv setting would imply that a topic exhibits greater lexical diversity at higher ranks, or else that it maintains greater semantic coherence further down the ranks. Either way, the property of semantic coherence with greater lexical diversity is an interesting one from the perspective of utility for tasks such as paraphrasing and automatic summarisation.

Fleiss' κ provides a slightly different perspective on topic coherence, as a measurement of how often the annotators agreed on their choice of intruder, serving also as a check on model accuracy since it rules out random success on intruder identification. Again, the higher the inter-annotator agreement, the more coherent the topic.

The results are given in Table 3. We observe that accuracy was consistenty lower for lexdiv than for top, which is unsurprising, since the task is much harder: in many cases for top5, all five top triples share at least one lexical item and sometimes more, while the intruder is often lexically distinct. For top5, IDist shows the highest accuracy (0.85), indicating that its topics are most coherent, or possibly that because they are the most *lexically* coherent, the intruder is easiest to iden-

Space	Accuracy top5	Accuracy lexdiv	Fleiss' κ top5	Fleiss' κ lexdiv
IDist	0.85	0.45	0.88	0.54
DDist	0.78	0.58	0.55	0.75
DVerb	0.75	0.58	0.82	0.63

Table 3: Triple intrusion task: model accuracy average over two (amalgamated) annotators and Fleiss' κ.

tify. However, IDist shows the lowest accuracy for lexdiv (0.45), as well as the greatest dropoff in accuracy from top5 to lexdiv, a drop of 0.40, compared to 0.20 for DDist and 0.27 for DVerb. It appears that when triples are restricted to be lexically diverse, DDist and DVerb are more semantically coherent, with an accuracy of 0.58. We note that DVerb results would likely improve with more data and more stringent triple selection. Since we allow triples that occur two or more times, there are some triples in DVerb that are extremely sparse, and occur with only one verb., e.g. *saint pray temple* which only co-occurs with *use*, or *man plug setup* which only co-occurs with *play*, and also appears to be a result of parser error. There is at least one topic where many such triples have been grouped together, making DVerb evaluation more difficult for annotators.

We observe similar effects for Fleiss' κ. Annotaters generally achieved much higher agreement on top5 than lexdiv. The exception is DDist-top5, where agreement was much lower than for lexdiv; since model accuracy was high, it appears that each annotator had trouble with different examples, a fact for which we find no obvious explanation. IDist-top5 again achieves the highest agreement (0.88), indicating the task is fairly easy, but there is a steep dropoff to lexdiv, whereas DVerb shows a much smaller dropoff, and DDist and DVerb both show higher agreement for lexdiv than IDist does

7 Conclusions

We have introduced and evaluated two distributional vector spaces based on extra-sentential contexts. Results on two standard similarity tasks demonstrate that these spaces are effective in modelling sentence meaning for SVO sentences. Furthermore, a qualitative analysis indicates that extra-sentential spaces differ from the standard intra-sentential space in ways that may not be captured by the similarity tasks. The next step, therefore, is to experiment on tasks where discourse plays a larger role, such as script induction or automatic summarisation.

We have also explored only a small fraction of the many possible contextual sentence spaces. At a minimum, the role of the size and symmetry of the extra-sentential context in the quality of sentence vectors should be investigated. Future work could also investigate other, more sophisticated models that go beyond simple sentence adjacency; for example, making use of the Penn Discourse Treebank (Prasad et al., 2008, 2014).

Acknowledgments

Tamara Polajnar and Stephen Clark are supported by ERC Starting Grant DisCoTex (306920). Laura Rimell and Stephen Clark are supported by EPSRC grant EP/I037512/1.

References

Marco Baroni, Raffaella Bernardi, and Roberto Zamparelli. 2014. Frege in space: A program for compositional distributional semantics. *Linguistic Issues in Language Technology*, 9:5–110.

Nathanael Chambers and Dan Jurafsky. 2008. Unsupervised learning of narrative event chains. In *Proceedings of ACL-HLT*.

Nathanael Chambers and Dan Jurafsky. 2009. Unsupervised learning of narrative schemas and their participants. In *Proceedings of ACL-IJCNLP*.

J. Chang, J. Boyd-Graber, S. Gerrish, C. Wang, and D. Blei. 2009. Reading tea leaves: How humans interpret topic models. In *Advances in Neural Information Processing Systems 21 (NIPS-09)*, page 288296, Vancouver, Canada.

Stephen Clark. Vector space models of lexical meaning. In Shalom Lappin and Chris Fox, editors, *Handbook of Contemporary Semantics second edition (to appear)*. Wiley-Blackwell, 2015.

Stephen Clark. Type-driven syntax and semantics for composing meaning vectors. In Chris Heunen, Mehrnoosh Sadrzadeh, and Edward Grefenstette, editors, *Quantum Physics and Linguistics: A Compositional, Diagrammatic Discourse*, pages 359–377. Oxford University Press, 2013.

Stephen Clark and James R. Curran. 2007. Wide-coverage efficient statistical parsing with CCG and log-linear models. *Computational Linguistics*, 33(4):493–552.

Bob Coecke, Mehrnoosh Sadrzadeh, and Stephen Clark. Mathematical foundations for a compositional distributional model of meaning. In J. van Bentham, M. Moortgat, and W. Buszkowski, editors, *Linguistic Analysis (Lambek Festschrift)*, volume 36, pages 345–384. 2010.

James R. Curran. *From Distributional to Semantic Similarity*. PhD thesis, University of Edinburgh, 2004.

Daniel Fried, Tamara Polajnar, and Stephen Clark. 2015. Low-rank tensors for verbs in compositional distributional semantics. In *Proceedings of the 53nd Annual Meeting of the Association for Computational Linguistics (ACL 2015)*, Bejing, China.

Edward Grefenstette. *Category-Theoretic Quantitative Compositional Distributional Models of Natural Language Semantics*. PhD thesis, University of Oxford, 2013.

Edward Grefenstette and Mehrnoosh Sadrzadeh. July 2011a. Experimental support for a categorical compositional distributional model of meaning. In *Proceedings of the 2011 Conference on Empirical Methods in Natural Language Processing*, pages 1394–1404, Edinburgh, Scotland, UK.

Edward Grefenstette and Mehrnoosh Sadrzadeh. 2011b. Experimenting with transitive verbs in a discocat. In *Proceedings of the GEMS 2011 Workshop on Geometrical Models of Natural Languge*, Edinburgh, Scotland, UK.

Edward Grefenstette, Georgiana Dinu, Yao-Zhong Zhang, Mehrnoosh Sadrzadeh, and Marco Baroni. 2013. Multi-step regression learning for compositional distributional semantics. *Proceedings of the 10th International Conference on Computational Semantics (IWCS 2013)*.

Kazuma Hashimoto and Yoshimasa Tsuruoka. 2015. Learning embeddings for transitive verb disambiguation by implicit tensor factorization. In *Proceedings of the 3rd Workshop on Continuous Vector Space Models and their Compositionality (CVSC)*, Beijing, China.

Dimitri Kartsaklis and Mehrnoosh Sadrzadeh. June 2014. A study of entanglement in a categorical framework of natural language. In *Proceedings of the 11th Workshop on Quantum Physics and Logic (QPL)*, Kyoto, Japan.

Dimitri Kartsaklis, Mehrnoosh Sadrzadeh, and Stephen Pulman. 2012. A unified sentence space for categorical distributional-compositional semantics: Theory and experiments. In *Proceedings of COLING*, pages 549–558.

Ryan Kiros, Yukun Zhu, Ruslan Salakhutdinov, Richard S. Zemel, Antonio Torralba, Raquel Urtasun, and Sanja Fidler. 2015. Skip-thought vectors. *CoRR*, abs/1506.06726. URL `http://arxiv.org/abs/1506.06726`.

Quoc Le and Tomas Mikolov. 2014. Distributed representations of sentences and documents. In *Proceedings of ICML*.

K. McRae, V. R. de Sa, and M. S. Seidenberg. Jun 1997. On the nature and scope of featural representations of word meaning. *Journal of experimental psychology. General*, 126(2):99–130. ISSN 0096-3445.

Dmitrijs Milajevs, Dimitri Kartsaklis, Mehrnoosh Sadrzadeh, and Matthew Purver. 2014. Evaluating neural word representations in tensor-based compositional settings. In *Proceedings of EMNLP*, Doha Qatar.

Guido Minnen, John Carroll, and Darren Pearce. 2001. Applied morphological processing of English. *Natural Language Engineering*, 7(3):207–223.

Tamara Polajnar and Stephen Clark. 2014. Improving distributional semantic vectors through context selection and normalisation. In *14th Conference of the European Chapter of the Association for Computational Linguistics, EACL'14*, Gothenburg, Sweden.

Tamara Polajnar, Luana Fagarasan, and Stephen Clark. 2014a. Reducing dimensions of tensors in type-driven distributional semantics. In *Proceedings of EMNLP 2014*, Doha, Qatar.

Tamara Polajnar, Laura Rimell, and Stephen Clark. 2014b. Using sentence plausibility to learn the semantics of transitive verbs. *CoRR*, abs/1411.7942. URL `http://arxiv.org/abs/1411.7942`.

R. Prasad, N. Dinesh, A. Lee, E. Miltsakaki, L. Robaldo, A. Joshi, and B.Webber. 2008. The Penn discourse TreeBank 2.0. In *Proceedings of LREC*, pages 2,9612,968.

Rashmi Prasad, Bonnie Webber, and Aravind Joshi. 2014. Reflections on the Penn discourse TreeBank, comparable corpora and complementary annotation. *Computational Linguistics*, 40(4):921–950.

Richard Socher, Eric H. Huang, Jeffrey Pennington, Andrew Y. Ng, and Christopher D. Manning. 2011a. Dynamic pooling and unfolding recursive autoencoders for paraphrase detection. In *Proceedings of NIPS*.

Richard Socher, Cliff Lin, Andrew Y. Ng, and Christopher D. Manning. 2011b. Parsing natural scenes and natural language with recursive neural networks. In *Proceedings of the 28th International Conference on Machine Learning (ICML 2011)*, Bellevue, Washington.

Richard Socher, Brody Huval, Christopher D. Manning, and Andrew Y. Ng. 2012. Semantic compositionality through recursive matrix-vector spaces. In *Proceedings of the Conference on Empirical Methods in Natural Language Processing*, pages 1201–1211, Jeju, Korea.

Richard Socher, John Bauer, Christopher D. Manning, and Andrew Y. Ng. 2013. Parsing with compositional vector grammars. In *Proceedings of ACL*.

Peter D. Turney and Patrick Pantel. 2010. From frequency to meaning: Vector space models of semantics. *Journal of Artificial Intelligence Research*, 37:141–188.

Matthew D. Zeiler. 2012. ADADELTA: an adaptive learning rate method. *CoRR*, abs/1212.5701.

Linking discourse modes and situation entity types in a cross-linguistic corpus study

Kleio-Isidora Mavridou[1] **Annemarie Friedrich**[1] **Melissa Peate Sørensen**[1]
Alexis Palmer[2,3] **Manfred Pinkal**[1]

[1]Department of Computational Linguistics, Universität des Saarlandes, Germany
{mavridou,afried,melissap,pinkal}@coli.uni-saarland.de

[2]Institute for Natural Language Processing, University of Stuttgart, Germany
[3]Department of Computational Linguistics, Heidelberg University, Germany
palmer@cl.uni-heidelberg.de

Abstract

The main contribution of this paper is a cross-linguistic empirical analysis of two interacting levels of linguistic analysis of written text: situation entity (SE) types, the semantic types of situations evoked by clauses of text, and discourse modes (DMs), a characterization of passages at the sub-document level. We adapt an existing annotation scheme for SEs in English to be used for German data, with a detailed discussion of the most important differences. We create the first parallel corpus annotated for SEs, and the first DM-annotated corpus. We find that: (a) the adapted scheme is supported by evidence from a large-scale experimental study; (b) SEs mainly correspond to each other in parallel text, and a large part of the mismatches are systematic; (c) the DM annotation task can be performed intuitively with reasonable agreement; and (d) the annotated DMs show the predicted differences in the distributions of SE types.

1 Introduction

There are complex and interwoven relationships between the nature of a text – whether construed as genre, register, text type, discourse mode, or something else – and the linguistic characteristics of the text (Werlich, 1975; Smith, 2003; Biber and Conrad, 2009; Passonneau et al., 2014, among others). Furthermore, these relationships involve phenomena at different levels, from lexical to structural, and from semantic to functional/pragmatic. In this paper we investigate correspondences across two levels of linguistic analysis, for phenomena spanning semantics and discourse, for two languages (English and German). Specifically, we conduct a corpus study on **discourse modes** (DMs), defined as types over passages of text, and **situation entity** (SE) types, defined as situation types evoked by clauses of text.

The theory of DMs (Smith, 2003) builds on the intuition that, in any genre, texts are made up of passages which have different functions. For example, a news article about student loan debt may begin with a NARRATIVE passage describing a particular student experiencing a difficult financial episode and then move on to a passage in INFORMATION mode giving background on relevant laws and policies. The different modes of discourse have different linguistic properties, one of which is the distribution of SE types predominant in the mode. (More details on DMs appear in Section 3.) We perform the first pilot annotation study of texts for DMs. Annotators label passages with their DM without referring to SEs, but only following a short manual providing prototypical examples of each DM. Our aim is to determine how easily modes can be distinguished in an intuitive setting, and to look at cross-linguistic correspondence of DM types per paragraph.

The SE types differentiate between clauses describing events, those describing states, and those conveying generic information (for more detail, see Section 4). While these semantic types are language-independent, they differ in their linguistic realizations. Here we perform the first detailed cross-linguistic study of SE types, aiming to understand both the differences in their linguistic characteristics across languages (Section 4.1) and how closely SE types correspond to each other cross-linguistically (Section 5.2). This requires adaptation of an existing annotation scheme for SEs in English (Friedrich and Palmer, 2014) to German. We discuss this adaptation (Section 4.1), including an experiment on the interpretation of

Proceedings of the EMNLP 2015 Workshop on Linking Models of Lexical, Sentential and Discourse-level Semantics, pages 12–21,
Lisboa, Portugal, 18 September 2015.

the German perfect (Section 4.2). During the development of the annotation scheme, we identified clauses with perfect tense as one of the most difficult cases for SE annotation in German. Our corpus study shows that SE types are mostly stable across translated segments, but that there are systematic SE type shifts.

Finally, we investigate the correspondence of DMs and SEs, and find that the intuitively labeled DMs mostly have the characteristic SE type distributions predicted by Smith (2003). This is the first empirical validation of this correspondence. Interestingly, some of the pairwise DM distinctions which seem to be most difficult for annotators to make also have similar SE distributions.

In this work, we study these two related levels of semantic and discourse analysis for two reasons. The first is to provide an empirical analysis for the linguistic theory of DMs; the second is their potential to support applications like summarization, information extraction, or question answering, all of which could benefit from sorting the information conveyed by texts into different categories and different modes of presentation. Further, we discuss the potential of this level of analysis for translation studies or application within machine translation.

Related Work. Unlike genre, a notion of text type for entire documents, DMs are an aspect of sub-document structure, and thus are similar to approaches such as Argumentative Zoning (AZ) (Teufel, 2010). AZ analyzes scientific research articles according to the rhetorical functions of their text passages, identifying and labeling passages with categories like *General scientific background* or *Contrastive/comparative statements*. The key difference is that AZ is a genre-specific approach, and DMs are relevant for most written text genres.

Liakata et al. (2013) use AZ to improve summarization of scientific articles, showing that subdocument structure can indeed be useful in downstream applications. Santini (2006) also employ types over passages of text (called simply "text types"), with labels that are partially similar to Smith's DMs. These text types are then used as building blocks for automatic web genre classification.

Palmer and Friedrich (2014), inspired by Webber (2009), investigate the distribution of SE types for various genres of text. In contrast, here we study the distribution of SE types per DM. Related work for the other subparts of the study is discussed in the relevant sections of the paper.

2 Corpus Data

This study requires aligned parallel data with different text types. We collect 11 parallel English-German texts from a variety of sources and produce clause- and paragraph-level alignments for the texts. Table 1 gives statistics on the number of segments, tokens, and paragraphs in each document, as well as aggregate statistics for the corpus. The translation direction differs across documents, and part of the data consists of translations from a third language into both English and German.[1] The corpus includes three documents from a version of Europarl customized for translation studies (Islam and Mehler, 2012), two documents from the news commentary corpus (WMT 2013 shared task training data[2]), sections from the novels *Alice in Wonderland* and *Anna Karenina* from the OPUS collection (Tiedemann, 2012),[3] and two texts from a multilingual news website.[4] These texts were segmented into clauses manually by one of the authors. English and German segments were also aligned manually.

In addition, we use two documents (*Sophie's world* and *economy*) from the Smultron corpus (Volk et al., 2010). We split the English part of Smultron into clauses using SPADE (Soricut and Marcu, 2003), and the German part using a syntax-based discourse segmenter for German.[5] The Smultron corpus provides alignments on a token-/phrase-level, but these phrases do not necessarily match the clause segmentation. To align clauses, we first identify the main verb of each English segment using dependency parses (Klein and Manning, 2002). We then align each segment to the German segment containing the verb to which the identified (English) main verb is aligned. For all texts, paragraph segmentation follows the paragraph breaks in the original source texts.

3 Annotating discourse modes

This exploratory study takes the first steps toward computational treatment of DMs, resulting in the first corpus of texts labeled with DMs.

[1] This metadata is available for each document pair.
[2] http://statmt.org/wmt13
[3] http://opus.lingfil.uu.se
[4] http://globalvoicesonline.org
[5] Publication in preparation.

source	text/excerpt	# tokens	# aligned tokens	# clauses	# aligned clauses	# aligned paragraphs
OPUS: novels	Alice in Wonderland (en) Alice in Wonderland (de)	764 690	684 647	106 98	90	10
OPUS: novels	Anna Karenina (en) Anna Karenina (de)	592 679	543 571	83 86	73	9
Europarl	Document1 (en) Document1 (de)	551 487	454 466	59 50	47	6
Europarl	Document2 (en) Document2 (de)	1879 1662	1669 1598	192 172	163	14
Europarl	Document3 (en) Document3 (de)	923 859	774 764	104 100	85	9
GlobalVoices	Heimkino (en) Heimkino (de)	816 734	689 647	102 95	84	16
GlobalVoices	Karneval (en) Karneval (de)	1014 827	847 756	89 78	72	25
NewsCommentary	Kernspaltung (en) Kernspaltung (de)	831 849	788 727	82 89	75	17
NewsCommentary	Musharraf (en) Musharraf (de)	751 770	667 714	82 78	72	12
Smultron	Sophie's World (en) Sophie's World (de)	7011 6389	5953 6825	931 937	557	188
Smultron	Economy (en) Economy (de)	10312 9532	4238 3894	863 740	471	184
TOTAL	English German	25444 23478	17306 17609	2693 2523	1789	490

Table 1: Size of English-German parallel corpus, with per-document statistics.

3.1 Annotation scheme and analysis

Annotating DMs involves two aspects: finding the boundaries between passages of different DMs and labeling those passages with the appropriate DM. In this study we take paragraphs as an approximation of DM segments, leaving the modeling of DM boundaries for future work. The DM types used in this study are described below, together with some of the linguistic characteristics of the modes identified by Smith. These characteristics are of two types: the distribution of SE types (Section 6) and the mode of progression through the text.

- NARRATIVE: mode used for telling stories; temporal progression is generally linear
- REPORT: typical mode of news articles; events are discussed with respect to a reference time
- INFORMATION: mode used for explanations; atemporal, often focuses on generalizations rather than specific entities or events
- DESCRIPTION: mode used to describe entities, locations, objects; temporally static, progression often spatially oriented
- ARGUMENT/COMMENTARY: mode used for persuasion or presenting opinions; atemporal
- OTHER: text types not covered by Smith's set of DMs, such as instructional texts
- NONE: paragraphs whose text serves primarily structural purposes, such as headlines or document section headings

One aim of this pilot annotation is to determine how intuitively clear these categories are to minimally-trained annotators. Annotators were given a short, simple annotation manual of just 2 pages, focusing on intuitive descriptions of the modes with a prototypical paragraph for each DM. The training phase consisted of labeling and getting feedback on 14 paragraphs of text, with 2 examples of each type. The training examples were selected to be clear cases, in order to give the annotators a strong intuitive sense of each DM. Once annotators had completed the training examples, they were given documents packaged in chunks of 30 consecutive paragraphs each. Ten different annotators each labeled from 3-7 such chunks. Each paragraph is labeled once, with five annotators labeling English text, and five labeling German text.

Agreement between annotators. Inter-annotator agreement is captured through an *agreement* chunk containing five 10-paragraph segments extracted from different texts, taking aligned paragraphs for the two languages. All 10 annotators labeled the agreement dataset, five for each language. For these 50 paragraphs, Fleiss' κ for the German-language annotators is 0.50, with κ of 0.46 for the English-language annotators.

		German						
		NARR.	REPORT	INF.	DESCR.	ARG./COMM.	OTHER	NONE
English	NARRATIVE	43	5	2	8	6	1	2
	REPORT	0	17	65	4	3	0	2
	INFORMATION	9	13	53	23	10	5	3
	DESCRIPTION	16	6	8	20	7	6	3
	ARG/COMM	4	1	5	3	48	5	4
	OTHER	2	0	0	1	2	2	12
	NONE	1	1	4	1	2	10	42

Table 2: Confusion matrix of DM paragraph labels for parallel English-German text. Lightly-shaded cells highlight the most prominent confusions.

During the annotation process, it quickly became clear that two distinctions in particular were difficult for annotators to make: DESCRIPTION vs. INFORMATION, and INFORMATION vs. REPORT. Below we show three passages with their true labels. Nearly all annotators agreed on their labels for the first two passages (A and B); the third passage (C) received a mix of the labels INFORMATION and DESCRIPTION, plus REPORT.

A. DESCRIPTION
The red house was surrounded by a large garden with lots of flowerbeds, fruit bushes, fruit trees of different kinds, a spacious lawn with a glider and a little gazebo that Granddad had built for Granny...

B. INFORMATION
The Group has three control functions, which are independent from the business operations: Internal Audit, Compliance and Risk control.

C. INFORMATION/REPORT
According to Chris Wille, the Rainforest Alliance's Chief of Sustainable Agriculture, technological advances and a more favorable market should facilitate a steady evolution toward ever better conditions on certified farms.

The intuitive descriptions we gave to the annotators intentionally avoided mentioning specific linguistic characteristics of the modes, and this may be one reason some distinctions were difficult to make. INFORMATION was frequently mentioned by annotators as the most confusing category and the most difficult to differentiate from the others. The choice to use paragraph boundaries instead of true DM boundaries also influenced the annotation process, as inspection of the most-disagreed-upon passages shows that many paragraphs in fact display a mix of DMs. Finally, several annotators seemed to have trouble making the distinction between labeling the DMs of individual passages rather than the genre of texts.

Cross-linguistic comparison. The next question to be addressed is to what extent DMs correspond across parallel aligned paragraphs of text for the language pair English-German. Given the differences between annotators, of course, these results can only be seen as suggestive. Table 2 shows the confusion matrix for DM annotations across languages, aggregated across all texts. Interestingly, the same mode pairs that were reported as being difficult to distinguish by individual annotators show the highest degree of confusability when we compare annotations across languages (light-grey shaded boxes in Table 2).

Additional annotations and more systematic investigation are needed in order to determine whether these patterns reflect preferences of individual annotators or rather differences in how the two languages realize discourse modes.

4 Situation entities: annotation scheme

The second focus of this study is the question of how *situation entity (SE) types*, as defined by Smith (2003), differ cross-linguistically, focusing on two closely-related languages, English and German. During annotation, we follow the existing scheme for English data (Friedrich and Palmer, 2014), and our own adapted scheme for German data (Section 4.1). Here, we give a brief description of the SE types relevant to this study (see the cited paper for more details).

- STATE: clauses introducing properties (*Mary is tall*); modalized clauses (*Mary can swim*); perfect tense (*Mary has submitted the paper)*
- EVENT: dynamic events, particular things that happened (*Mary ate a cupcake)*
- GENERALIZING SENTENCE: clauses reporting on regularities related to particular individuals (*Mary cycles to work*)
- GENERIC SENTENCE: clauses making statements about kinds (*Monkeys like bananas*)
- QUESTION: *Do you really need an example?*
- IMPERATIVE: *Hand me the pen!*

In the remainder of this section, we describe (a) our adaptation of this scheme to German, and (b) an experiment studying the interpretation of the German perfect as having stative or event readings, as this is a crucial difference when determining the SE types for English or German text.

4.1 Annotation scheme for German

For adapting the scheme, we first asked several annotators, German native speakers, to apply the existing English scheme to German data and report on problems they found. In addition, disagreements between the annotators were carefully analyzed. The scheme was then adapted to German in order to account for the identified differences between the two languages, outlined below.

Perfect tense. Possibly the most striking relevant difference between English and German is the interpretation of perfect tense. While in English, all clauses in perfect tense are interpreted as stative (Katz, 2003), the German perfect can have a stative or an event reading (fulfilling a function similar to the English simple past), or even be underspecified depending on the context. In English, SE annotators are instructed to label all clauses in perfect tense as STATES; in German, annotators can label them as EVENT or STATE, depending on what they find to be appropriate. We introduce a new label EVENT-PERF-STATE for underspecified cases. In Section 4.2, we conduct an experiment studying in detail the interpretation of the German perfect with regard to stative/event readings; the findings there validate our choice to allow variable SE annotations for the German perfect.

Genericity of main referent. A clause's main referent is the entity 'the clause is about.' GENERIC SENTENCES have *generic* main referents, which are defined as references to kinds, and all other SE types have *non-generic* main referents. In English clauses, the main referent usually coincides with the grammatical subject, but this simple heuristic does not always apply for German. We identify the following cases where it can be difficult in German to select the main referent.

Examples (1) and (2) illustrate usages of the *impersonal passive*, which can be formed in German (unlike English) for intransitive verbs. The pronoun *es* is a grammatical placeholder, and annotators have to infer the main referent from the clause's discourse context. In (1), the first clause introduces a particular situation, and we can infer in the second clause that some particular group of people is talking again. In (2), again context determines the habitual/generic reading of the second clause.

(1) *(a) Jetzt ist Pause, (non-generic,* STATE*)*
(b) es wird wieder geredet. (non-generic, EVENT*)*
There's a break now, people are talking again.

(2) *(a) Früher gab es keine Nähmaschinen, (generic,* GENERIC SENTENCE*)*
(b) heute wird anders genäht. (generic, GENERIC SENTENCE*)*
In the past, there were no sewing machines, today one sews differently / sewing is done differently.

In addition, there is a group of impersonal perception verbs which are usually expressed with stative verbs, and require an argument either in dative, as in (3a), or accusative, as in (3b). In both cases, the argument in dative or accusative is considered to be the main referent of the clause.

(3) *(a) Es graut mir vor morgen. (non-generic,* STATE*)* *I dread tomorrow.*
(b) Mich friert es oft. (non-generic, GENERALIZING SENTENCE*)* *I often freeze.*

Statal passive. The statal passive (4a), in contrast to the processual passive (4b), focuses on the result or the "state" reached after a process, and are marked as STATES.

(4) *(a) Die Tür ist geöffnet. (*STATE*)*
*(b) Die Tür wurde geöffnet. (*EVENT*)*
(a) The door is open. / (b) The door was opened.

Modal constructions. Modalized clauses describe, among others, possibilities, necessities or conditions rather than actual events, and are therefore marked as STATES.[6] In German, two common constructions indicating necessity are *haben/sein + zu + infinitive*; these are similar to the English *have to + infinitive / is to be + past participle*. The *sich lassen* construction (5) indicates possibility.

(5) *Dieser Konflikt* ***lässt sich*** *ohne Gewalt* ***lösen****. (*STATE*)*
This conflict ***can be*** *solved without violence.*

[6]The coercions described here and in the following two paragraphs (subjunctive and *damit*) do not apply to GENERALIZING or GENERIC SENTENCES.

Subjunctive mood. The German *Konjunktiv* expresses doubt, possibility, speculations or conditionality. The verb construction *wir gehen in Urlaub* in (6) is dynamic, but the subjunctive mood coerces the SE type to be STATE.

(6) *(a)* ***Hätten*** *wir das Geld,* (STATE)
(b) ***gingen*** *wir morgen schon in Urlaub.* (STATE)
If we had the money, we ***would*** *go on holiday tomorrow.*

Final clauses with "damit". Final clauses (7) describe a purpose, an intention or a goal rather than an actual event, and are coerced to STATEs.

(7) *Erinnere mich nochmal,* (IMPERATIVE)
damit ich pünktlich komme. (STATE)
Remind me again so I will be on time.

Interim summary. We have now described the major differences identified when applying the English SE annotation scheme to German data. How clauses of each SE type are expressed is clearly language-dependent. However, our main finding is that the SE categories *are* applicable to German, and that the SE level of discourse analysis is cross-linguistically applicable. In the following section, we drill down on the most striking difference, the annotation of clauses in perfect tense.

4.2 Experiment on the interpretation of the German perfect by many annotators

German clauses in perfect tense may have either a temporal reading (past event, as in (8a)) or an aspectual reading indicating completedness of an event, as in (8b) (Klein, 2000).

(8) *(a) Gestern sind wir ins Kino gegangen.* (EVENT) *Yesterday we went to the movies.*
(b) Ich habe schon gegessen. (STATE)
I have eaten.

The above examples clearly emphasize either the event or its result, but in some sentences, such as (9), it is hard to say which is more important; the construction is underspecified. For such cases, we introduce the label EVENT-PERF-STATE.

(9) *Sie haben mir den Job gegeben.*
(EVENT-PERF-STATE)
They gave me the job. / They have given me the job.

The focus of the experiment described in this section is to investigate to what extent German native speakers are able to agree on the relative salience of the state/event information. We conduct a large-scale experiment involving a large number of participants. To the best of our knowledge, interpretation of the perfect has not been investigated in this way for German before.

Experiment. The experimental data are 73 German sentences collected from several multilingual web sites. Two authors of this paper collaborated to provide reference labels for the sentences, marking 24 as STATE, 24 as EVENT and 25 as EVENT-PERF-STATE. We ask participants to give a rating for whether they think the state or the event matters more for a target word in a sentence (sentences are presented in their context, usually a very short paragraph). The rating scale is 1-5, where 1 means that only the event is important, and 5 means that only the state matters.

We recruit voluntary annotators via mailing lists of computational linguistics students at several German universities. We randomize the presentation of experimental items, ensuring that each annotation batch contains 1/3 STATE items, 1/3 EVENT items and 1/3 EVENT-PERFECT-STATE items. Each annotator is also shown four 'sample' items, two of which are clearly STATEs and two of which are clearly EVENTs. A total of 2,347 annotations were made by 102 German native speakers. To control for whether the participants read the short instructions carefully, we additionally exclude the data of participants who did not mark the two STATE samples with a score between 1-3, or the two EVENT samples as 3-5 on the scale. This reduced the data set to 1,611 annotations by 63 people. Each annotator marked 18 or more sentences (average: 25), and each sentence was annotated 13 or more times (average: 18).

Results. The averaged scores for each item can be seen in Figure 1. Towards either end of the scale, standard deviation is low, validating our hypothesis that some cases clearly have a preferred interpretation. For underspecified cases (i.e. those with means around 3), standard deviation is also high: many annotators only see one reading.

Most of the reference labels match the mean of the scores given by the annotators. However, there are some noticeable outliers. The EVENT item seen around the 70 mark on the x-axis is the

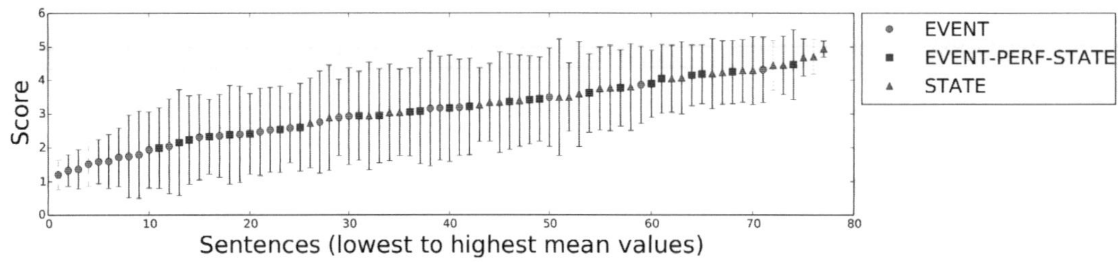

Figure 1: Perception of German perfect: mean and standard deviations for scores given to sentences. Semantics of scores: 1=EVENT, 3=EVENT-PERF-STATE, 5=STATE. Orange dotted lines: sample items.

sentence *Warum haben wir eigentlich geheiratet? (Why did we get married?)* – here, the state of being married is apparently quite prominent to our participants. The EVENT outlier seen around the 60 mark is *welches wir oben beschrieben haben (which we (have) described above)*, which probably should have been marked as EVENT-PERF-STATE.

Related work. A corpus study by de Swart (2007) analyzes the usage of the perfect in translations of the French novel *L'étranger* by Albert Camus. They show that the present perfect can be used to tell a story in French or German, but not in English or Dutch. Nishiyama and Koenig (2006) assess the role that the English perfect plays in discourse by examining the interpretations of 605 present perfect examples. Scheifele (2014) uses a picture-sentence-verification task to study the activation of the resultant state of sentences in the German perfect.

5 Situation entities: corpus study

With the annotation scheme established, we now compare the SE annotations on the parallel corpus.

5.1 Agreement

Each segment of the corpus data described in Section 2 is separately marked by three different annotators. Most annotations were done by paid, trained annotators, with some labels provided by one of the authors. Annotators were given the written manuals and trained on a few documents not included in the corpus. We create a gold standard via majority voting. The Smultron part of the data was labeled by a different combination of annotators than the rest of the documents. As Table 3 shows, substantial agreement was achieved. The categories (SE types) apply equally for both languages, but the mapping from linguistic structures to these types is language-dependent. The agreement numbers show that the two sets of guidelines work equally well for German and English.

corpus section	English	German
Smultron	0.63	0.62
other	0.61	0.67

Table 3: Agreement for SE type labels, Fleiss' κ.

5.2 Cross-lingual comparison of SE types

In this section, we move on to the cross-lingual comparison of the SE types of parallel texts. Our main questions are: do SE types in the texts of one language usually correspond to translated segments of the same SE type; and what are the cases in which aligned segments have different SE types? We use the subset of segments which have an aligned counterpart in the respective other language for this analysis.

As the confusion matrix of SE type labels in Table 4 shows, in most cases, the aligned segments receive the same SE type labels. This level of linguistic discourse analysis holds across languages and can potentially be relevant for improving or evaluating machine translation or translations of language learners: mismatches could be indicators for bad translations. However, mismatches can also occur for *good* translations in certain circumstances. In the following, we present a qualitative analysis of the non-matching cases with regard to whether they represent errors in annotation or patterns of SE type shift across languages.

Table 5 shows the counts of various mismatch types we identified for the aligned segments whose SE type labels differ. We found about 40% of mismatches to be results of disagreements, as they would occur in a monolingual setting as well.

		German							
		STATE	EVENT	EVT-PERF-ST	GENERAL.	GENERIC	IMP.	QUEST.	–
English	STATE	642	85	27	14	47	0	4	34
	EVENT	40	304	14	10	5	1	0	9
	GENERALIZING	9	5	0	38	49	1	0	6
	GENERIC	33	0	0	1	143	0	0	3
	IMPERATIVE	2	1	0	0	0	9	0	2
	QUESTION	2	0	0	0	1	0	62	5
	–	57	32	2	8	41	0	4	37

Table 4: Confusion matrix of SE type labels for parallel English-German text.

mismatch type	#
systematic disagreements	259
- involving German perfect	62
- lexical choice	79
- grammatical structure	5
- segmentation	113
language-independent disagreements	184
- genericity	125
- lexical aspectual class	17
- other	42

Table 5: Reasons identified for SE type mismatch.

For example, we find mismatches between judging the main referent of a segment as generic or non-generic, which has been found to be a difficult decision before (Friedrich et al., 2015). Most of these cases seem to be language-independent, however, there are cases where a certain form of the noun phrase primes a particular reading. The GENERIC SENTENCE *Terrorists may also benefit* has been translated as *Auch die Terroristen könnten profitieren* (STATE), in which the noun phrase *die Terroristen* primes the non-generic reading in this context. Further cross-linguistic study of the expression of generic noun phrases is needed.

About 60% of the disagreements were identified as resulting from cross-lingual differences. As expected, the German perfect causes confusion between STATEs and EVENTs. Additional confusion between these two types results from lexical choice, presenting the same matter of affairs as either a STATE or an EVENT, as in *She was startled* (STATE) vs. *Sie fuhr zusammen* (EVENT). Similarly, the lexical aspectual class of the English verb *support* can be interpreted as stative or dynamic, but the German translation *fördern* has a stronger preference for a dynamic interpretation.

Some clauses are marked as a segmentation error in one language, meaning the clause does not contain a full verb constellation. This occurs for example if a clause contains only an infinitive. If the other language did not use an infinitive construction, the segment receives a label.

In addition, requests can be formulated in different ways and lead to mismatches, as the following example shows: *Take a look at...* (IMPERATIVE) vs. *Hier können Sie ... sehen* (STATE).

This paper presents a small pilot study, but it shows clearly that some SE type shifts are systematic for this closely related language pair. As future work, we suggest investigating whether these SE type shifts can be predicted with an automatic classifier. This in turn could be a valuable resource for translation studies or for improving or evaluating machine translation.

6 Discourse modes and situation entities

We have studied the cross-linguistic correspondences of SE types and DMs above. The final step in the study brings these two levels of analysis together by looking at the distributions of SE types for paragraphs of different DM types. According to Smith, SE distributions should be one of the distinguishing features between text passages of different DM types: NARRATIVE and DESCRIPTION passages contain large numbers of EVENTs and STATEs; REPORT passages contain these two types plus GENERALIZING and GENERIC SENTENCES; INFORMATION and ARGUMENT/COMMENTARY should contain higher proportions of the latter two SE types.

Annotators were not told which SE types to expect in DMs; DM annotation was done purely intuitively. Note that the SE annotations were created via majority voting using established annotation schemes, and are thus quite reliable, but the DM labels are the results of the pilot study on DM annotation as described in Section 3. Table 6 shows the percentage of clauses labeled with a given SE type for each DM. We exclude clauses that the SE annotators marked as segmentation errors but include those which received no SE label

DM	# clauses	% STATE	% EVENT	% EV-PRF-ST	% GNRL.	% GENERIC	% IMP.	% QST.	% –
NARR.	288 / 341	57 / 53	25 / 29	0 / 1	2 / 6	8 / 4	1 / 3	0 / 1	6 / 4
REPORT	503 / 220	59 / 54	26 / 29	0 / 2	5 / 7	5 / 5	1 / 1	0 / 0	4 / 2
INF.	613 / 726	58 / 46	14 / 25	0 / 1	5 / 20	15 / 4	1 / 0	1 / 0	6 / 3
DESCR.	280 / 341	61 / 46	21 / 23	0 / 1	4 / 18	5 / 6	2 / 2	1 / 0	6 / 4
ARG/COM	552 / 553	57 / 46	19 / 20	0 / 2	12 / 24	7 / 4	1 / 1	1 / 0	3 / 3
OTHER	19 / 101	90 / 48	11 / 19	0 / 7	0 / 16	0 / 4	0 / 2	0 / 1	0 / 4
NONE	70 / 72	36 / 38	23 / 29	0 / 6	27 / 13	6 / 5	3 / 4	3 / 0	3 / 6

Table 6: Distribution of SE type labels per DM, as **percentage (%)** of all clauses per DM: *(En / De)*

due to annotator disagreements (marked as –).

Discussion. The distribution of SE types largely matches the predictions of Smith (2003). In all DMs, the predominant SE type is STATE.[7] The reason is possibly that STATE marks several different types of coerced cases (e.g., perfect, negation, modals). In future work, we are planning to investigate the different types of STATEs per mode. There is already a clear path for this investigation: for each clause, we also annotated features such as the type of main referent, the lexical aspectual class of the main verb, and habituality (as described in the original annotation scheme by Friedrich and Palmer (2014)). These features will allow us to quickly sub-type clauses labeled STATE. EVENT-PERF-STATE of course appears only in the German data.

The most interesting differences show up in the distributions of the SE types which convey general rather than specific information: both GENERALIZING SENTENCE and GENERIC clauses figure more prominently in the modes of INFORMATION, DESCRIPTION, and ARGUMENT/COMMENTARY than they do in NARRATIVE or REPORT.

It should also be noted that the distributions shown here could to some extent be affected by problems with automatically aligning clauses across languages. The non-Smultron portion of the corpus is manually aligned, and there we retain from roughly 80-90% of the annotated clauses. The Smultron data is automatically aligned, and there we drop to below 60% of the clauses.

7 Conclusion and future work

The present corpus study shows that discourse analysis at the level of DMs and semantic analysis at the level of SEs are quite robust across the two closely related languages German and English. Both of these phenomena have been investigated from a theoretical perspective for other languages (Smith, 2003), with a small empirical study for Mandarin (Smith and Erbaugh, 2001), and further empirical analysis of additional languages is certainly warranted.

The DM annotation pilot study confirmed the expectation that paragraph boundaries as signaled by white space in the original documents do not correspond cleanly to actual DM borders, and these mixed paragraphs were especially difficult for annotators to label. Another question for future work is whether to allow one passage to have a mixture of DMs (for example, sometimes NARRATIVE passages have many background INFORMATION sentences), or whether additional DMs should be introduced.

Finally, as future work, we plan to create computational models of SEs and DMs, and exploit their relationship as empirically ascertained in Section 6. These computational models could then in turn be used to improve NLP applications as mentioned in the introduction.

Acknowledgments

First and foremost, thanks to the fleet of volunteer annotators who gave their time for either the discourse modes pilot annotation study or the German perfect study, as well as our excellent situation entity annotators. We also thank Alessandra Zarcone for invaluable help with experimental design, and the anonymous reviewers for their feedback. This work is funded in large part by the Cluster of Excellence *Multimodal Computing and Interaction* and in smaller part through the Leibniz ScienceCampus *Empirical Linguistics and Computational Language Modeling*. The second author is supported by an IBM PhD Fellowship.

[7] Although the proportion of STATEs appears to be unusually high for English paragraphs with the DM label OTHER, investigation of this data revealed no particular patterns. Instead, this is an anomaly due to the very small sample size.

References

Douglas Biber and Susan Conrad. 2009. *Register, Genre, and Style*. Cambridge University Press, Cambridge.

Henriëtte de Swart. 2007. A cross-linguistic discourse analysis of the perfect. *Journal of pragmatics*, 39(12):2273–2307.

Annemarie Friedrich and Alexis Palmer. 2014. Situation entity annotation. In *Proceedings of the 8th Linguistic Annotation Workshop*.

Annemarie Friedrich, Alexis Palmer, Melissa Peate Sørensen, and Manfred Pinkal. 2015. Annotating genericity: a survey, a scheme, and a corpus. In *Proceedings of the 9th Linguistic Annotation Workshop*.

Zahurul Islam and Alexander Mehler. 2012. Customization of the Europarl Corpus for Translation Studies. In *Proceedings of the Eighth International Conference on Language Resources and Evaluation (LREC'12)*.

Graham Katz. 2003. On the stativity of the English perfect. *Perfect explorations*, pages 205–234.

Dan Klein and Christopher D Manning. 2002. Fast exact inference with a factored model for natural language parsing. In *Advances in neural information processing systems*, pages 3–10.

Wolfgang Klein. 2000. An analysis of the German Perfekt. *Language*, pages 358–382.

Maria Liakata, Simon Dobnik, Shyamasree Saha, Colin Batchelor, and Dietrich Rebholz-Schuhmann. 2013. A discourse-driven content model for summarising scientific articles evaluated in a complex question answering task. In *Proceedings of EMNLP*.

Atsuko Nishiyama and Jean-Pierre Koenig. 2006. The perfect in context: A corpus study. *University of Pennsylvania Working Papers in Linguistics*, 12(1):22.

Alexis Palmer and Annemarie Friedrich. 2014. Genre distinctions and discourse modes: Text types differ in their situation type distributions. In *Proceedings of the Workshop on Frontiers and Connections between Argumentation Theory and NLP*.

Rebecca J. Passonneau, Nancy Ide, Songqiao Su, and Jesse Stuart. 2014. Biber Redux: Reconsidering Dimensions of Variation in American English. In *Proceedings of COLING*.

Marina Santini. 2006. Towards a zero-to-multi-genre classification scheme. In *Proceedings of ATALA*.

Edith Scheifele. 2014. The German Perfekt: Activation of the Resultant State? In *Linguistic Evidence 2014, Empirical, Theoretical, and Computational Perspectives*, Tübingen.

Carlota S. Smith and Mary S. Erbaugh. 2001. Temporal Information in Sentences of Mandarin. In Xu Liejiong and Shao Jingmin, editors, *New Views in Chinese Syntactic Research – International Symposium on Chinese Grammar for the New Millenium*.

Carlota S Smith. 2003. *Modes of discourse: The local structure of texts*. Cambridge University Press.

Radu Soricut and Daniel Marcu. 2003. Sentence level discourse parsing using syntactic and lexical information. In *Proceedings of the 2003 Conference of NAACL-HLT*. Association for Computational Linguistics.

Simone Teufel. 2010. *The Structure of Scientific Articles: Applications to Citation Indexing and Summarization*. CSLI Publications.

Jörg Tiedemann. 2012. Parallel Data, Tools and Interfaces in OPUS. In *Proceedings of the Eight International Conference on Language Resources and Evaluation (LREC'12)*, Istanbul, Turkey.

Martin Volk, Anne Göhring, Torsten Marek, and Yvonne Samuelsson. 2010. SMULTRON (version 3.0) — The Stockholm MULtilingual parallel TReebank.

Bonnie Webber. 2009. Genre distinctions for discourse in the Penn TreeBank. In *Proceedings of ACL*.

Egon Werlich. 1975. *Typologie der Texte*. Quelle & Meyer, Heidelberg.

Recovering discourse relations: Varying influence of discourse adverbials

Hannah Rohde **Anna Dickinson** **Chris Clark** **Annie Louis** **Bonnie Webber**
University of Edinburgh
[hannah.rohde, bonnie.webber]@ed.ac.uk
[anna.y.dickinson, chrisclark272, annieplouis]@gmail.com

Abstract

Discourse relations are a bridge between sentence-level semantics and discourse-level semantics. They can be signalled explicitly with discourse connectives or conveyed implicitly, to be inferred by a comprehender. The same discourse units can be related in more than one way, signalled by multiple connectives. But multiple connectives aren't necessary: Multiple relations can be conveyed even when only one connective is explicit. This paper describes the initial phase in a larger experimental study aimed at answering two questions: (1) Given an explicit discourse adverbial, what discourse relation(s) do naive subjects take to be operative, and (2) Can this be predicted on the basis of the explicit adverbial alone, or does it depend instead on other factors?

1 Introduction

Semantics comes both explicitly and implicitly from a text. One bridge between sentence-level semantics and discourse semantics consists of relations between sentences and/or clauses, called variously *discourse relations* (Prasad et al., 2014), *coherence relations* (Kehler, 2002) or *rhetorical relations* (Mann and Thompson, 1988). Such relations between what we will call here *discourse spans* can be signaled explicitly via discourse connectives or specific lexico-syntactic contructions, or conveyed implicitly, via inference on the part of a comprehender. But **when** does the latter happen? Previously, it was assumed that relations are conveyed implicitly when they are **not** signalled explicitly. But consider Ex. 1a-b, each with two explicit connectives conveying distinct relations:

(1) a. Let's eat dinner now because otherwise we'll miss the film.

b. I can't walk 5 miles, so instead I'll take a taxi.

In Ex. 1a, *because* signals the REASON for eating dinner now, while *otherwise* signals the CONDITION under which we'll miss the film. In Ex. 1b, *so* signals the RESULT of my inability to walk so far, while *instead* signals the CHOSEN ALTERNATIVE to taking a taxi.[1]

However, both relations may still be conveyed, even if only one is signalled explicitly, as in Ex. 2a–c:

(2) a. Let's eat dinner now. Otherwise we'll miss the film.

b. I can't walk 5 miles. Instead I'll take a taxi.

c. I can't walk 5 miles, so I'll take a taxi.

d. Let's eat dinner now because we'll miss the film.

So it is not the case that implicit discourse relations only arise when discourse relations are **not** signalled explicitly. (Ex. 2d shows that a CHOSEN ALTERNATIVE is not achieved with the single connective *because*.)

The potential availability of multiple concurrent discourse relations raises important questions for both Language Technology (LT) and psycholinguistics: When a discourse relation is signalled with an explicit connective, should a LT system also look for a distinct implicit relation? From the perspective of psycholinguistics, implicit co-occurring relations raise fundamental questions about how comprehenders infer discourse relations and which contexts allow such relations to be understood without an explicit linguistic signal.

[1] The sense labels used here (in small caps) are short forms of the labels used in the PDTB 2.0 (Prasad et al., 2008; Prasad et al., 2014).

Proceedings of the EMNLP 2015 Workshop on Linking Models of Lexical, Sentential and Discourse-level Semantics, pages 22–31, Lisboa, Portugal, 18 September 2015.

Despite multiple explicit connectives being observed in Catalan and Spanish (Cuenca and Marin, 2009) as well as Turkish (Zeyrek, 2014) and English, questions about multiple relations in the presense of only a single connective have not yet been addressed (Section 2). To address them, we have embarked on a large crowd-sourcing experiment, the first phase of which is described in Sections 3–5. Section 6 discusses our results to date, with further phases described in Section 7.

2 Background

This is not the first work to call attention to multiple co-occurring connectives. Webber and colleagues (1999) used them to argue that discourse spans could be related by both adjacency relations and anaphoric relations. Similary, in the context of Catalan and Spanish oral narrative, Cuenca and Marin (2009) used them to argue for different patterns and degrees of discourse cohesion. Oates (2000) considers how multiple discourse connectives should be used in Natural Language Generation, noting that the order in which they occur correlates with the hierarchy of discourse connectives presented in (Knott, 1996). Fraser (2013) considers the order in which multiple CONTRASTIVE connectives co-occur, describing their patterning in terms of *general contrastive* discourse markers and *specific contrastive* discourse markers. For Turkish, Zeyrek (2014) describes patterns of multiple co-occuring connectives that signal CONTRASTIVE and/or CONCESSIVE relations.

These efforts have all been directed at providing an account of the existence of multiple connectives and their patterning. As for the phenomenon illustrated in Ex. 2a–c, the only work we are aware of is an MSc project supervised by the first co-author (Rohde). This study, by Xi Jiang (2013), involved four discourse adverbials (*after all, instead, in fact, in general*) that can occur alone or following a conjunction. Jiang presented participants in a crowd-sourcing experiment with a set of fill-in-the-gap passages such as the following

(3) Logically, she should be dead / _____ instead / she feels fine, caring for her daughters and walking a pedometer-measured two miles a day.

(4) He suspected he shouldn't say that / _____ instead / he lied.

asking the participants to either insert one of five conjunctions (*and, because, but, or, so*) into the gap or choose *None*.[2] In half the passages (10 per adverbial), the author had used one of these conjunctions before the adverbial (which Jiang then removed), and in the other half (including Ex. 3–4), the author had used no conjunction before the adverbial. The only criteria used in selecting these passages were brevity (i.e., could the passage be read quickly?) and clarity (i.e., did the passage make sense when presented out of context?).

Jiang's study was aimed at answering two questions: (1) When the author had used an explicit conjunction before the discourse adverbial, did participants always fill the gap with the same conjunction; and (2) where the original passage lacked an explicit conjunction, did participants choose to omit an explicit conjunction (i.e., did they chose *None*).

Each of the 80 passages (20 per adverbial) was annotated by the same 52 participants. Jiang's results showed some interesting patterns. In the gap preceding *after all*, participants tended to insert *because*, indicating that they interpreted the content of the second span as a REASON for the content of the first span, independent of whether the original text contained *because* or a different conjunction or *None*. In contrast, in the gap preceding *instead*, the choice made by participants varied from passage to passage: For instance, they reliably inserted *but* in Ex. 3 and *so* in Ex. 4, even though the original text contained no conjunction.

The data that Jiang collected suggested that the answer to both of her questions was **no**, but stopped there. One reason is that the response *None* was ambiguous: Participants could have used it to mean "I can't insert any of these conjunctions to express the sense I get", or "The sense I get cannot be expressed with a conjunction", or "I don't get any additional sense". Secondly, in using only brevity and clarity as her criteria for selecting passages from COCA, Jiang did not assess whether all the conjunction-less passages she selected might have been similar in terms of how their clauses/sentences related and hence would all draw the same response from participants. Finally, Jiang only considered four adverbs, so could not draw more general conclusions. The current, much larger enterprise attempts to avoid these problems.

[2] All passages were taken from the Corpus of Contemporary American English (COCA) `corpus.byu.edu/coca/`.

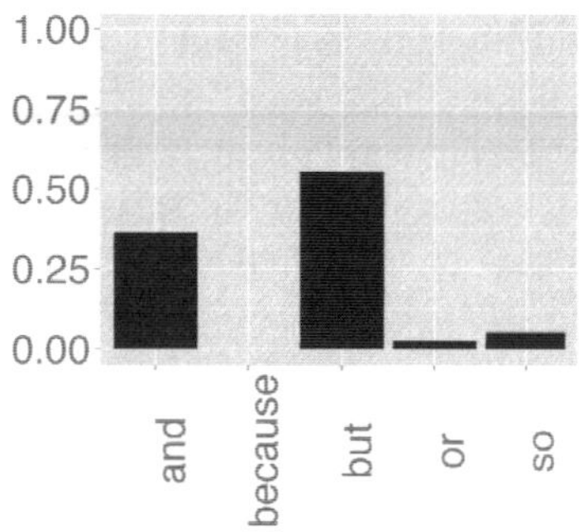

Figure 1: The distribution of ⟨conjunction⟩ immediately preceding *instead* tokens in Google NGRAMS, with or without a comma after the conjunction, excluding cases where *instead* was followed by *of*.

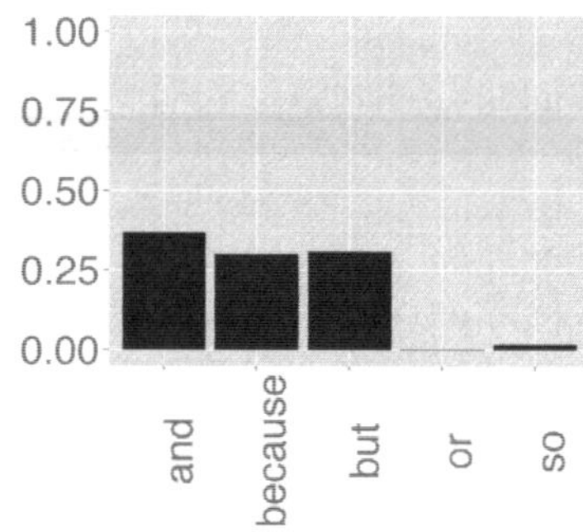

Figure 2: The distribution of ⟨conjunction⟩ immediately preceding *after all* tokens in Google NGRAMS.

3 Task Definition

We have embarked on a large-scale study of discourse adverbials, attempting to gather evidence that will help answer two specific questions:

1. Given an explicit discourse adverbial in a passage, what discourse relation(s) do naive subjects take to be operative?

2. Can the relation(s) be predicted on the basis of the explicit adverbial alone, or does it depend on the arguments to the relation or on everything in the passage?

Note that the discourse relations that subjects take to be operative may corroborate the sense conveyed by the discourse adverbial or they may be distinct.

In this paper we describe Phase I of the study, carried out between August 2014 and June 2015. We began with a survey of Google NGRAMs to first establish the overall frequency and preferred conjunction(s) of a wide range of adverbials. In the long term, our study aims to examine both common and rarer adverbials (see Section 7) and those with a single preferred co-occurring conjunction and those with a flatter distribution. As Figures 1 and 2 show, the distribution of conjunctions is neither uniform for a given adverbial nor equivalent across adverbials. Since all four adverbials (*after all*, *instead*, *in general* and *in fact*) used in (Jiang, 2013) had different distributions, we decided to target the same adverbials in our Phase I study.

Also following (Jiang, 2013), we wanted to see whether subjects responded differently to passages in which the author explicitly used a pair of connectives (i.e. ⟨conjunction⟩–⟨adverbial⟩) compared with those in which the author only used an explict adverbial. The former we call *explicit passages* and the latter, *implicit passages*.

4 Phase I Experiment

Each participant in Phase 1 saw 50 passages, each containing a gap between two spans of text, the second beginning with a discourse adverbial, as in Ex. 3–4. With *expicit passages*, we replaced the conjunction with a gap, while with *implicit passages*, we inserted a gap before the adverbial. For each passage, participants were instructed to fill in the gap with the word of their choice (from a randomly ordered list of the six conjunctions *and*, *because*, *before*, *but*, *or*, *so*) that "best reflects the **meaning** of the connection" between the spans. They also had the option of choosing either *None at all* (for cases where they felt that no conjunction was possible) or *Other word or phrase* (for cases where they felt that only some option other than the six presented conjunctions was appropriate). These were intended to correct for the ambiguity of *None* in Jiang's study.

At a coarse sense level, all six conjunctions are relatively unambiguous: Table 1 shows the frequency of their main sense in the Penn Discourse TreeBank (The PDTB Research Group, 2008). As such, there are grounds for believing that the experiment targeted the participants' inferred relation through choosing a conjunction that realizes it, even if the sense is only a coarse one.

	# tokens	sense label	overall %
and	3000	CONJUNCTION	91.0%
because	858	REASON	99.5%
before	326	PRECEDENCE	99.0%
but	3308	COMPARISON[3]	90.7%
or	98	ALTERNATIVE	86.7%
so	263	RESULT	99.6%

Table 1: Proportion of explicit tokens of each conjunction having its most frequent sense label

4.1 Interface

Working with a group of researchers and a pilot group of participants, we iteratively designed and evaluated an interface and a set of instructions aimed at encouraging participants to choose a conjunction that identified the sense of the connection between the two spans of text in a passage — the span before the gap and the span following it. Instructions for the task could be reviewed when necessary by clicking on a button labelled "Show Instructions", to the right of the heading "Trial" (Figure 3).

During pilot testing, it emerged that participants sometimes chose *None at all* when it sounded more fluent and less awkward to them than did an explicit conjunction. In order to avoid this, we explicitly instructed participants to choose the conjunction that best conveyed the sense of the connection, "even if the resulting text sounds awkward", but also offered them the opportunity to record whether they would in fact use the chosen conjunction, or whether it sounded odd to them in that context (Figure 4).

To avoid order effects, the stimuli were pseudo-randomised for each participant such that each participant only saw each excerpt once, they never encountered more than three of the same adverbial in a row, and for explicit passages, they never saw excerpts expecting the same conjunction more than three times in a row. In addition, the list of conjunctions appeared in a different order for each participant, to avoid the risk of skewing the results, should participants prefer conjunctions presented at the top of the list.

After a participant had read the instructions, three practice items were presented.

4.2 Stimuli

Of the 50 passages used in Phase 1, 38 replicated those previously used in (Jiang, 2013). Of the remaining twelve, eight came from a large set of possible stimuli we collected from the New York Times Annotated Corpus (NYTAC) (Sandhaus, 2008) for use in later phases of the experiment, while four were "catch trials", intended to ensure participants were paying attention. Table 2 shows the number of *explicit passages* for each of the four adverbials (where the explicit conjunction before the adverbial was deleted, leaving a gap) and *implicit passages* (where a gap was simply inserted before the adverbial).

	explicit	implicit
after all	7	5
in fact	7	4
in general	7	5
instead	6	5

Table 2: Explicit/implicit passages per adverbial

The 38 excerpts from Jiang were chosen based on the responses they had received during her study. For example, for the *instead* implicits, two showed a range of responses, one showed participant agreement on *but*, one showed agreement on *because*, and one showed agreement on *so*. The eight new stimuli from NYTAC (two per adverbial) were longer and more complex than those used in (Jiang, 2013). The purpose of these stimuli, besides providing more data, was to identify participants who were discouraged or confused by these passages, since later phases of the experiment would use stimuli drawn only from NYTAC.

4.3 Participants

Seventy participants, all with addresses in the United States, completed the trial through Amazon Mechanical Turk. Demographic data collected in a short questionnaire before the main trial showed that participants were aged 20-67 (mean 37), 71% read newspapers at least twice a week, and half were female. All were English speakers. Each participant was paid $8 for their contribution.

5 Phase 1 Results

All participants paid attention to the task, as indicated by their selection of sensible responses for the four catch trials, while they varied in how long the task took them and how often they agreed with the choices made by other participants. As we required fewer participants to complete Phase 2 of the task, we reduced the participant number based on their performance in Phase 1. Specifically, we removed data from 12 participants with very short completion rates and high rates of disagreement

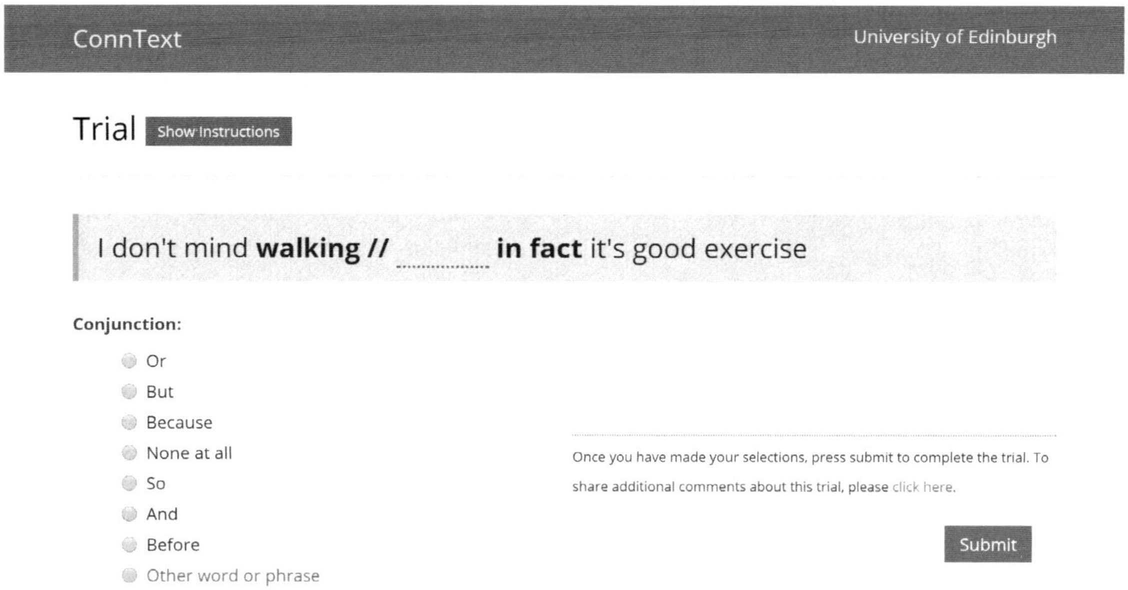

Figure 3: Screen shot of passage presentation

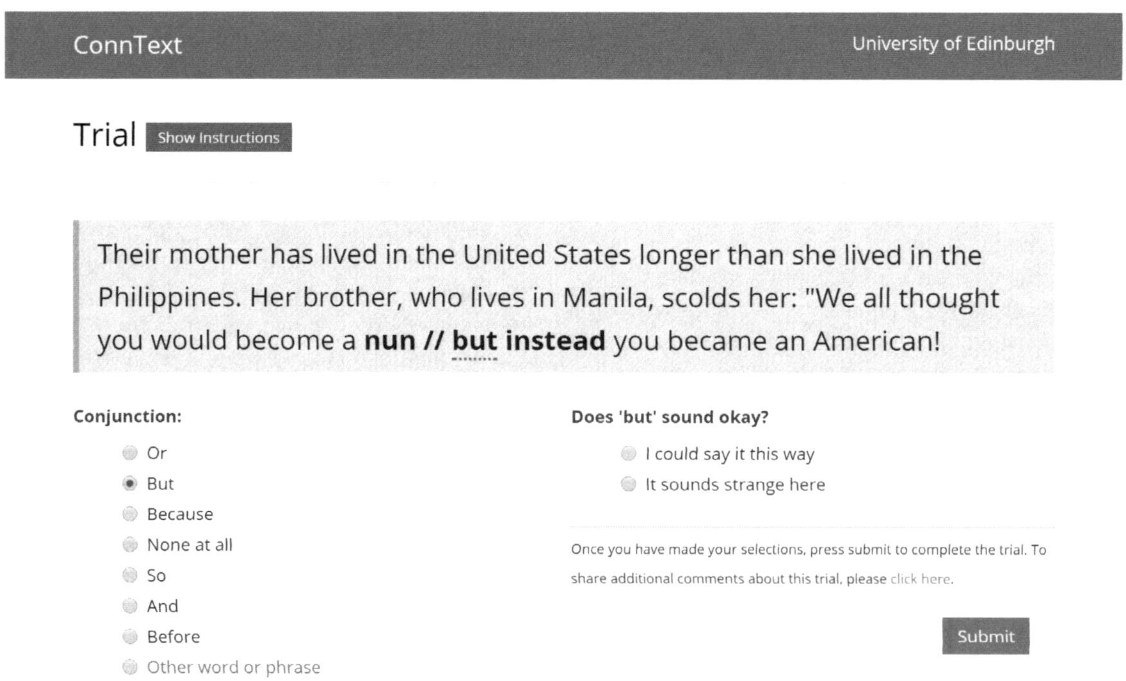

Figure 4: Screen shot of a participant being asked to indicate whether or not their choice of a conjunction that fits with respect to its sense — in this case, "but" — sounds natural

with other participants, as well as 3 trials in which a participant selected the response *before*, which was intended for use in only the catch trials. The resulting dataset of responses from 58 participants comprises 2665 judgments over the 46 target passages (ignoring the four catch trials). The results reported below are raw counts, and do not yet take account of potential participant bias (Passonneau and Carpenter, 2014).

Considering the dataset as a whole, we can ask how often a participant's response matched the author's original choice. (Note that this can only be assessed on *explicit passages* – that is, ones where the author expicitly used a pair of co-occurring connectives, cf. Section 3). Table 3 shows the pattern of participant responses for passages for which the authors themselves had included an explicit conjunction before the adverbial. Recall that participants always saw a gap before the discourse adverbial, regardless of the author's original choice to use or not use a conjunction, meaning the explicit and implicit passages were indistinguishable.

	AND	BECAUSE	BUT	OR	SO
and	189	14	81	5	33
because	60	105	60	2	9
but	68	48	497	7	9
or	2	0	2	35	0
so	125	1	25	2	56
other	3	1	8	2	0
none at all	17	4	23	5	9

Table 3: Confusion matrix for explicit passages. Rows show participant responses (participants' selected conjunctions in lower case) for passages whose authors had used the explicit conjunctions in the columns (in CAPS).

The values on the diagonal in Table 3 show a high degree of convergence between participant and author choices: The largest value for any column and any row is the value indicating participant$\sim$author agreement. A conjunction like *and* notoriously underspecifies the relation sense since it is compatible with many senses. The results in Table 3 allow us to ask what more specific senses participants infer in cases in which the original author used *and*. Although participants overall favor 'and' for author 'AND' (189 instances out of 464 'AND' trials), they also show a preference for the inference of causality with their selection of *so* (125 instances out of the 464 'AND' trials).

Table 4 shows the pattern of responses for passages in which the author did not include a conjunction. In only a small number of cases (69 instances out of 1158 'NONE' trials) did a participant choose *None at all*. Therefore, in answer to question (1) from Section 3, participants are able to reliably select an explicit conjunction that realizes the relation(s) they take to be operative. The next section considers participants' behavior for each of the 4 adverbials in turn.

	author=NONE
and	275
because	404
but	252
or	1
so	147
other	10
none	69

Table 4: Response distribution (implicit passages)

5.1 Variation across adverbials for explicit passages

To address the second question raised in Section 3, we analyzed participant responses to each adverbial. Tables 5-7 show the responses for *after all*, *in fact*, *in general* and *instead* respectively, when the original author included an explicit conjunction.

	AND	BECAUSE	BUT
and	18	6	30
because	9	51	51
but	25	0	128
or	0	0	0
so	0	0	3
other	1	0	3
none	5	1	17

Table 5: Explicit *after all* response distribution. Participant responses in lower case, versus author choice in CAPS. (Six explicit *after all* passages — 1 AND, 1 BECAUSE, 4 BUT)

For *after all* (Table 5), participants assigned a meaning of *because* not only for author BECAUSE but frequently for author BUT and AND. This is particularly odd for BECAUSE and BUT, since however underspecified one might take these two conjunctions to be, the senses they convey are still different. This suggests that the adverbial itself may be biasing the inferred relation.

For *in fact* (Table 6), the responses track the authors with two notable exceptions. First, the responses show that author BUT and author SO passages are frequently labelled by participants with

	AND	BECAUSE	BUT	OR	SO
and	53	8	27	5	29
because	1	54	4	2	1
but	1	48	74	7	6
or	0	0	0	35	0
so	0	1	4	2	15
other	0	1	5	2	0
none	3	3	2	5	7

Table 6: Explicit *in fact* response distribution. Participant responses in lower case versus author choice in CAPS. (Seven explicit *in fact* passages — 1 AND, 2 BECAUSE, 2 BUT, 1 OR, 1 SO)

the less specific conjunction *and*. This may reflect the fact that the conjunction that most frequently appears left-adjacent to *in fact* is *and*, according to our study of the Google NGRAM corpus (cf. Section 3). Second, cases of author BECAUSE are split closely between responses of *because* and *but*. The alternation between "because" and "but" responses is surprising (as already noted above), given that they are not typically understood to be synonyms or even hyponyms or hypernyms. Nor does this variation appear to simply reflect a scenario in which, of the two BECAUSE passages, one favored *because* while the other favored *but*: Rather, each BECAUSE passage (such as Ex. 5) received a mix of *because* and *but* responses.

(5) Americans' big-is-better mentality is a shame in the case of artichokes ________ in fact the small ones are much easier to clean, cook more quickly and can be purchased spontaneously because they don't take any more time than any other vegetables.

	AND	BUT	SO
and	102	23	4
because	50	4	8
but	36	85	3
or	2	0	0
so	33	1	41
other	2	0	0
none	7	3	2

Table 7: Explicit *in general* response distribution. Participant responses in lower case versus author choice in CAPS. (Seven *in general* passages — 4 AND, 2 BUT, 1 SO)

For *in general* (Table 7), the responses track the author, suggesting that the adverbial itself is not biasing the inferred relation, but that responses depend on properties of the adjacent clauses or the larger context.

	AND	BUT
and	16	1
because	0	1
but	6	210
or	0	2
so	92	17
other	0	0
none	2	1

Table 8: Explicit *instead* response distribution. Participant responses in lower case versus author choice in CAPS (Six *instead* passages — 4 AND, 2 BUT)[5]

Like the data for *in fact*, the data for *instead* (Table 8) highlight a link between *and* and *so*, but in the opposite direction. For *in fact*, author SO received many *and* responses, whereas for *instead*, it was the reverse: Author AND received many *so* responses. This is in keeping with the observation that *and* is underspecified but is compatible with, and often implicates, a temporal or causal relationship between the eventualities denoted by the adjacent clauses (Gazdar, 1979). With *in fact*, participants are selecting a less specific conjunction (*and*) rather than the more specific *but* or *so*, whereas for *instead*, they are selecting the more specific *so*. It is possible that this can be explained as a frequency-induced bias: Compared with *in fact*, our Google NGRAM estimates show *instead* to have proportionally more co-occurrences with *so*, potentially leading participants to posit "so instead" for passages whose author had used AND.

5.2 Variation across adverbials for implicit passages

As noted earlier, Jiang's (2013) study leaves open the question of how to interpret a *None* response from a participant: Does it mean the participant believed there was no relation to infer, or that none of the available conjunctions were appropriate, or that there was an inferred relation but the resulting passage simply sounded awkward? Our experiment was designed to eliminate this ambiguity. That is, *None* can be understood to convey "no relation to infer", given that participants could choose *Other* if they wanted to fill in an alternative conjunction or they could mark the meaning they inferred but then tag it as awkward with the "would not say" button. Note that in Jiang's study, 15.7% of the responses were *None*. In our study, the proportion was comparable, with 15.2% of responses being one of our variants of *None*, i.e.

None (7.7%), *Other* (1.0%) or marked as something the participant would not say (6.4% of responses).

Our data on implicit passages therefore provides a clearer picture of how frequently participants assign a conjunction even when the author had used no conjunction. The results in Table 9 show that no adverbial favors *None* in these cases: *after all* had only 26/348 judgments; *in fact*, only 20/231; *in general*, only 13/290, and *instead*, only 10/290.

	after all	in fact	in general	instead
and	50	87	118	20
because	245	35	86	38
but	16	83	50	103
or	1	0	0	0
so	4	3	21	119
other	5	3	2	0
none	26	20	13	10

Table 9: Response distribution for implicit passages by adverbial (20 unique passages: 6 "after all", 4 "in fact", 5 "in general", 5 "instead")

Table 9 also confirms some of the behavior observed in the responses to explicit passages. First, *after all* shows a preference for the response *because*, whereas *in fact*, *in general* and *instead* all show more variability. This variability suggests that participants are responding to the content of the conjoined arguments to identify the sense, rather than associating the adverbial with one preferred connective. According to our Google NGRAM estimates, *after all* differs from the other three adverbials insofar as *because* is one of its most frequent co-occurring conjunctions. In contrast, *in fact*, *in general* and *instead* rarely cooccur with *because*. So participant behavior may reflect their sensitivity to the affinity of *after all* for *because*.

Finally, we can check how consistent participants were in selecting their response to each implicit passage. For each passage, we identify the most frequent response and the proportion of participants who selected that response. For all passages, the most frequent response was neither *None* nor *Other*. Table 10 shows the mean agreement for each adverbial, collapsed across passages, revealing whether different adverbials demonstrate different degrees of inter-annotator consistency. Table 10 shows that the agreement rate for two adverbials (*after all* and *instead*) is higher than for the other two: *After all* consistently favored *because*, while *instead* showed more variability in inferred conjunctions but nevertheless had a similar agreement rate. So while the four adverbials have different degrees of overall interannotator consistency on *implicit passages*, none of them shows random selection over the five non-None/non-Other responses, which would yield an agreement rate of just over 0.2.

after all	in fact	in general	instead
0.706	0.581	0.503	0.717

Table 10: Participant agreement rates by adverbial

6 Discussion

We draw two conclusions from Phase 1 of our study: (1) It is possible for naive subjects to infer an implicit conjunction alongside an explicit discourse adverbial, even for passages in which the original author used only an explicit adverbial, and (2) subjects do so reliably and systematically, depending on the adverb. Our subjects had the option on each trial to decline to add a conjunction, but they did not. Rather, they endorsed meaning-bearing conjunctions and did so in a way that is not explainable from the adverbial alone. In other words, it is not the case that any of these four adverbials is uniformly associated with a single conjunction whose meaning is linked directly to that of the adverbial itself. That would not explain the fact that, across passages, different conjunctions were endorsed as plausible insertions for the same adverbial. What's more, the selection of a conjunction for a given passage shows a strong degree of consistency, particularly for *after all* and *instead*.

The second point is that discourse adverbials themselves are not indiscriminate with regard to the conjunction that they appear to favor. The analysis of *after all* showed that participants selected a causal interpretation (*because*) more often than would be expected based on the conjunction provided by the original author and with a bias that was more pronounced than in passages with any other adverbial. This highlights potential differences among adverbials (either individually or by class): Not all adverbials may be compatible with all conjunctions. Even where variation is permitted, the adverbial may bring its own preference to bear on the inference of an additional co-occuring relation. This point was made by Jiang (2013) as well, and our data are in keeping with the range of behavior she reports across these four adverbials. The new study goes beyond prior work by ensuring that participants who preferred to communicate that none of the available conjunctions should be inserted had recourse to three distinct responses: a stylistic rejection of the selected conjunction ("does it sound okay?"), an option to insert an alternative conjunction (*Other*), or simply the response *None at all* (to reject insertion of any explicit connective to link the two spans of text).

So how do participants identify the conjunction they insert into these passages? One hypothesis might be that the purported lexical semantics of the adverbial is what determines its co-occurrences with conjunctions. Under that account, *instead* might be expected to favor a conjunction that expresses contrast, i.e., *but*. The distribution of responses for explicit passages with *instead* shows that *but* was indeed the preferred response when the author chose to use *but*. However, when the author used *and*, participants favored *so*, which generally conveys RESULT. For implicit passages with *instead*, the response choice *but* was likewise frequent, but not as frequent as *so*. On the other hand, the results for *after all* do suggest that the inference of *because* is common when that adverbial is present. This pattern is there for the explicit passages, and is even more evident for the implicit passages (for which 245 of 348 responses were *because*). This finding could suggest that *after all* either conveys a single sense itself or is used frequently in contexts in which a REASON relation is operative. The other adverbials show no such preference, implying that it is properties of the clauses themselves and the rest of the discourse that allow a consistent meaning to be identified for each passage.

7 Future work

Building on the results of Phase 1, we have begun to run a larger Phase 2 study with twenty adverbials, using 976 excerpts. The 58 participants whose results are reported here for Phase 1, have been invited to complete further Amazon Turk hits. In the longer term, we hope to explore the other common case of non-adjacent co-occuring discourse connectives, as in

(6) They cut few trees in the summer, when they prefer to feed more on fresh grasses, tubers, and saplings, **but** autumn, **however**, is a period of intensive logging for beavers. (`hawriver.org/peaceful-coexistence-with-beavers`)

and to extend the research cross-linguistically.

Acknowledgments

This research has been supported by the Nuance Foundation. The authors would also like to acknowledge advice and support from researchers on the Penn Discourse TreeBank and helpful comments from our three anonymous reviewers.

References

M.J. Cuenca and M.J. Marin. 2009. Co-occurrence of discourse markers in Catalan and Spanish oral narrative. *Journal of Pragmatics*, 41(5):899–914.

Bruce Fraser. 2013. Combinations of contrastive discourse markers in english. *International Review of Pragmatics*, 5:318–340.

G. Gazdar. 1979. *Pragmatics: Implicature, Presupposition, and Logical Form*. Academic Press, London.

Xi Jiang. 2013. Predicting the use and interpretation of implicit and explicit discourse connectives. Master's thesis, Linguistics and English Language, University of Edinburgh. MSc in English Language.

Andrew Kehler. 2002. *Coherence, Reference, and the Theory of Grammar*. CSLI Publications, Stanford.

Alistair Knott. 1996. *A Data-driven Methodology for Motivating a Set of Coherence Relations*. Ph.D. thesis, Department of Artificial Intelligence, University of Edinburgh.

William C. Mann and Sandra A. Thompson. 1988. Rhetorical Structure Theory: Toward a functional theory of text organization. *Text*, 8(3):243–281.

Sarah Oates. 2000. Multiple discourse marker occurrence: Creating hierarchies for natural language generation. In *Proceedings, ANLP-NAACL 2000 Student Research Workshop*, pages 41–45, Seattle WA.

Rebecca Passonneau and Bob Carpenter. 2014. The benefits of a model of annotation. *Transactions of the Association of Computational Linguistics*, 2(1):311–326.

Rashmi Prasad, Nikhil Dinesh, Alan Lee, Eleni Miltsakaki, Livio Robaldo, Aravind Joshi, and Bonnie Webber. 2008. The Penn Discourse TreeBank 2.0. In *Proceedings, 6th International Conference on Language Resources and Evaluation*, pages 2961–2968, Marrakech, Morocco.

Rashmi Prasad, Bonnie Webber, and Aravind Joshi. 2014. Reflections on the penn discourse treebank, comparable corpora and complementary annotation. *Computational Linguistics*, 40(4):921–950.

Evan Sandhaus. 2008. New York Times corpus: Corpus overview. LDC catalogue entry LDC2008T19.

The PDTB Research Group. 2008. The Penn Discourse TreeBank 2.0 Annotation Manual. Available at http://www.seas.upenn.edu/˜pdtb/, or as part of the download of LDC2008T05.

Bonnie Webber, Alistair Knott, and Aravind Joshi. 1999. Multiple discourse connectives in a lexicalized grammar for discourse. In *Third International Workshop on Computational Semantics*, pages 309–325, Tilburg, The Netherlands.

Deniz Zeyrek. 2014. On the distribution of contrastive-concessive discourse connectives *ama* (but/yet) and *fakat* (but) in written Turkish. In P. Suihkonen and L.J. Whaley, editors, *On Diversity and Complexity of Languages Spoken in Europe and North and Central Asia*.

Semantics and Discourse Processing for Expressive TTS

Rodolfo Delmonte, Rocco Tripodi
Department of Linguistic Studies & Department of Computer Science
Ca' Foscari University of Venice
Email: delmont@unive.it

Abstract

In this paper we present ongoing work to produce an expressive TTS reader that can be used both in text and dialogue applications. The system has been previously used to read (English) poetry and it has now been extended to apply to short stories. The text is fully analyzed both at phonetic and phonological level, and at syntactic and semantic level. The core of the system is the Prosodic Manager which takes as input discourse structures and relations and uses this information to modify parameters for the TTS accordingly. The text is transformed into a poem-like structures, where each line corresponds to a Breath Group, semantically and syntactically consistent. Stanzas correspond to paragraph boundaries. Analogical parameters are related to ToBI theoretical indices but their number is doubled.

1 Introduction

In this paper we present ongoing work to produce an expressive TTS reader that can be used both in text and dialogue applications. The system has been previously used to read (English) poetry and we now decided to apply it to short stories. The text is fully analyzed both at phonetic and phonological level, and at syntactic and semantic level. In addition, the system has access to a restricted list of typical pragmatically marked phrases and expressions that are used to convey specific discourse function and speech acts and need specialized intonational contours.

Current TTS systems are dull and boring and characterized by a total lack of expressivity. They only take into account information coming from punctuation and in some cases, from tagging and syntactic constituency. Few expressive synthetic speech synthesizers are tuned to specific domains and are unable to generalize. They usually convey specific emotional content linked to a list of phrases or short utterances – see below. In particular, comma is a highly ambiguous punctuation mark with a whole set of different functions which are associated with specific intonational contours. In general, question and exclamative marks are used to modify the prosody of the previous word. We use the word "expressivity" in a specific general manner which includes sensible and sensitive reading that can only be achieved once a complete syntactic and semantic analysis has been provided to the TTS prosodic manager.

From a general point of view, the scientific problem can be framed inside the need to develop models that are predictive for a speech synthesizer to be able to sound natural and expressive, getting as close as possible to human-like performance. This can only be achieved manipulating prosody so that the text read aloud sounds fully natural, informative and engaging or convincing. However, in order to achieve something closer to that, text understanding should be attained or some similar higher level semantic computation. As Xu(2011) puts it, " It will probably be a long time before anything close to that is developed, of course"(ibid:94). Similar skeptical or totally negative opinions are expressed by Marc Huckvale (2002), when summarizing work he and his group have been carrying out for a long period over the project for an articulatory TTS called ProSynth. The goal of speech synthesis, in his perspective would be that of "understanding how humans talk" rather than the one of replicating a human talker (ibid. 1261).

Linguistically based work on emotions has been documented by the group working at Loquendo (now acquired by Nuance). They report their approach based on the selection of Expression which is related to a small inventory of what they call "speech acts" which coincide partly with dialogue, conversational and argumentative categories (Zovato et al. 2008; see also Campbell, 2002; Hamza et al. 2004). They implemented the acoustic counterpart of a limited, but rich, set of such categories, including: refuse, approval/ disapproval, recall in proximity, announce, request of information, request of confirmation, request of action/ behaviour, prohibition, contrast, disbelief, surprise/astonishment, regret, thanks, greetings, apologies, and compliments. In total, they

Proceedings of the EMNLP 2015 Workshop on Linking Models of Lexical, Sentential and Discourse-level Semantics, pages 32–43,
Lisboa, Portugal, 18 September 2015.

managed to label and model accordingly some 500 different (expressive) utterances that can be used domain and context independently.

Work related to what we are trying to do is to be found in the field of storytelling and in experiments by the group from Columbia University working at MAGIC a system for the generation of medical reports. Montaño et al. [1] present an analysis of storytelling discourse modes and narrative situations, highlighting the great variability of speech modes characterized by changes in rhythm, pause lengths, variation of pitch and intensity and adding emotion to the voice in specific situations.

However, the approach most closely related to ours is the one by the group of researchers from Columbia University, where we can find Julia Hirschberg and Kathy McKeown. In the paper by S.Pan,K.McKeown & J.Hirschberg they highlight the main objectives of their current work, as "Prosody modeling" which is the task of "associating variations of prosodic features with changes in structure, meaning, intent and context of the language spoken." This requires "identifying correlations between this information and prosodic parameters through data exploration, and using learning algorithms to build prosody models from these data."(ibid. 1419) In fact, their attempt at using machine learning for prosody modeling has been only partially achieved. In their work on the concept-to-speech manager "the content planner uses a presentation strategy to determine and order content. It represents discourse structure, which is a hierarchical topic structure in MAGIC, discourse relations, which can be rhetorical relations, and discourse status, which represents whether a discourse entity is given, new or inferable and whether the entity is in contrast with another discourse entity."(ibid. 1420) As the authors affirm further on, the discourse level is where prosody is mostly affected. They then report previous work on discourse structure which can affect pitch range, pause and speaking rate by Grosz & Hirschberg, 1992; given/new/inferable information can affect pitch-accent placement by Hirschberg 1993; a shift in discourse focus can affect pitch-accent assignment (in Nakatani 1998); and contrastive entities can bear a special pitch accent (Prevost 1995). Further work towards predicting prosodic structure was published by Bachenko & Fitzpatrick, 1990, Delmonte & Dolci, 1991, and Wang & Hirschberg, 1992.

The objective of their experiment was modeling ToBI prosody features, i.e. pitch accents, phrase accents, boundary tones and break indices. Given the fact that there are six pitch-accent classes, five break-index classes, three phrase-accent classes, and three boundary-tone classes, they come up with a total of 17 different features organized in four separate classes. The experiment was carried out on a corpus of spontaneous speech with some 500 dialogues on medical issues, which ended up by being reduced to 250 annotated dialogues. In fact the features they managed to annotate are just surface syntactic and semantic ones[1].

The most disappointing fact was that they attempted to carry out a complete annotation but didn't succeed. In the paper they report their annotation efforts on the spontaneous-speech corpus which was automatically annotated with POS information, syntactic constituent boundaries, syntactic functions, and lexical repetitions, using approximations provided by POS taggers and parsers. It was also manually labelled with given/new/inferable information. But when it comes to semantic and discourse level information they say that they "are still working on manually labelling discourse structure, discourse relations, and semantic abnormality... We are currently annotating the speech corpus with features closely related to meaning and discourse."(ibid. 1426)

No further publication reports experiments with the complete annotation. And this is clearly due to difficulties inherent in the task. Now, this is what our system allows us to do, i.e. using discourse structure and relation to instruct the prosody manager to introduce the appropriate variation of prosodic parameters. According to ToBI features, this implies the ability to achieve: juncture placing prediction; phrase boundary tone prediction; prominence prediction; intonational contour movement prediction. To be more specific, given an input text the "Ideal

---

[1] and they are: (1) ID: the ID of a feature vector; (2) Lex: the word itself; (3) Concept: the semantic category of a content word; (4) SynFunc: the syntactic function of a word; (5) SemBoundary: the type of semantic constituent boundary after a word; (6) SemLength: the length, in number of words, of the semantic constituent associated with the current SemBoundary; (7) POS: the part-of-speech of a word; (8) IC: the semantic informativeness of a word(???), where in particular, the latter is – in our opinion – wrongly computed as a "semantic feature", being constitute by the logarithm of the relative frequency of a term in the corpus.

System" will read it aloud using naturally sounding prosody, where: phrasing is fully semantically consistent; intonation varies according to structural properties of clauses in discourse and speaker intention; prominence is assigned on the basis of novelty of topics and related events. In addition, expressivity conveys variations of attitude and mood as they are derived from deep subjective and affective analysis.

Our reformulation of ToBI (see Silverman et al. 1992) features from general/generic into concrete and implemented analogical parameters for natural and expressive TTS will be shown in a section at the end of the paper. The correspondence between prosodic features and linguistic representation is the issue to cope with and will be presented here.

Lieske et al.(1997) and Bos & Rupp(1998) documented their work on the generation system produced by the research project **Verb***mobil*. In particular the Verbmobil Interface Term which had responsibility for the interaction between different linguistic modules, including a TTS and an ASR modules. These linguistic modules included a SynSem component, i.e. a syntactic, a semantic and discourse component, which was meant to drive the generation of appropriate utterance with the appropriate prosody. The prosody component of Verbmobil is related to semantics and can influence segmentation, sentence mood and focus. The ad-hoc formalism they created allowed the parser to take into account prosodic information already from the start. However, the Verbmobil system did not allow to communicate stress patterns to the TTS. Here we are dealing with a much simpler effort which also has semantics and other discourse level information available from the generator. On the contrary, SPARSAR is a system that can be used with any English text or poem and has to derive its information directly from the words.

2 Semantic Representation for TTS

Systems that can produce an appropriate semantic representation for a TTS are not many at an international level but they can be traced from the results of a Shared Task organized by members of SigSem and are listed here below in the corresponding webpage http://www.sigsem.org/w/index.php?title=STEP_2008_shared_task:_comparing_semantic_representations (see Bos & Delmonte, 2008).

State of the art semantic systems are based on different theories and representations, but the final aim of the workshop was reaching a consensus on what constituted a reasonably complete semantic representation. Semantics in our case not only refers to predicate-argument structure, negation scope, quantified structures, anaphora resolution and other similar items, it refers essentially to a propositional level analysis. Propositional level semantic representation is the basis for discourse structure and discourse semantics contained in discourse relations. It also paves the way for a deep sentiment or affective analysis of every utterance, which alone can take into account the various contributions that may come from syntactic structures like NPs and APs where affectively marked words may be contained. Their contribution needs to be computed in a strictly compositional manner with respect to the meaning associated to the main verb, where negation may be lexically expressed or simply lexically incorporated in the verb meaning itself.

In Fig. 1 we show the architecture of our deep system for semantic and pragmatic processing, in which phonetics, prosodics and NLP are deeply interwoven.

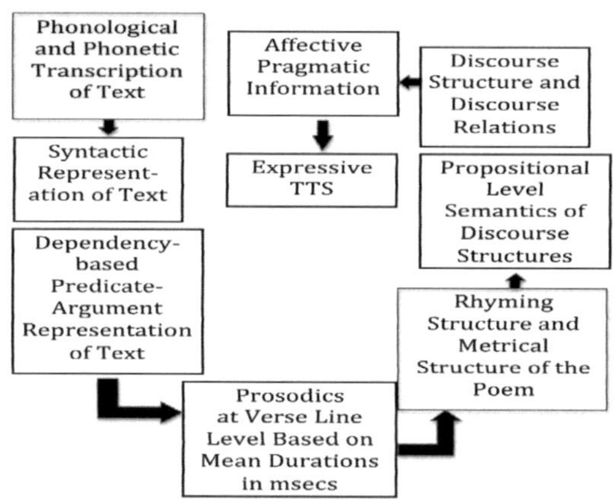

Figure 1. System Architecture Modules for SPARSAR

The system is based on VENSES a shallow version of GETARUNS. All these versions have been extensively tested and results published in a number of international publications and collected in two books (Delmonte 2007;2009)[1].

[1] In more detail here: Parser evaluation has been documented in Delmonte(2002;2004); Anaphora Resolution in Delmonte(2002a), Delmonte et al.(2006a), Delmonte & Tonelli(2006); Discourse Relations in

The current system may take any English text and produce an output to be used for TTS. All components of the system have undergone evaluation in particular discourse level analysis has been shown to be particularly effective (see Delmonte, 2007). The system does low level analyses before semantic modules are activated, that is tokenization, sentence splitting, multiword creation from a large lexical database. Then chunking and syntactic constituency parsing which is done using a rule-based recursive transition network. The parser works in a cascaded recursive way to include always higher syntactic structures up to sentence and complex sentence level. These structures are then passed to the first semantic mapping algorithm that looks for subcategorization frames in the lexica made available for English, including VerbNet, FrameNet, WordNet and a proprietor lexicon with most frequent verbs, adjectives and nouns, containing also a detailed classification of all grammatical or function words. This mapping is done following LFG principles, where c-structure is turned into f-structure obeying uniqueness, completeness and coherence grammatical principles. The output of this mapping is a rich dependency structure, which contains information related also to implicit arguments, i.e. subjects of infinitivals, participials and gerundives. It also has a semantic role associated to each grammatical function, that is used to identify the syntactic head lemma uniquely in the sentence. Finally it takes care of long distance dependencies for relative and interrogative clauses.

Now that fully coherent and complete predicate argument structures have been built, pronominal binding and anaphora resolution algorithms can be fired. Also coreferential processed are activated at the semantic level: they include a centering algorithm for topic instantiation and memorization that we do using a three-place stack containing a Main Topic, a Secondary Topic and an Potential Topic. In order to become a Main Topic, a Potential Topic must be reiterated and become persistent in the text.

Discourse Level computation is done at propositional level by building a vector of features associated to the main verb complex of each clause. They include information about tense, aspect, negation, adverbial modifiers, modality. These features are then filtered through a set of rules which have the task to classify a proposition as either objective/subjective, factual/nonfactual, foreground/background. In addition, every lexical predicate is evaluated with respect to a class of discourse relations. Eventually, discourse structure is built, according to criteria of clause dependency in which a clause can be classified either as coordinate or subordinate. As a result, we have a set of four different moves to associate to each clause: root, down, level, up. We report here below semantic and discourse structures related to the poem by Sylvia Plath "Edge" which you can find here, http://www.poetryfoundation.org/poem/178970.

PROPOSITIONAL SEMANTICS

Clause No.	Funct/ Role	View	Factivity	Change	Relevance	Aspect	Pred	Tense	Disc_ Rel_	Subject_
39,	main/prop,	external,	factive,	null,	background,	activity,	crackle,	pres,	narration,	objective
38,	main/prop,	external,	factive,	null,	background,	activity,	drag,	pres,	narration,	objective
31,	main/prop,	external,	factive,	culmintd,	foregrnd,	activity,	use,	perf,	cause,	objective
25,	xcomp/prop,	internal,	factive,	null,	background,	activity,	moon,	pres,	narration,	objective
24,	main/prop,	external,	factive,	null,	background,	activity,	have,	pres,	narration,	objective
23,	main/prop,	external,	factive,	culmintd,	foregrnd,	activity,	stare,	past,	result,	objective
18,	main/prop,	external,	factive,	culmintd,	foregrnd,	activity,	bleed,	past,	narration,	objective
17,	main/prop,	external,	factive,	null,	background,	activity,	fold,	perf,	narration,	objective
16,	adj/temp_coinc,	external,	factive,	null,	background,	activity,	stiffen,	pres,	narration,	objective
11,	main/prop,	internal,	factive,	null,	background,	activity,	it,	pres,	narration,	objective
10,	main/prop,	external,	factive,	culmintd,	foregrnd,	activity,	come,	perf,	result,	objective
7,	main/prop,	external,	factive,	null,	background,	activity,	flow,	pres,	result,	objective
6,	main/prop,	external,	factive,	culmintd,	foregrnd,	activity,	perfect,	perf,	result,	objective
5,	main/prop,	external,	factive,	culmintd,	foregrnd,	activity,	say,	past,	narration,	objective
4,	main/prop,	external,	factive,	null,	background,	activity,	seem,	pres,	narration,	objective
3,	main/prop,	external,	factive,	null,	background,	activity,	wear,	pres,	narration,	objective
1,	xcomp/prop,	internal,	factive,	null,	background,	state,	edge,	nil,	setting,	objective

Figure 2. Propositional semantics for Edge

In Fig.2, clauses governed by a copulative verb like BE report the content of the predication to the subject. The feature CHANGE can either be set to NULL, GRADED or CULMINATED: in this case Graded is not used seen that there no progressive or overlapping events.

In the representation of Figure.3, we see topics of discourse as they have been computed by the coreference algorithm, using semantic indices characterized by identifiers starting with ID. Every topic is associated to a label coming from the centering algorithm: in particular, WOMAN which is assigned ID id2 reappears as MAIN topic in clauses marked by no. 15. Also BODY reappears with id7. Every topic is associated to

---

Delmonte et al.(2007a;2007b); Recognizing Textual Entailment evaluations in Delmonte et al.(2005), Delmonte et al.(2006b), Delmonte, Bristot, Piccolino, Tonelli, (2007), Delmonte et al.(2009); Implicit Entities and Events in Delmonte & Pianta(2009), Delmonte(2009a;b;c), Delmonte & Tonelli(2010); Tonelli & Delmonte(2011); Delmonte(2013)

morphological features, semantic inherent features and a semantic role.

DISCOURSE SEMANTICS

Topic Type	Clause No.	Pred	Semant_ Id_	M-Feats Per,Gen,Num	Semantic Inherent Feats	Semantic Role
main,	1,	edge,	id1,	[3, neu, sing,	[abstrct, legal, nquant, objct],	theme_bound]
poten,	3,	illusion,	id2,	[3, nil, nil,	[abstrct, inform, danger],	theme_bound]
poten,	3,	scroll,	id3,	[3, mas, sing,	[abstrct, tecno],	goal]
poten,	3,	foot,	id4,	[3, nil, nil,	[animat, body_part, objct],	theme_bound]
poten,	3,	smile,	id5,	[3, mas, sing,	[activ, inform],	goal]
poten,	3,	toga,	id6,	[3, nil, nil,	[body_part, objct],	theme_bound]
poten,	3,	dead_body,	id7,	[3, mas, sing,	[objct, hum],	goal]
poten,	3,	necessity,	id8,	[3, nil, nil,	[place, inform, state],	theme_bound]
poten,	3,	accomplishment,	id10,	[3, mas, sing,	[abstrct, chang,state],	goal]
main,	3,	woman,	id2,	[3, fem, sing,	[any, relat, social, hum],	theme]
second,	15,	garden,	id11,	[3, neu, plur,	[instit, objct, instrum],	agent]
poten,	15,	child,	id12,	[3, neu, sing,	[any, activ, body_part, objct, relat, social, instrum, hum],	actor]
poten,	15,	serpent,	id13,	[3, neu, sing,	[animt, objct, instrum],	theme]
poten,	15,	throat,	id14,	[3, neu, plur,	[body_part, objct, instrum, hum],	loc_origin]
poten,	15,	stiffen,	id16,	[3, neu, plur,	[instit],	goal]
poten,	15,	body,	id7,	[3, neu, sing,	[abstrct, activ, body_part, inform, instit, place, objct, instrum, hum],	loc_direct]
poten,	15,	pitcher,	id15,	[3, mas, sing,	[activ, inform, nquant, objct, relat, social, instrum, hum],	specif]
poten,	15,	milk,	id17,	[3, neu, sing,	[body_part, edible, objct, hum],	specif]
poten,	15,	petal,	id18,	[3, neu, plur,	[plant],	agent]
poten,	15,	flower,	id19,	[3, neu, sing,	[plant, time],	theme]
poten,	15,	night,	id20,	[3, neu, sing,	[state, time],	specif]
main,	21,	hood,	id21,	[3, mas, sing,	[objct, instrum, hum],	loc_origin]
poten,	21,	moon,	id22,	[3, neu, sing,	[event, place, objct, time],	experiencer]
poten,	29,	sort_of,	id23,	[3, nil, nil,	[abstrct, activ, inform, relat, social, state, tecno, hum],	attr]

Figure 3. Discourse level Semantics for Topic Hierarchy

Eventually, the final computation concerning Discourse Structure is this one:

DISCOURSE SEMANTICS

Sent_ No.	Clause No.	Subject_	Disc_ Rel_	Tense	Pred	Relevance	Disc_ Move	Disc_Struct_ Attach_Node
edge_7,	39,	objective,	narration,	pres,	crackle,	background,	level,	down(31-39)).
edge_7,	38,	objective,	narration,	pres,	drag,	background,	level,	down(31-39)).
edge_6,	31,	objective,	cause,	perf,	use,	foreground,	up,	to(1-31)).
edge_5,	25,	objective,	narration,	pres,	moon,	background,	level,	down(18-25)).
edge_5,	24,	objective,	narration,	pres,	have,	background,	level,	down(18-24)).
edge_5,	23,	objective,	narration,	pres,	stare,	foreground,	down,	down(18-23)).
edge_4,	18,	objective,	narration,	past,	bleed,	foreground,	up,	to(1-18)).
edge_4,	17,	objective,	narration,	perf,	fold,	background,	level,	level(11-17)).
edge_4,	15,	objective,	circumstance,	pres,	stiffen,	background,	level,	level(11-16)).
edge_3,	11,	objective,	narration,	pres,	it,	background,	level,	level(7-11)).
edge_3,	10,	objective,	narration,	pres,	come,	foreground,	level,	level(7-10)).
edge_2,	7,	objective,	result,	pres,	flow,	background,	down,	down(1-7)).
edge_2,	5,	objective,	narration,	past,	say,	foreground,	up,	to(1-5)).
edge_2,	4,	objective,	narration,	pres,	seem,	background,	level,	level(1-4)).
edge_2,	3,	objective,	narration,	pres,	wear,	background,	level,	level(1-3)).
edge_2,	6,	objective,	narration,	perf,	perfect,	foreground,	down,	down(1-6)).
edge_1,	1,	objective,	setting,	nil,	edge,	background,	up,	down(nil-1)).

Figure 4. Discourse Semantics for Discourse Structures

Movements in the intonational contours are predicted to take place when FOREGROUND and UP moves are present in the features associated to each clause.

2.1 From Poetry to Story Reading

We referred to a poem in the previous section because in fact we will be using rules associated to poetry prosodic mapping in our work on story reading. We assume that reading a story aloud requires the reader to organize pauses in such a way that expressivity and meaning is preserved. This process is usually referred to as Breath Group organization. Since a breath group is a well-formed group of words conveying a concept or a meaning we decided to compare it to a line in a poem. Poems are organized into lines and stanzas, while stories usually have punctuation to mark main concepts and introduce pauses. Punctuation however is not sufficient in itself and does not always guarantee meaning coherence. In particular, Commas are highly ambiguous and may be used for a whole set of different functions in discourse. So eventually what we can actually trust are Breath Groups. Continuing our comparison with poems, lines may be end-stopped or enjambed when they run on the following line or stanza. The same may happen with Breath Groups, they may be end-stopped or enjambed and require a different prosodic setup.

We will then define Breath Groups as syntactically and semantically coherent units coinciding with an Intonation Phrase in ToBI terms: IPs are characterized by different tones, possible boundary tones and break indices. On the contrary, pitch Accents are associated to word stresses which are present in our phonetic representation: except that only syntactic heads are associated with Pitch Accents, dependents are demoted.

2.2 Implementing the Rules for Expressive TTS

Let's now look at one example, a short story by Aesop, "Bellying the Cat" that can be found here, http://www.taleswithmorals.com/aesop-fable-belling-the-cat.htm. At first we show the decomposition of the story into Breath Groups and then the mapping done by the Prosodic Manager.

long_ago ß
the mice had a general council ß
to consider what measures they could take ß
to outwit their common enemy ß
the cat ß
some said this ß
and some said that ß
but at_last a young mouse got_up ß
and said he had a proposal ß
to make ß
which he thought would meet the case ßß
you will all agree ß
said he ß
that our chief danger consists in the sly ß
and treacherous manner ß
in which the enemy approaches us ßß
now ß

if we could receive some signal of her approach ß
we could easily escape from her ß
i venture ß
therefore ß
to propose that a small bell be procured ß
and attached by a ribbon round the neck of the cat ß
by_this_means ß
we should always know when she was about ß
and could easily retire ß
while she was in the neighborhood ßß
this proposal met with general applause ß
until an old mouse got_up ß
and said ßß
that is all very_well ß
but who is to bell the cat ßß
the mice looked at one_another ß
and nobody spoke ß
then the old mouse said ßß
it is easy ß
to propose impossible remedies ßß

Table 1. Decomposition of the text into Breath Groups

2.3 Breath Group Creation Rules

A first set of the rules to map the story into this structures are reported below. The rules are organized into two separate sets: low level and high level rules. Here are low level ones:

- Follow punctuation first, but check constituent length; look for Coordinate Structures;
- look for Subordinate Clauses;
- look for Infinitival Complements;
- look for Complement Clauses; look for Relative Clauses;
- look for Subject and VerbPhrase juncture;
- look for AdverbialPhrase but only when beginning of Clause;
- look for Obligatory complements followed by adjuncts - with long constituents (Constituent length is at first checked in no. of words but also by phonetic length in no. of phones and their average duration in msec).

The high level corresponds to the recursive level. Recursive rules are associated with complex sentences and with Coordinate, Subordinate and Complement clauses. In Appendix 1 we show the mapping into Analogical phonetic acoustic correlates of pitch, speaking rate and intensity, and pauses for the text above. They can be copy/pasted into a TextEdit file and spoken aloud by Apple TTS.

3 The Prosodic Manager or ToBI features re-implemented

We will now discuss the use of Pierrehumbert's inventory of Tones and Break Indices, in relation to its actual application in real texts reading. We shall start from Break Indices which amount to 5, starting from 0 to 4 included. We assume that BI 0 is in a sense very special and peculiar and covers an aspect of prosody which has no general and practical application. As for BI 2 we will use label it to cover one of the phenomena indicated in the manual, that the idea to indicate a stronger sense of disjuncture than 1, for careful deliberation (see manual online).

So we come up with two types of BIs: those that are simple pauses, and those that also induce an intonation curve reset. BI 3 and 4 are intonationally related and regard phrase and sentence level prosody. BI 1 and B 2 are to be regarded as pertaining to word level and to possible internal constituent or internal phrase. The latter BIs have no effect on the intonational contour. In terms of our analogical parameterization, the former two indices require a ***reset*** at the end that accompany the ***silence***, the latter two have no ***reset***. However, our list is much longer:

[[slnc 300]],[[rset 0]]	**BI 4**
[[slnc 200]],[[rset 0]]	**BI 3**
[[slnc 100]]	**BI 2**
[[slnc 30]],[[rset 0]]	**BI 32**
[[slnc 50]],[[rset 0]]	**BI 33**
[[slnc 100]],[[rset 0]]	**BI 23**
[[slnc 300]]	**BI 22**
[[slnc 400]]	**BI 44**
[[rate 110; volm +0.3]]	**<slow down**
[[rate 130; volm +0.5]]	**<slow down**

In our representation, there are additional different 2 and 3 breaks: the reason for that is due to the use of the break in presence of end of Breath Group, with punctuation (BI 3) and without punctuation. The latter case is then split into two subcases, one in which the last word – a syntactic head – is followed or not by a dependent word, hence 33 and 32 respectively are the indices used. We also use 44 for the separation of the title from the text. Finally 23 is a break with a reset between constituents of a specific type, quantifiers. Then we have two slow down commands, one that precedes again quantifiers, and the other for all syntactic heads, end of Breath Groups (hence BGs). Quantifiers are treated in a special manner by the system if they are syntactic heads. For instance consider "Nothing" which is a subject head,

[[rate 110; volm +0.3]]	**<slow down**
[[slnc 100]],[[rset 0]]	**BI 2 %**

Coming now to tones and pitch accents, we assume the original list is again insufficient to cover the phenomena we found in our texts. We show the list of additional labels in Table 2 in Appendix 2.

3.1 The algoritm of the Prosodic Manager

The algorithm of the Prosodic Manager (hence PM) is a continuation of work carried out by Delmonte (1985). It receives information from the syntactic level - all heads with their grammatical function; from the semantic level - all discourse relations and structures with their relevance function foreground/background; from the metrical level - all end of line (Breath Groups) words with their relative line number plus all end of stanza lines again with relative line number; all phonetically translated words at each line level. And of course all sentences into which the text has been automatically split.
The PM receives one sentence at a time from the list of sentences and passes it down to the recursive algorithm that has the task of transforming all these rules into analogical parameters for the TTS. The first sentence coincides with the title and author and is computed in a standardized way. The computation starts from the first line of the first stanza: now the PM has to match the information available at sentence level with the subdivision of the text into lines or BGs. Sentences do not coincide with lines nor with stanzas. In some cases, when lines are end-stopped with a period as punctuation it may be the case that they coincide with a single sentence. However this is usually rare. Three indices are then needed to keep trace of what the recursive algorithm is doing and where in the text it is positioned. This is due to the fact that the end of line position may contain words that may occur in multiple places, both at the end and line internally. In order to help with recognizing where the PM is positioned, we collect all stanza markers with their indices, taken from the list of end of line last words.

So, the PM keeps note of each word in a sentence with an internal index; it then keeps note of the end of stanza by removing stanza markers both in the list of end of line words and in the list of end of stanzas. The input string is the one coming from the list of words contained in the sentence. When we meet a word which is recognized as end of line, we then check to see whether this word is followed by punctuation or not. In case it is not followed by punctuation we check to see whether the rest of the sentence contains other identical words and whether these are end of line. If the current word is not present in the rest of the sentence then is last, else if it is present more than once in the list of LAST words again is last. Now the system knows at what Stanza it is positioned and can verify whether the current word matches the last of the current stanza. To do this, we find all the N-stanzas that have the N lower than the index associated to the LAST word found - this should match with the current stanza number.
The PM has 35 high level recursive rules, these in turn contain the following associated rules:
- discourse level rules: removeforeground ; removebackground five different calls. They fire a specific intonational control parametric combination, for FOREGROUND discourse structures, and for BACKGROUND discourse structures;
- discourse level rules: direct speech is fired by a first sentence and is then continued in one or more following sentence/s thus requiring the downstep intonation to be in place. This has to continue until the final sentence of direct speech is detected. If downstep was not in place, the sentence would be computed with a normal reset and a possible declarative simple declination line with no relation whatsoever with the previous sentence in discourse.
- syntactic-phonological rules : these rules check to see whether the current word or the pair of current words are end-of-line and if yes whether they are syntactic heads or not ;
- this will trigger the parameter [[rate 130; volm +0.5]] for BI and possible boundary tones depending on position with respect to stanza ending;
- rules for multiwords are needed to restructure these words and see whether they are part of the list of affective words ;
- rules for affective words and phrases : they have to be treated differently according to whether they are heads or dependents, line final or not; they are associated with a descending tone;
- semantic rules devised for exclamatives and questions, their tone is raised and the speaking rate is also raised;
- exceptions rules: these have been created to account for the role of specific items in the sentence which have been previously computed like discourse markers introducing coordination and comparisons; a short list of conjunction with a concessive or adversative content. Finally a list

which contains words that Apple TTS cannot pronounce correctly and need our phonetic reconversion. Then just exceptions constituted by quantifiers which have been computed as syntactic heads and require to be set apart by introducing a specific BI.

- pragmatic rules : for lexically frozen expression and for particular emotionally and conversationally related phrases and utterances. These have been organized as rules to modify the phrase or utterance, depending on the specific dialogue act, emotion or conversational turn it refers to subdividing the tone sequence possibily in bitonal pitch accent.

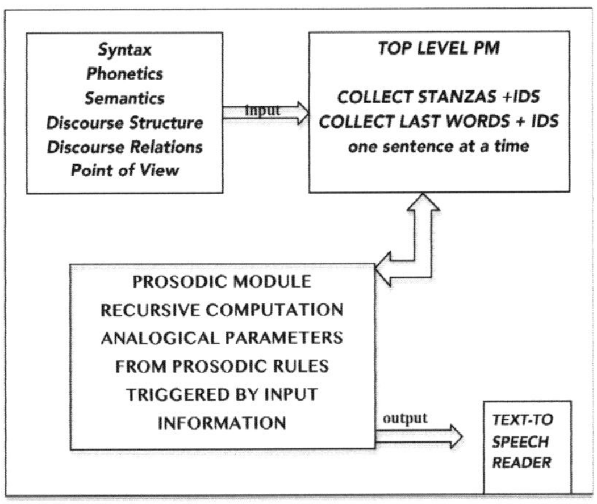

Figure 5: The Algorithm of the Prosodic Manager

3.2 One specific case: downstepped Direct Speech

Consider now the case of another of the fables by Aesop we worked on – The Fox and the Crow, that can be found here, http://www.taleswithmorals.com/aesop-fable-the-fox-and-the-crow.htm. In this story the main character introduced by the narrator, starts his speech with an exclamative sentence and then continues with some explanation and elaborations. These discourse structures need to be connected to the previous level of intonation. This requires receiving information at clause level from the discourse level, in order to allow for the appropriate continuation. In particular, this is done by:

- detecting the presence of Direct Speech by both verifying the presence of a communication verb governor of a sentence started by the appropriate punctuation mark, inverted commas. This same marker will have to be detected at the end of direct speech. The end may coincide with current sentence or a number of additional sentences might be present as is the case at stake. The current reported speaker continues after the exclamative with a series of apparently neutral declarative sentences, which can be computed as explanations and elaborations. But they all depend from the exclamative and need to be treated accordingly at discourse level.

To work at discourse level, the system has a switch called "point of view" which takes into account whose point of view is reported in each sentence. The default value for a narrative text would be the "narrator" whenever the sentence is reported directly with no attribution of what is being said. When direct speech appears, the point of view is switched to the character whom the sentence has been attributed to. This switch is maintained until the appropriate punctuation mark appears. So eventually, it is sufficient for the PM to take the current point_of_view under control. If it is identical to the previous one, nothing happens. If it changes to a new holder and it is marked with direct speech, the algorithm will be transferred to a different recursive procedure which will continue until point_of_view remains identical. This new procedure allows the PM to assign downstepped intonational contours as shown here below. In this fragment, we also mark the presence of a word – HUE - which is wrongly pronounced by Apple synthesizer and requires activating the exceptional phonetic conversion.

"What a noble bird I see **BI-3** above me **BI-22 H*-H-1** ! **BI-2 H-!H*-1**
Her beauty is without **H*-L%** equal **BI-3** ,
H*-L the [[inpt PHON]]hUW[[inpt TEXT]] of her plumage **H*-H-3** exquisite **BI-2** .
H-!H*-1 If only her voice is **BI-2** as sweet **BI-2** as her **BI-2 H-!H*-1** looks are **H*-L** fair **BI-3** , she **BI-2 H-H*-2** ought **L*-L%** without doubt [[rset 0]] to be Queen of the **H*-L%-2** Birds **BI-3** . "

In case this information was not made available to the PM, the result would have been the following.

" What a noble bird I see **BI-3** above me **BI-22 H*-H-1** ! **BI-2 H-!H*-1**!
Her beauty is without **H*-L%** equal **BI-3** ,

H*-L the [[inpt PHON]]hUW[[inpt TEXT]] of her plumage **H*-H-3** exquisite **BI-2** .
If only her voice is **BI-2** as sweet **BI-2**
as her **BI-2 H-!H*-1** looks are **H*-L** fair **BI-3** ,
she **BI-2 H-H*-2** ought **L*-L%** without doubt [[rset 0]] to be Queen of the **H*-L%-2** Birds **BI-3** . "
We started lately to experiment with Google Chrome addon TTS which is included in the system SpeakIt© and contains iSpell TTS. Some of the voices are particularly well equipped and we tested English UK female. The TTS requires a fee to be paid and the use of an XML interface based on SSML, Speech Synthesis Markup Language adopted by W3C, Version 1.1. The authors of the specification unclude well-known experts of speech synthesis and prosody, like Paolo Baggia from Loquendo, Paul Bagshaw from France Telecom. The excerpt from Aesop's story converted into this new language is given here below. Note that the conversion has been done using the new ToBI labels:

What a noble <prosody pitch="medium">bird I see</prosody><break time="100ms"/>
<prosody pitch="default" rate="slow" volume="-0.2">above me </prosody><break time="200ms"/>
<prosody pitch="medium" rate="medium" volume="+1.1">Her beauty is without </prosody> <prosody pitch="-10Hz" rate="default" volume="medium"> equal ,</prosody> <break time="200ms"/>
<prosody rate="default" volume="medium">the hue of her plumage</prosody>
<prosody pitch="medium" rate="default" volume="+1.1">exquisite</prosody><break time="200ms"/>
<prosody pitch="low" rate="default" volume="loud">If only her voice </prosody><break time="5ms"/><prosody pitch="low" rate="default" volume="loud">is as sweet </prosody> <break time="10ms"/>
<prosody pitch="medium" rate="default" volume="loud">as her looks are fair</prosody><break time="200ms"/>
<prosody pitch="medium" rate="default" volume="medium">she <break time="5ms"/> </prosody><prosody pitch="high" rate="slow" volume="loud">ought</prosody><prosody pitch="medium" rate="slow" volume="soft">without doubt to be Queen of the</prosody>
<prosody pitch="high" rate="default" volume="loud">Birds</prosody></speak>

5 Evaluation and Conclusion

The system has undergone extensive auditory evaluation by expert linguists. It has also been presented at various demo sessions always receiving astounded favourable comments (Delmonte & Bacalu, 2013; Delmonte & Prati, 2014; Delmonte 2015). The evaluation has been organized in two phases, at first the story is read by Apple TTS directly from the text. Then the second reading has been done by the system and a comparison is asked of the subject listening to it. In the future we intend to produce an objective evaluation on a graded scale using naïve listeners English native speakers. We will be using the proposal in Xu (2011:95), called MOS, or Mean Opinion Score, with a five-level scale: 5-Excellent, 4-Good, 3-Fair, 2-Poor, 1-Bad, with the associated opinions: 5-Imperceptible, 4-Perceptible but not annoying, 4-Slightly annoying, 2-Annoying, 1-Very annoying.
In this paper we presented a prototype of a complete system for expressive and natural reading which is fully based on internal representations produced by syntactic and semantic deep analysis. The level of computation that is mostly responsible for prosodic variations is the discourse level, where both discourse relations, discourse structures, topic and temporal interpretation allow the system to set up an interwoven concatenation of parameters at complex clause and sentence level. Pragmatically frozen phrases and utterances are also fully taken into account always at a parameterized level. Parameters have been related to ToBI standard set and a new inventory has been proposed. The system is currently working on top of Apple TTS but we already started to port it to other platforms. It is available for free download at a dedicated website.

References

Balyan, Archana, S. S. Agrawal, Amita Dev, Speech Synthesis: A Review, International Journal of Engineering Research & Technology (IJERT), Vol. 2, Issue 6, 57-75.

Bachenko, J. & Fitzpatrick, E. 1990. A computational grammar of discourse-neutral prosodic phrasing in English. *Comp. Ling.* 16, 155{170.

Bos, Johan and C.J. Rupp, Bianka Buschbeck-Wolf and Michael Dorna, Managing information at linguistic interfaces, 1998. Proceedings of the 36th Annual Meeting of the Association for Computational Linguistics and 17th International

Conference on Computational Linguistics, Volume 1, ACL-COLING, pp. 160-166.

Bos Johan & Rodolfo Delmonte (eds.), 2008. Semantics in Text Processing (STEP), Research in Computational Semantics, Vol.1, College Publications, London.

Campbell N., 2002. Towards a grammar of spoken language: incorporating paralinguistic information. In: 7th ISCA International Conference on Spoken Language Processing, Denver, Colorado, USA, September 16-20, 2002.

Campbell's Conclusion for SSW6 TALK on Towards Conversational Speech Synthesis; "Lessons Learned from the Expressive Speech Processing Project".http://www.isca-speech.org/ archive_open/archive_papers/ssw6/material/ ssw6_022/ ssw6_022.ppt

Raúl Montaño, Francesc Alías, Josep Ferrer, 2013. Prosodic analysis of storytelling discourse modes and narrative situations oriented to Text-to-Speech synthesis, 8th ISCA Speech Synthesis Workshop.

Cahn, J.E., 1990. The generation of affect in synthesized speech.Journal of the American Voice I/O Society, 8, 1–19.

Delmonte R., 1982. Automatic Word-Stress Patterns Assignment by Rules: a Computer Program for Standard Italian, Proc. IV F.A.S.E. Symposium, 1, ESA, Roma, 153-156.

Delmonte R., G.A.Mian, G.Tisato, 1984. A Text-to-Speech System for the Synthesis of Italian, Proceedings of ICASSP'84, San Diego(Cal), 291-294.

Delmonte R., 1986. A Computational Model for a text-to-speech translator in Italian, Revue - Informatique et Statistique dans les Sciences humaines, XXII, 1-4, 23-65.

Delmonte R., G.A.Mian, G.Tisato, 1986. A Grammatical Component for a Text-to-Speech System, Proceedings of the ICASSP'86, IEEE, Tokyo, 2407-2410.

Delmonte R., R. Dolci, 1991. Computing Linguistic Knowledge for text-to-speech systems with PROSO, Proceedings 2nd European Conference on Speech Communication and Technology, Genova, ESCA, 1291-1294.

Delmonte R., 2002. GETARUN PARSER - A parser equipped with Quantifier Raising and Anaphoric Binding based on LFG, Proc. LFG2002 Conference, Athens, pp.130-153, at http://cslipublications.stanford.edu/hand/miscpubs online.html.

Delmonte R., 2002a. From Deep to Shallow Anaphora Resolution:, in Proc. DAARC2002 , 4th Discourse Anaphora and Anaphora Resolution Colloquium, Lisbona, pp.57-62.

Delmonte R., 2004. Evaluating GETARUNS Parser with GREVAL Test Suite, Proc. ROMAND - 20th International Conference on Computational Linguistics - COLING, University of Geneva, 32-41.

Delmonte R., S.Tonelli, M.A. Piccolino Boniforti, A. Bristot, E.Pianta, 2005. VENSES – a Linguistically-Based System for Semantic Evaluation, in Joaquin Quiñonero-Candela, et al., 2005, Machine Learning Challenges. Evaluating Predictive Uncertainty, Visual Object Classification, and Recognising Textual Entailment.: MLCW 2005, UK, 344-371.

Delmonte R., A.Bristot, M.A. Piccolino Boniforti and S.Tonelli, 2006a. Another Evaluation of Anaphora Resolution Algorithms and a Comparison with GETARUNS' Knowledge Rich Approach, ROMAND 2006, 11th EACL, Trento, Association for Computational Linguistics, 3-10.

Delmonte R., A. Bristot, M.A. Piccolino Boniforti and S. Tonelli, 2006b. Coping with semantic uncertainty with VENSES, in Bernardo Magnini, Ido Dagan(eds.), Proceedings of the Challanges Workshop - The 2nd PASCAL Recognizing Textual Entailment Challenge, Università Ca' Foscari, Venezia, 86-91.

Delmonte R., A.Bristot, M.A.Piccolino Boniforti, S.Tonelli, 2007. Entailment and Anaphora Resolution in RTE3, in Proc. ACL Workshop on Text Entailment and Paraphrasing, Prague, ACL Madison, USA, pp. 48-53.

Delmonte R., G. Nicolae, S. Harabagiu (2007b), A Linguistically-based Approach to Detect Causality Relations in Unrestricted Text, in Proc. MICAI-2007, IEEE Publications, 173-185.

Delmonte R., G. Nicolae, S. Harabagiu, (2007a), A Linguistically-based Approach to Discourse Relations Recognition, in B.Sharp & M.Zock(eds.), Natural Language Processing and Cognitive Science, Proc. 4th NLPCS, Funchal, Portugal, INSTICC PRESS, pp. 81-91.

Delmonte, R, & S. Tonelli, 2009. Knowledge-poor and Knowledge-rich Approach in Anaphora Resolution Algorithms : a Comparison, In Linguistica e modelli tecnologici di ricerca : atti del XL Congresso internazionale di studi della Società di linguistica italiana (SLI), Roma, Bulzoni, pp.1-7.

Delmonte R., S.Tonelli, R. Tripodi, (2009), Semantic Processing for Text Entailment with VENSES, in Proceedings of Text Analysis Conference (TAC) 2009 Workshop - Notebook Papers and Results, NIST, Gaithersburg MA, pp. 453-460.

Delmonte R., E. Pianta, 2009. Computing Implicit Entities and Events for Story Understanding, in H.Bunt, V.Petukhova and S.Wubben(eds.), Proc. Eighth International Conference on Computational Semantics IWCS-8, Tilburg University Press, pp. 277-281.

Delmonte R., 2009a. Computing Implicit Entities and Events with Getaruns, in B.Sharp and M.Zock (eds.), Natural Language Processing and Cognitive Science 2009, Insticc Press, Portugal, 23-35.

Delmonte R., 2009b. A computational approach to implicit entities and events in text and discourse, in International Journal of Speech Technology (IJST), Springer, pp. 1-14.

Delmonte R., 2009c. "Understanding Implicit Entities and Events with Getaruns," IEEE International Conference on Semantic Computing, Berkeley, pp. 25-32.

Delmonte R. & S. Tonelli, 2010. VENSES++-UNIVE: Adapting a deep semantic processing system to the identification of null instantiations, Proceedings of the 5th International Workshop on Semantic Evaluation, ACL, pp. 296–299.

Tonelli S., R. Delmonte, 2011. "Desperately seeking Implicit arguments in text", in RELMS'2011, Workshop on Relational Models of Semantics at ACL 2011 Portland, pp.54-62.

Delmonte R., 2013. Coping With Implicit Arguments And Events Coreference, in E. Hovy, T. Mitamura, M. Palmer, (eds.), Proceedings of the Conference The 1st Workshop on EVENTS: Definition, Detection, Coreference, and Representation, HLT-NAACL, Atlanta, pp. 1-10.

Delmonte R. & C. Bacalu. 2013. SPARSAR: a System for Poetry Automatic Rhythm and Style AnalyzeR, SLATE 2013 - Demonstration Track, Grenoble.

Delmonte R. & A.M. Prati. 2014. SPARSAR: An Expressive Poetry Reader, Proceedings of the Demonstrations at the 14th Conference of the EACL, Gotheborg, 73–76.

Delmonte R., 2015. Visualizing Poetry with SPARSAR - Poetic Maps from Poetic Content, Proceedings of NAACL-HLT Fourth Workshop on Computational Linguistics for Literature, Denver, Colorado, ACL, pp. 68–78.

Delmonte R., 2007. Computational Linguistic Text Processing – Logical Form, Semantic Interpretation, Discourse Relations and Question Answering, Nova Science Publishers, New York.

Delmonte R., 2009. Computational Linguistic Text Processing – Lexicon, Grammar, Parsing and Anaphora Resolution, Nova Science Publishers, New York.

Grosz, B. & Hirschberg, J. 1992. Some intonational characteristics of discourse structure. In *Proc. Int. Conf. Spoken Language Processing, Banff , Canada, 1986*, vol. 1, pp. 429-432.

Hamza W., Bakis, R., Eide, E.M., Picheny, M. A., & Pitrelli, J. F. (2004), The IBM Expressive Speech Synthesis System. In: Proceedings of the International Conference on Spoken Language Processing (ICSLP), Jeju, South Korea, October, 2004.

Hirschberg, J. 1993. Pitch accent in context: predicting intonational prominence from text. Artificial Intell. 63, 305-340.

Huckvale M. 2002. Speech synthesis, speech simulation and speech science. In *Proceedings of the International Conference on Speech and Language Processing 2002*, pp. 1261– 1264.

Lakshmi Saheer, Blaise Potard, 2013. Understanding Factors in Emotion Perception, At 8° Speech Synthesis Workshop.

Lieske, C., J. Bos, M. Emele, B. Gamback, and C.J. Rupp 1997. Giving Prosody a Meaning, In Proceedings of the 5th European Conference on Speech Communication and Technology (EuroSpeech'97), Rhodes, Greece, 1431-1434.

Murray, I. R., & Arnott, J. L., 1993. Towards the simulation of emotion in synthetic speech: A review of the literature on human vocal emotion. Journal of the Acoustic Society of America, 93(2), pp. 1097–1108.

Nakatani, C. 1998. Constituent-based accent prediction. In *Proc. COLING-ACL '98, Montreal, Canada*, pp. 939-945.

Pierrehumbert, J. and J. Hirschberg (1990). The meaning of intonational contours in the interpretation of discourse. In P. Cohen, J. Morgan, and M. Pollack (Eds.), *Intentions in Communication*, pp. 271–311. Cambridge, Mass.: MIT Press.

Polzehl, T., S. Möller, and F. Metze, 2011. "Modeling speaker personality using voice," in Proc. INTERSPEECH, ISCA.

Prevost, S. 1995 A semantics of contrast and information structure for specifying intonation in spoken language generation. PhD thesis, University of Pennsylvania, Philadelphia, PA, USA.

Shaikh, M. A.M., Molla, M. K. I., and Hirose, K., 2008. Assigning suitable phrasal tones and pitch accents by sensing affective information from text to synthesize human-like speech. In Proceedings of InterSpeech, pp. 326–329, Brisbane.

Shaikh, M. A. M., Prendinger, H., and Ishizuka, M., 2008. Sentiment assessment of text by analyzing linguistic features and contextual valence assignment. Applied Artificial Intelligence, vol.22, issue 6, pp.558-601, Taylor & Francis.

Shimei Pan and Kathleen McKeown. 1997. Integrating language generation with speech synthesis in a Concept-to-Speech system. In *Proc. of ACL/EACL'97 Concept to Speech Workshop*, Madrid, Spain.

Shimei Pan and Kathleen McKeown. 1998. Learning intonation rules for concept to speech generation. In *Proc. of COLING/ACL'98*, Montreal, Canada.

Shimei Pan and Kathleen McKeown. 1999. Word informativeness and automatic pitch accent modeling. In *Proc. of the Joint SIGDAT Conference on Empirical Methods in Natural Language Processing and Very Large Corpora.*

Silverman, K., Beckman, M., Pierrehumbert, J., Ostendorf, M., Wightman, C., Price, P., And Hirschberg, J. 1992. ToBI: A standard scheme for labelling prosody. In Proceedings of the International Conference on Speech and Language Processing 1992.

Steidl, S., T. Polzehl, T. Bunnell, Y. Dou, P. Muthukumar, D. Perry, K. Prahallad, C. Vaughn, A. Black, and F. Metze, 2012. Emotion identification for evaluation of synthesized emotional speech, in Proc. Speech Prosody.

Wang, M. & Hirschberg, J. 1992. Automatic classiˉcation of intonational phrase boundaries. Comp. Speech Lang. 6, 175-196..

Zovato, E., Francesca Tini-Brunozzi and Morena Danieli, 2008. Interplay between pragmatic and acoustic level to embody expressive cues in a Text to Speech system, in AISB Proceedings - Affective Language in Human and Machine, vol.2, 88-91.

Semantically Enriched Models for Modal Sense Classification

Mengfei Zhou[1] **Anette Frank**[1,2] **Annemarie Friedrich**[3] **Alexis Palmer**[1]

[1]Department of Computational Linguistics, Heidelberg University, Germany
[2]Research Training Group AIPHES, Dept. of Computational Linguistics, Heidelberg University
{zhou,frank,palmer}@cl.uni-heidelberg.de
[3]Department of Computational Linguistics, Universität des Saarlandes, Germany
afried@coli.uni-saarland.de

Abstract

Modal verbs have different interpretations depending on their context. Previous approaches to modal sense classification achieve relatively high performance using shallow lexical and syntactic features. In this work we uncover the difficulty of particular modal sense distinctions by eliminating both distributional bias and sparsity of existing small-scale annotated corpora used in prior work. We build a semantically enriched model for modal sense classification by novelly applying features that relate to lexical, proposition-level, and discourse-level semantic factors. Besides improved classification performance, especially for difficult sense distinctions, closer examination of interpretable feature sets allows us to obtain a better understanding of relevant semantic and contextual factors in modal sense classification.

1 Introduction

Factuality recognition (de Marneffe et al., 2011) is an important subtask in information extraction. Beyond bare filtering aspects of veridicality recognition, classification of **modal senses** plays an important role in text understanding, plan recognition, and the emerging field of argumentation mining. Communication revolves about *hypothetical, planned, apprehended or desired states of affairs*. Such 'extrapropositional' meanings are often linguistically marked using modal verbs, adverbs, or attitude verbs, as in (1) for hypothetical situations.

(1) a. He *must*'ve hurt himself.
b. He has *certainly* found the place by now.
c. We *anticipate* that no one will leave.

Following Kratzer (1991)'s seminal work in formal semantics, recent computational approaches such as Ruppenhofer and Rehbein (2012) distinguish different modal 'senses', most prominently, *epistemic* (2.a), *deontic/bouletic* (2.b) and *circumstantial/dynamic* (2.c) modality.

(2) a. Geez, Buddha *must* be so annoyed!
(epistemic – possibility)
b. We *must* have clear European standards.
(deontic – permission/request)
c. She *can*'t even read them.
(dynamic – ability)

Modal sense tagging is typically framed as a supervised classification task, as in Ruppenhofer and Rehbein (2012), who manually annotated the modal verbs *must, may, can, could, shall* and *should* in the MPQA corpus of Wiebe et al. (2005). The obtained data set comprises 1340 instances. Maximum entropy classifiers trained on this data yield accuracies from 68.7 to 93.5 for the different lexical classifier models. While these accuracies seem high, we note a strong distributional bias in their data set. Due to the small data set size (200-600 instances per modal verb) and its distributional bias, classifiers trained on this corpus are prone to overfitting and hardly beat the majority baseline. Indeed, none of the classification models in Ruppenhofer and Rehbein (2012) (henceforth R&R) is able to beat the baseline with uniform settings across all modal verb types.

Of particular concern in our work are specific sense ambiguities that are difficult to discriminate, such as dynamic vs. deontic readings of *can* (3.a), epistemic vs. dynamic readings of *could* (3.b) or epistemic vs. deontic readings of *should* (3.c).

(3) a. You *can* do this, if you want.
ability (dy) vs. permission (de)
b. He *could* have arrived in time.
possibility (ep) vs. ability (dy)
c. He *should* be aware of the issue.
possibility (ep) vs. obligation (de)

Proceedings of the EMNLP 2015 Workshop on Linking Models of Lexical, Sentential and Discourse-level Semantics, pages 44–53,
Lisboa, Portugal, 18 September 2015.

In this paper we reexamine prior work on modal sense classification and show that specific distinctions are difficult for state-of-the art models. We show that modal sense classification is a challenging problem that profits from lexical, proposition-level and discourse-level semantic information.

Our goals and contributions are as follows:

(i) We investigate the impact of **semantic and discourse-related factors for modal sense classification**, looking in particular at difficult modal sense distinctions. Accordingly, we define a range of semantically inspired linguistic feature classes. The feature groups are related to lexical and propositional semantics, as well as discourse-level semantics, ranging from tense and aspect to speaker/hearer orientation.

As an example, one of our hypotheses is that aspectual event types play a decisive role in deontic vs. epistemic sense disambiguation for modal verbs such as *must*. Our intuition is that events are more likely to co-occur with the deontic sense of *must* (4.a,b), whereas statives are more likely to co-occur with the epistemic sense (4.c).

(4) a. The prisoners *must* return their weapons.
b. Prisoners of war *must* be returned to their home countries.
c. They *must* be so scared.

(ii) As a precondition for the aims of this work, we construct a large corpus that is balanced for modal sense distribution and less prone to overfitting compared to prior work. To this end we apply a **paraphrase-driven cross-lingual modal sense projection approach** using parallel corpora. We show that this automatic acquisition method yields modal sense annotations of very high accuracy.

(iii) Using this corpus as training data, we devise a **novel, semantically enriched model for modal sense classification**. We assess the impact of diverse feature groups for modal sense classification in unbiased classification settings and analyze to what extent they contribute to solving difficult disambiguation problems.

Overview. We review related work in Section 2. Section 3 outlines an automatic modal sense projection approach using parallel corpora. We apply this method to bilingual corpora and evaluate the quality of the obtained data set. Section 4 motivates and describes semantic and discourse-oriented features for modal sense classification. These are examined in classification experiments in Section 5. We reconstruct the modal sense classifier of Ruppenhofer and Rehbein (2012) to compare against prior work. We evaluate the performance of different models in unbiased classification experiments, using the harvested sense-labeled corpora for training. We analyze the impact of different feature groups on disambiguation performance and relate them to specific difficult disambiguation classes. Section 6 concludes.

2 Related Work

Most relevant to our work is the state of the art in modal sense classification in Ruppenhofer and Rehbein (2012). They manually annotated modal verbs in the MPQA corpus of Wiebe et al. (2005). Their annotation scheme departs from both the earlier setting in Baker et al. (2010) and a more recent proposal in Nissim et al. (2013). Baker et al. (2010) distinguish 8 categories. Next to *requirement, permissive, want* and *ability*, they include *success, effort, intention* and *belief*. They measured precision in automatic tagging of 86.3% by examining 249 modality-tagged sentences. Nissim et al. (2013) propose a fine-grained hierarchical modality annotation scheme that can be applied cross-linguistically. It includes (subtypes) of factuality, as well as speaker attitude. To our knowledge their annotation scheme has not been used for computational tagging.

Ruppenhofer and Rehbein (2012) apply the well-established modal sense categories of Kratzer (1991): *epistemic, deontic/bouletic* and *circumstantial/dynamic* modality. They add the categories: *concessive, conditional* and *optative*. Their annotation scheme proves reliable both in inter-annotator agreement, which ranges from $\mathcal{K}$=0.6 to 0.84 for the different modal verbs, and classification performance, which yields accuracies between 68.7 and 93.5, depending on the verb. However, the sense distributions of their data set are heavily biased (cf. Table 2, Section 5), and as a consequence, the majority sense baselines are hard to beat. The classification model of Ruppenhofer and Rehbein (2012) employs a mixture of target and contextual features, taking into account surface, lemma and PoS information, as well as syntactic labels and path features linking targets to their surrounding words and constituents. These features are able to capture very diverse contextual factors, but it is difficult to interpret their impact for distinguishing modal senses.

3 Paraphrase-driven Sense Projection

Given the sparsity and distributional bias in existing modal sense annotated corpora such as the MPQA, we propose a method for cross-lingual sense projection to alleviate the manual annotation bottleneck. Our approach exploits the paraphrasing behaviour of modal senses, which holds across modal verbs, modal adverbs and certain attitude verbs. As illustrated in (5) and (6), this paraphrasing behaviour is applicable across languages.

(5) a. He *may* be home by now. (possibility)
b. You *may* enter this building. (permission)
c. *May* you live 100 years. (wish)

(6) a. *Vielleicht* ist er schon zu Hause.
MAYBE IS HE ALREADY AT HOME.
b. Es ist *gestattet*, das Gebäude zu betreten.
IT IS PERMITTED THE BUILDING TO ENTER
c. *Hoffentlich* werden Sie 100 Jahre.
HOPEFULLY BECOME YOU 100 YEARS

Capitalizing on the paraphrasing capacity of such expressions, we apply a semi-supervised cross-lingual projection approach, similar to prior work in annotation projection (Yarowsky and Ngai, 2001; Diab and Resnik, 2002):

(i) we select a seed set of cross-lingual sense indicating paraphrases,
(ii) we extract modal verbs in context that are in direct alignment with one of the seed expressions in word-aligned parallel corpora, and
(iii) we project the label of the sense-indicating paraphrase to the aligned modal verb.

Experimental setup and annotation scheme. German is our source language, and we project into English. We adopt R&R's annotation scheme, which is grounded in Kratzer's modal senses *epistemic, deontic* and *dynamic*. While R&R add the novel categories *conditional, concessive* and *optative*,[1] we subsume the former two as cases of *epistemic* and optative as a subtype of *deontic*.

Seed selection. The seeds were manually selected from PPDB (Ganitkevitch et al., 2013) and parallel corpora from OPUS (Tiedemann, 2012). The major criterion, besides frequency of occurrence, was non-ambiguity regarding the modal sense. We chose 30 seed phrases. Examples are adverbs like *wahrscheinlich* (probably – epistemic), *hoffentlich* (hopefully – deontic), adjectives like *erforderlich* (necessary – deontic), verbs like *gelingen* (succeed – dynamic), *erlauben* (admit – deontic) or affixes such as *-bar* (-able) as in (*lesbar* (readable) – dynamic). For projection we employed the word-aligned Europarl (Koehn, 2005) and OpenSubtitles parallel corpora.

Projection and validation. We extracted 11,610 instances with direct alignment of modal sense paraphrase and modal verb. 80.6% were labeled epistemic, 8.2% deontic, 11.2% dynamic.

In order to assess the quality of the heuristically sense-labeled modal verbs we performed manual annotation on a balanced subset of the acquired data consisting of 420 sentences. We established annotation guidelines that ask the annotators to consider four paraphrasing possibilities for modal verbs: *possibility (epistemic), request (deontic), permission (deontic)*[2] and *ability (dynamic)*. We performed annotation by two linguistically trained experts. They also annotated a balanced subset of 103 instances from R&R's MPQA data set, in order to calibrate our annotation quality against the MPQA gold standard.

On the automatically acquired data (from Europarl and Open Subtitles) we obtain high annotator agreement at $\mathcal{K}$=0.87.[3] Evaluating projected sense labels against ground truth, we observe high accuracy of .92. Agreement for MPQA is lower. There we achieve moderate agreement: $\mathcal{K}$ of 0.66 and 0.77 against the gold standard and 0.78 between annotators. In R&R, agreement averaged over the different modal verbs was 0.67. Our annotation reliability is largely comparable.

4 Semantic Features for Modal Sense Classification

In our work we expand the feature inventory used for modal sense classification to incorporate semantic factors at various levels. An overview of our semantic features is given in Table 1. We define specific feature groups for focused experimental investigation in Section 5. Feature extraction is performed using Stanford's CoreNLP (Manning et al., 2014) and Stanford parser (Klein and Manning, 2002) to obtain syntactic dependencies.

[1]Examples: "Should anyone call, please take a message" (conditional), "But, fool though he may be, he is powerful" (concessive), and "Long may she live!" (optative). (R&R)

[2]We split permission and request to make the task more accessible and merged them to deontic later.

[3]Cohen's Kappa, Cohen (1960)

VB: Lexical features of the embedded verb. The *embedded verb* in the scope of the modal plays an important role in determining modal sense. For instance, with the embedded verb *fly* in (7.a), we prefer a dynamic reading of *can*, whereas with *eat* in (7.b) we find a deontic reading.

(7) a. The children *can* **fly** (if they just believe, says Peter Pan)!
b. The children *can* **eat** (ice cream) now.

We extract the `lemma` of the embedded verb and its `part-of-speech` tag in the sentence. We also extract whether the verb has a `particle` (e.g. *the plane could take **off***), and if yes, which.

SBJ: Subject-related features. These features capture syntactic and semantic properties of the subject of the modal construction. In (8) a non-animate, abstract subject favors an epistemic reading for *could*, whereas with an animate subject, a dynamic reading is preferred. Other factors involve speaker/hearer/third party distinctions (9).

(8) (The conflict | He) *could* now move to a next stage. (ep | dy)

(9) a. I *must* be home by noon. (deontic only)
b. He *must* be home by noon. (de or ep)

We extract `person` and `number` of the subject and the `noun_type` (common, proper, pronoun). Person is identified via personal pronoun features, and the other features are extracted from POS tags. The `countability` of the noun is obtained from the Celex database (Baayen et al., 1996).

Lexical semantic features for the subject NP are extracted from WordNet (Fellbaum, 1999). Following Reiter and Frank (2010), we take the most frequent sense of the noun in WN (`subject_sense0`), add the direct hypernym of this sense, the direct hypernym of that hypernym, etc., resulting in features `subject_sense[1-3]`. We also extract the top sense in the WN hierarchy `subject_sense_top` (e.g. *entity*) and the WN `lexical_filename` (e.g. *person*).

TVA: Tense/voice/grammatical aspect features. These features capture tense and grammatical aspect of the embedded verb complex. LA below notes how grammatical aspect influences modal sense. At the same time, tense is an important factor for modal sense disambiguation. (10) clearly favors an epistemic reading, as the event is located in the past, whereas deontic sense is favored with future events in indicative mood as in (4.a).

Embedded verb		
VB	lemma part-of-speech particle	lemma of head POS of head *up, off, on,...*
TVA	tense progressive perfect voice	present / past true / false true / false active / passive
LA	lexical aspect	dynamic / stative
NEG	negation	true / false
WNV	WN sense $[0-2]$ WN senseTop	WN senses (head+hypernyms) top sense in hypernym hierarchy
Subject noun phrase		
SBJ	number person countability noun type WN sense $[0-2]$ WN senseTop WN lex. fn.	sg, pl 1, 2, 3 from *Celex*, e.g. count common, proper, pronoun WN senses (head+hypernyms) top sense in hypernym hierarchy person, artifact, event, ...
Sentence structure		
S	conjunct clause adjunct clause relative clause temporal mod.	true / false true / false true / false true / false

Table 1: Individual features and feature groups.

We restrict the `tense` feature to the values `{past, present}`, determined via patterns of POS tags. We capture grammatical aspect features using sequences of POS tags of the verbal complex, following Loaiciga et al. (2014). The boolean features `perfect` and `progressive` indicate the respective grammatical aspect; `voice` indicates active or passive voice.

LA: Lexical aspectual class. Verbs can be used in a *dynamic* or *stative* sense, e.g. *I **ate** an apple* vs. *I **like** apples* (Vendler, 1957). The lexical aspect of a verb in context influences modal sense in some cases. In contrast to (4.a), for example, where the eventive verb *return* triggers the deontic sense, perfect aspect in (10) coerces the clause to stative, triggering the epistemic sense of *must*.

(10) The prisoners *must* have returned their weapons.

We label the lexical aspectual class of the embedded verb following Friedrich and Palmer (2014), who make use of both syntactic-semantic contextual features and linguistic indicators (Siegel and McKeown, 2000), which are patterns of usage for verb types estimated over a large parsed but otherwise unlabeled corpus. Accuracy for this prediction task is reported as around 84%.

NEG: Negation. Negation is a semantic feature at the proposition level that can have reflections in modal sense selection. *Should*, e.g., seems to favor a deontic meaning when negated in (11.a). Also, negation can interact with disambiguation of epistemic vs. deontic readings depending on propositional or discourse context. In (11.b), the favored reading is deontic in the negative sentence.

(11) a. He *should* (not) have returned.
(ep/de (pos) vs. de (neg))

b. He *may* (not) drink more gin tonight.
(ep/de (pos) vs. de (neg))

The `negation` feature captures the presence or absence of negation in the modal construction. We use the dependency label `NEG` to identify negation.

WNV: Lexical semantic features of the embedded verb. This feature group encourages semantic generalization for lexical features of the embedded verb. It can play a role in interaction with other features, such as lexical and grammatical aspect and proposition-level features such as negation or the combined lexical semantic features described below (WN). The features in this group are parallel to the WordNet features described for the SBJ feature group above (minus `lexical_filename`), but apply to the embedded verb instead of the subject NP.

S: Features of sentence structure. When modals appear as part of a complex sentence, certain structural configurations can reflect thematic or temporal relations between the proposition modified by the modal and dependent clauses. An example are telic clauses that can favor a deontic over a dynamic or epistemic reading (12).

(12) You *could* use a shortcut to save time.

We extract features from the constituent tree to capture such effects: whether the modal clause is conjoined to the main clause (`embedded ConjunctSentence`), whether it embeds adjunct clauses (and if so, the conjunction) (`adjunctSentence`), and whether it is in a relative clause (`relativeSentence`). Finally, `has_tmod` indicates the presence of a temporal modifier.

WN: All WordNet features. This feature group aims to capture aspects of proposition-level semantics by combining semantic features of the subject NP with those of the embedded verb. This feature group simply includes both the WordNet features described in SBJ and those in WNV.

The intuition is that certain subject-predicate combinations may have a preference for certain modal senses. In (13), for example, *can* appears with a proposition that is subject to specific prescriptions or "laws": soldiers are subject to restrictions with respect to consuming alcohol.

(13) a. Soldiers *can* drink when off duty.

TVA/LA: Features of the verb complex. Finally, this feature group uses both lexical aspect (LA) and tense, voice, and grammatical aspect (TVA) features. The goal is to investigate whether these two views of the verb complex are more effective separately or in combination.

5 Experiments & Results

Our experiments have several objectives:

(i.) We aim to show that modal sense classification, especially difficult sense distinctions, can profit from semantic and discourse-oriented features. To this end we construct **contrasting classifier models** with different feature sets: R&R's shallow lexical and syntactic path features ($F_{R\&R}$), a feature set consisting of only our newly designed semantic features (F_{Sem}), and a combined set F_{all} consisting of both $F_{R\&R}$ and F_{Sem}.

However, any classifier trained only on the highly unbalanced MPQA data set will have difficulty separating the effect of distributional bias in the training data from the predictive force of its feature set. A classifier that follows the majority class in the training data will neutralize the potential impact of its feature set. In order to counterbalance the distributional bias and also the sparsity inherent in the data, we evaluate the different classifier models in **different classification settings**:

(ii.) We extend the training set using **heuristically labeled instances** obtained from modal sense projection (cf. Section 3), thereby eliminating sparsity and reducing distributional bias.

(iii.) We further evaluate classifiers trained on perfectly **balanced data**. This eliminates the distributional bias in training and will allow us to carve out the impact of the different feature sets.

(iv.) Finally we measure the impact of **individual feature groups** via ablation (Section 5.3).

A note on **notation**: Subscripts on classifier names indicate the source of the training data. CL_M denotes a classifier trained only on MPQA data; CL_{MH} combines MPQA and heuristically-tagged data; CL_H is a classifier trained only on heuristically-tagged data. Superscripted $+b$ or $-b$ indicates a balanced vs. unbalanced training set.

5.1 Experimental settings

Replicating R&R's modal sense classifier. We replicate R&R's classifier by reimplementing their feature set,[4] a mixture of target and contextual features that take into account surface, lemma and PoS information, as well as syntactic labels and path features linking targets to surrounding words and constituents (cf. R&R, Table 5).

We train one classifier per modal verb, using R&R's best feature setting (context feature window=3 tokens left and right of target, target-specific features). Averaged accuracies for the replicated classifiers appear in Table 4 as CL_M^{-b} (feature set $F_{R\&R}$). Our scores are very similar to their published results, which appear in the same table in the column headed "R&R".[5]

Extending and balancing training data sets. From the 11,610 heuristically sense tagged instances (Section 3), we construct balanced ($+b$) training corpora for each modal verb. The composition of this data is shown in Table 2. To alleviate training data sparsity, we add this data to the (unbalanced) MPQA data; this configuration results in CL_{MH}^{-b}. Finally, we re-balance both CL_M and CL_{MH} by under- and oversampling.[6]

Classification setup and test data. Training on balanced data reduces distributional bias, but evaluating performance on an unbalanced, naturally-distributed data set gives us a more realistic picture. To this end, and in order to compare to prior work, our test data is drawn exclusively from MPQA. For CL_H^{+b}, we evaluate on R&R's full data set; the composition of the test set appears in the

	CL_H^{+b} train			Full MPQA test		
	ep	de	dy	ep	de	dy
must	800	800	0	11	183	0
may	950	950	0	130	9	0
can	150	150	150	2	115	271
could	40	40	40	156	17	67
should	150	150	0	26	248	0
shall	0	5	5	0	11	2

Table 2: Heuristic ($+b$) training data and MPQA ($-b$) training and test data

right-hand side of Table 2. The other two models (CL_M and CL_{MH}) are evaluated in a 5-fold CV setting, with testing on the naturally distributed MPQA instances. For each CV setting, only the training section is adapted, by addition of heuristic data, and/or balancing. Table 3 exemplifies one run of our cross-validation setting. First, we split MPQA into 80% train (CL_M^{-b}) and 20% test, then we add the heuristically-tagged data (CL_{MH}^{-b}) and re-balance (to produce CL_M^{+b} and CL_{MH}^{+b}).

Baselines. For unbalanced classifiers, we compare to the MFS baseline (BL_{Maj_M}), taking the most frequent sense for each modal verb from the MPQA training data. For balanced classifiers, we compare to the random baseline (BL_{Ran}), determined by the (evenly distributed) number of class labels seen in training for each modal verb.

5.2 Comparative performance evaluation

Table 4 compares accuracy of classifiers trained on ±balanced data, from different sources, and with different feature sets. We report results for individual classifiers (per modal verb) and macro- and micro-average across all verbs. The two bold-faced numbers per table row indicate the best models for unbalanced and for balanced data. For the balanced classifiers, where we find more interesting differences, we test significance using McNemar's test ($p<0.05$) (McNemar, 1947). Within a row (for $+b$ classifiers and micro-averages), a superscript on a number indicates which classifier is significantly outperformed by the result. Across feature sets, we compare micro-averages and mark significance by subscripts (R=$F_{R\&R}$, S=F_{Sem}).

We first discuss the classifiers trained on **unbalanced data**. With $F_{R\&R}$, CL_M^{-b} yields performance comparable to R&R's results, at 84.44% accuracy, 1.02pp below the majority baseline. Individual lexical classifiers also approach R&R's performance, though never beating the baseline.[7]

[4] Following R&R we use the Stanford parser for processing and induce maximum entropy models using OpenNLP with default parameter settings.

[5] R&R performed 10-fold cross-validation (CV) for evaluation. We perform 5-fold cross-validation instead.

[6] When doing oversampling, we generally perform a mixture of over- and undersampling, targeting about half the size of the larger class. The data sets are available at http://projects.cl.uni-heidelberg.de/modals.

[7] We report individual results, while R&R aggregated

	CL_M^{-b} train			CL_{MH}^{-b} train			CL_M^{+b} train			CL_{MH}^{+b} train			MPQA test		
	ep	de	dy	ep	de	dy	ep	de	dy	ep	de	dy	ep	de	dy
must	6	149	0	806	949	0	70	70	0	870	870	0	5	34	0
may	105	6	0	1055	956	0	50	50	0	999	1000	0	25	3	0
can	1	98	212	151	248	362	100	100	100	250	250	250	1	17	60
could	120	15	57	160	55	97	54	54	54	94	94	94	36	2	10
should	21	196	0	171	355	0	100	100	0	250	250	0	5	52	0
shall	0	9	1	0	14	6	0	10	10	0	15	15	0	2	1

Table 3: Cross-validation, one run: representative class distributions of training and test data.

$F_{R\&R}$	R&R	CL_M^{-b}	BL_{Maj_M}	CL_{MH}^{-b}	CL_M^{+b}	CL_{MH}^{+b}	CL_H^{+b}	BL_{Ran}
must	93.50	**94.32**	**94.32**	82.00	**76.25**	73.24	71.65	50.00
may	81.43	**93.57**	**93.57**	90.71	79.29	88.57^{M}	$\mathbf{90.71}^{M}$	50.00
might		100.00	100.00	100.00	100.00	100.00	100.00	100.00
can	68.70	66.56	**69.92**	64.25	49.86	53.19	**57.84**	33.33
could		62.50	**65.00**	59.17	41.25	44.17	**49.17**	33.33
should	91.29	90.77	**90.81**	90.77	80.21	$\mathbf{85.83}^{H}$	76.33	50.00
shall		83.33	84.61	**90.00**	70.00	**90.00**	53.85	50.00
macro-avg.	83.73	84.44	**85.46**	82.41	70.98	**76.43**	71.36	52.38
micro-avg.		78.71^{MH}	$\mathbf{80.22}^{M,MH}$	75.22	62.59	$\mathbf{66.24}^{M}$	66.08^{M}	41.54

F_{Sem}	R&R	CL_M^{-b}	BL_{Maj_M}	CL_{MH}^{-b}	CL_M^{+b}	CL_{MH}^{+b}	CL_H^{+b}	BL_{Ran}
must	93.50	93.28	**94.32**	88.11	85.48	**87.07**	86.08	50.00
may	81.43	92.86	**93.57**	87.14	83.57	**87.14**	84.29	50.00
might		100.00	100.00	100.00	100.00	100.00	100.00	100.00
can	68.70	65.03	**69.92**	61.43	58.38	**58.61**	55.78	33.33
could		**72.08**	65.00	69.17	**59.17**	57.50	50.00	33.33
should	91.29	89.71	**90.81**	90.79	**82.68**	81.97	79.15	50.00
shall		83.33	**84.61**	66.67	**76.67**	66.67	46.15	50.00
macro-avg.	83.73	85.18	**85.46**	80.47	**77.99**	76.99	71.64	52.38
micro-avg.		79.59^{MH}	$\mathbf{80.22}^{MH}$	76.57	71.17^{H}_{R}	$\mathbf{71.32}^{H}_{R}$	67.67	41.54

F_{All}	R&R	CL_M^{-b}	BL_{Maj_M}	CL_{MH}^{-b}	CL_M^{+b}	CL_{MH}^{+b}	CL_H^{+b}	BL_{Ran}
must	93.50	**94.32**	**94.32**	92.27	86.02	**90.72**	88.66	50.00
may	81.43	**93.57**	**93.57**	92.14	87.86	**92.14**	**92.14**	50.00
might		100.00	100.00	100.00	100.00	100.00	100.00	100.00
can	68.70	65.28	**69.92**	65.27	54.50	58.60	**63.50**	33.33
could		**66.67**	65.00	65.42	**63.33**	59.58	54.17	33.33
should	91.29	90.77	**90.81**	90.77	84.09	$\mathbf{90.79}^{M,H}$	84.09	50.00
shall		83.33	84.61	**90.00**	83.33	**90.00**	53.85	50.00
macro-avg.	83.73	84.85	**85.46**	85.12	79.88	**83.12**	76.63	52.38
micro-avg.		79.11	$\mathbf{80.22}^{MH}$	78.47_{R}	71.73_{R}	$\mathbf{75.06}^{M}_{R,S}$	$73.31_{R,S}$	41.54

Table 4: Classifier accuracy for various training data and feature sets. See text for details.

Changing from $F_{R\&R}$ to F_{Sem} and F_{All}, classifier CL_M^{-b} for *could* is now able to beat the baseline. The effect is stronger for F_{Sem}, which reflects the impact of the semantic features. Interestingly, accuracy of F_{Sem} is comparable to $F_{R\&R}$, even though the classifiers learn **only** on the basis of semantic features. Combining the two feature sets (F_{All}) produces minimal differences for CL_M^{-b}, but yields stronger gains for CL_{MH}^{-b}.

may/might and shall/should.

The addition of heuristically-tagged data in CL_{MH}^{-b} helps for some verbs, but hurts for others. Despite the larger training set size, individual classifier performances tend to drop, meaning they do not profit much from the reduced training bias.

For classifiers trained on **balanced data**, the picture changes. Accuracies on balanced data are lower, reflecting the lack of distributional bias. But all results are well above the random BL.[8]

[8]All comparisons to the random baseline are significant

Compared to CL_M^{+b} and CL_H^{+b}, we observe the best results for CL_{MH}^{+b}, which mixes MPQA and out-of-domain data. Here, the best performance is obtained with F_{All}. In fact, CL_{MH}^{+b} with 83.12% on balanced mixed data closely approaches the performance of the classifiers trained on biased training data and their majority baseline, with about 2pp difference, and being almost identical to R&R's published results.

Looking at **individual modal classifiers**, we see even more interesting results. *can* and *could*, both with 3-fold sense distinctions and lowest performance overall, suffer the greatest loss in the balanced setting, in ranges of 41-57% for $F_{R\&R}$. These verbs are hard to classify, and here we see a marked performance rise as the training data changes (from CL_M^{+b} to CL_H^{+b}), though these differences are not significant. Comparing F_{Sem} to $F_{R\&R}$, we obtain better results overall, always above 50% accuracy. With F_{All} we reach a range of 54-63%, achieving strong gains of more than +20pp for *could*, and about +5pp for *can*. We also note an almost continous rise for *should* with a final +5pp gain over $F_{R\&R}$. Across different feature sets, CL_{MH}^{+b} performs best, that is, combining MPQA and out-of-domain data is effective.

To summarize, with increasingly refined models and a tendency of CL_{MH} and CL_H outperforming CL_M, we obtain a coherent picture: semantic features contribute important information and reach their best performance with a mixture of training sets. We also note that F_{Sem} and F_{All} jointly yield significant gains over $F_{R\&R}$ for *could, must, should, can* and *may*.[9]

5.3 Impact of feature groups

A confusion analysis of the predictions made by CL_H^{+b} using $F_{R\&R}$ yields some insight into the most difficult sense distinctions for specific modal verbs. Table 5 highlights the most prominent misclassification classes: for instance, deontic *can* is misclassified as *dynamic* in 106 cases; epistemic *could* is misclassified as dynamic in 53 cases, etc.

For a deeper analysis of the impact of our semantic features, particularly on specific sense distinctions, we conducted a quantitative and qualitative evaluation by ablating individual feature groups (FGs) from the full feature sets F_{Sem} and F_{All}, for all balanced classifiers.

except: CL_M^{+b} and CL_{MH}^{+b} with F_{Sem} for *should*, and anything involving *shall*.

[9]Cross-feature set significance for individual verbs is not marked in Table 4.

can	ep	de	dy	*could*	ep	de	dy
ep	1	0	1	ep	92	11	**53**
de	8	1	**106**	de	6	2	9
dy	**28**	**21**	223	dy	**30**	6	31

must	ep	de	*should*	ep	de
ep	5	6	ep	4	**22**
de	**43**	140	de	**48**	209

Table 5: Confusion analysis: CL_H^{+b} using $F_{R\&R}$

It turns out that precisely for the modal verbs that exhibit prominent confusion classes in Table 5 we observe a significant performance drop when omitting individual feature groups (FGs): Table 6 reports all configurations where omitting a particular FG yielded a significant accuracy loss. In the following we analyze these cases in more detail.

Analysis. *Gains* (or *rescues*) due to FG_x are cases in which including FG_x turns a wrong classification into a correct one, compared to a model that ablates FG_x. *Losses* record the opposite: a correct classification made without FG_x becomes incorrect when FG_x is active.

Overall, for both models F_{Sem} and F_{All} we observe **more gains than losses** due to the FGs SBJ, NEG, TVA(/LA) and WN: 140 vs. 41 (29% losses) for F_{Sem} and 195 vs. 42 (22% losses) for F_{All}. For *must* there are only gains and no losses at all.

We observe different performance for correction of misclassifications for the different modal verbs, and we see clearly distinct contribution of FGs for the individual modal verb classifiers.

The most clear-cut positive effects are obtained for ***must***, with the highest number of gains (62/81 for F_{Sem}/F_{All}) and no losses. Here, exclusively the FGs TVA and TVA/LA are effective, leading to a majority of rescues of *deontic* readings that otherwise would be misclassified as *epistemic*. 5 rescues in the other direction occur, only with F_{Sem}.

Rescues for ***must*** through FG TVA/LA all meet the assumption that dynamic event readings of the verb go along with *deontic* sense (14.a), while stative readings (14.b) go along with *epistemic* sense.

(14) a. "Everything *must* be **done** by everyone to bring about de-escalation" [..]

b. And as all *must* now **know** [..] Mugabe has no chance of winning any ballot [..]

A particularly strong effect is seen for TVA, which avoids misclassification of up to 12% of all instances of ***must*** as *epistemic*. All cases follow the pattern in (15.a): the verb is not in past tense, and we prefer a deontic interpretation, whereas past tense in (15.b) indicates epistemic usage.

(15) a. [..] whoever is on the other side is the evil that must **be** destroyed [..]
b. The event must **have** rocked the halls of power [..]

should displays similar sense ambiguities and confusion patterns, but here the picture is less clear: as with *must* we obtain rescues of *deontic* readings, but here the WN features are most effective, jointly with SBJ. In contrast to *must*, we observe a mixture of gains (30/13) and losses (11/7) due mostly to over-correction. While for the other modal verbs, the gains/losses ratio is best for the F_{All} model, *should* performs best with F_{Sem}.

For ***could***, with a 3-way ambiguity, a different feature set is active: SBJ and NEG. Most rescues to *epistemic* are due to including SBJ features, and a strong effect is also seen for NEG. For both FGs we also observe gains of *dynamic* readings from *epistemic* misclassifications, while this effect is stronger for NEG, also in avoiding overcorrection. On the losses side, we observe 32% of losses as opposed to gains for F_{All}.

SBJ features apparently capture a preference for inanimate, abstract subjects for *epistemic* as opposed to deontic (or dynamic) readings, as with *the message* or propositional anaphora in (16.a,b). The same pattern is observed with ***should*** (16.c).

(16) a. "**the message** *could* not be clearer."
b. [..] officials said **this** *could* prompt industries to change behavior ....
c. [..] if **that** *should* prove necessary, De Winne will [..] pilot the space ship.

For NEG we see a clear effect that ***could***, if negated, is correctly analyzed as *dynamic*, while non-negated instances are classified as *epistemic*.

(17) a. Baghdad insisted [..] it *could* **not** be a threat to the United States.
b. Two basic principles *could* still, perhaps, make it possible.

Finally, ***can*** is our most difficult case. We obtain moderate gains (15) by rescues of *dynamic* readings from *epistemic/deontic*, through the SBJ feature. As we see no gains with F_{Sem}, this means we are still lacking precise features that can differentiate epistemic and dynamic readings.

verb	FG	comp. to	impact CL_M^{+b}	CL_{MH}^{+b}	CL_H^{+b}
can	SBJ	F_{All}			2.83*
could	SBJ	F_{Sem}		12.50**	
		F_{All}		6.25*	11.25**
	NEG	F_{Sem}		4.58*	
		F_{All}	6.25**		
must	TVA	F_{Sem}		5.69**	9.79**
		F_{All}		10.32**	11.86**
	TVA	F_{Sem}		6.21**	10.31**
	/LA	F_{All}	3.09*	10.32**	
					12.37**
should	SBJ	F_{Sem}			10.60**
		F_{All}			5.64**
	WN	F_{Sem}	6.01*		

**: p=0.01; *: p=0.05

Table 6: Accuracy loss by FG omission. $3rd$ column specifies from which feature set we ablate.

6 Conclusion

We show that difficult problems in modal sense disambiguation can be addressed with semantically enriched classification models that draw upon lexical, propositional and discourse-level semantic information. Our model obtains significant improvements, especially for difficult sense distinctions, in balanced training setups. This will prove advantageous when applying the classifiers to documents with sense distributions that differ from training. We further presented a method for automatic induction of training corpora that helps to alleviate sparsity and can be used to tailor training data to specific genres and domains.

The insights we gain from analyzing the impact of feature groups indicate avenues for future work: The sensitivity of modal senses to semantic properties of the subject calls for integration of antecedent information with pronominal subjects. The dependence on temporal information calls for temporal resolution. Our current model offers only a simple approximation of propositional semantics. We expect further improvements with a more effective representation of propositional content and addition of more training data.

Acknowledgements This work has been partially funded through the Leibniz ScienceCampus *Empirical Linguistics and Computational Language Modeling*, supported by the Leibniz Association under grant no. SAS-2015-IDS-LWC and by the Ministry of Science, Research, and Art (MWK) of the state of Baden-Württemberg. The third author is supported in part by the MMCI Cluster of Excellence. We thank the anonymous reviewers for helpful comments.

References

Baayen, H. R., Piepenbrock, R., and Gulikers, L. (1996). CELEX2. Philadelphia: Linguistic Data Consortium.

Baker, K., Bloodgood, M., Dorr, B. J., Filardo, N. W., Levin, L., and Piatko, C. (2010). A Modality Lexicon and its use in Automatic Tagging. In *Proceedings of LREC*, pages 1402–1407.

Cohen, J. (1960). A coefficient for agreement for nominal scales. *Education and Psychological Measurement*, (20):37–46.

de Marneffe, M.-C., Manning, C. D., and Potts, C. (2011). Veridicality and Utterance Understanding. *2011 IEEE Fifth International Conference on Semantic Computing*, pages 430–437.

Diab, M. and Resnik, P. (2002). An unsupervised method for word sense tagging using parallel corpora. In *Proceedings of ACL 2002*, pages 255–262, Philadelphia, Pennsylvania, USA.

Fellbaum, C. (1999). *WordNet*. Wiley Online Library.

Friedrich, A. and Palmer, A. (2014). Automatic prediction of aspectual class of verbs in context. In *Proceedings of the ACL 2014*.

Ganitkevitch, J., Van Durme, B., and Callison-Burch, C. (2013). PPDB: The Paraphrase Database. In *Proceedings of the ACL-HLT 2013*, pages 758–764, Atlanta, Georgia.

Klein, D. and Manning, C. D. (2002). Fast exact inference with a factored model for natural language parsing. In *Advances in neural information processing systems*, pages 3–10.

Koehn, P. (2005). Europarl: A parallel corpus for statistical machine translation. In *Proceedings of Machine Translation Summit X*, pages 79–86.

Kratzer, A. (1991). Modality. In von Stechow, A. and Wunderlic, D., editors, *Semantics: An International Handbook of Contemporary Research*, pages 639–650. Berlin: de Gruyter.

Loaiciga, S., Meyer, T., and Popescu-Belis, A. (2014). English-French Verb Phrase Alignment in Europarl. In *Proceedings of LREC 2014*.

Manning, C. D., Surdeanu, M., Bauer, J., Finkel, J., Bethard, S. J., and McClosky, D. (2014). The Stanford CoreNLP natural language processing toolkit. In *Proceedings of ACL 2014: System Demonstrations*, pages 55–60.

McNemar, Q. (1947). Note on the sampling error of the difference between correlated proportions or percentages. *Psychometrika*.

Nissim, M., Pietrandrea, P., Sanso, A., and Mauri, C. (2013). Cross-linguistic annotation of modality: a data-driven hierarchical model. In *Proceedings of the 9th Joint ISO - ACL SIGSEM Workshop on Interoperable Semantic Annotation*, pages 7–14, Potsdam, Germany.

Reiter, N. and Frank, A. (2010). Identifying Generic Noun Phrases. In *Proceedings of the ACL 2010*, pages 40–49, Uppsala, Sweden.

Ruppenhofer, J. and Rehbein, I. (2012). Yes we can !? Annotating the senses of English modal verbs. In *Proceedings of the LREC 2012*, pages 1538–1545.

Siegel, E. V. and McKeown, K. R. (2000). Learning methods to combine linguistic indicators: Improving aspectual classification and revealing linguistic insights. *Computational Linguistics*, 26(4):595–628.

Tiedemann, J. (2012). Parallel Data, Tools and Interfaces in OPUS. In Calzolari, N., Choukri, K., Declerck, T., Doğan, M. U., Maegaard, B., Mariani, J., Odijk, J., and Piperidis, S., editors, *Proceedings of LREC-2012*, pages 2214–2218, Istanbul, Turkey.

Vendler, Z. (1957). *Linguistics in Philosophy*, chapter Verbs and Times, pages 97–121. Cornell University Press, Ithaca, New York.

Wiebe, J., Wilson, T., and Cardie, C. (2005). Annotating expressions of opinions and emotions in language. *Language resources and evaluation*, 39(2-3):165 – 210.

Yarowsky, D. and Ngai, G. (2001). Inducing Multilingual POS Taggers and NP Bracketers via Robust Projection Across Aligned Corpora. In *Proceedings of the Second Meeting of ACL 2001*, pages 200–207.

Identification and Disambiguation of Lexical Cues of Rhetorical Relations across Different Text Genres

Taraneh Khazaei
Department of Computer Science
University of Western Ontario
London, ON, Canada
tkhazae@uwo.ca

Lu Xiao
Faculty of Information & Media Studies
University of Western Ontario
London, ON, Canada
lxiao24@uwo.ca

Robert E. Mercer
Department of Computer Science
University of Western Ontario
London, ON, Canada
mercer@uwo.ca

Abstract

Lexical cues are linguistic expressions that can signal the presence of a rhetorical relation. However, such cues can be ambiguous as they may signal more than one relation or may not always function as a relation indicator. In this study, we first conduct a corpus-based analysis to derive a set of n-grams as potential lexical cues. These cues are then utilized in graph-based probabilistic models to determine the syntactic context in which the cue is signaling the presence of a particular relation. Evaluation results are reported for various cues of the CIRCUMSTANCE relation, confirming the value of syntactic features for the task of cue disambiguation in the context of Rhetorical Structure Theory. Moreover, using a graph to encode syntactic information is shown to be a more generalizable and effective approach compared to the direct usage of syntactic features.

1 Introduction

A semantically sound text consists of discourse units that are connected through discourse relations, which are also referred to as rhetorical relations. Despite the efforts to build robust theoretical foundations and taxonomies for such relations (Hobbs, 1990; Knott and Sanders, 1998; Lascarides and Asher, 1993; Mann and Thompson, 1988), current methods for their automatic analysis and discovery in written discourse have yet to improve. However, providing robust models to analyze and identify rhetorical relations can benefit various research directions in computational linguistics such as text generation (Hovy, 1993) and summarization (Marcu, 2000), and machine translation (Meyer et al., 2011).

One of the widely accepted frameworks for discourse analysis and understanding is Rhetorical Structure Theory (RST) (Mann and Thompson, 1988). In RST, discourse structure has a form of a tree, where the leaves correspond to elementary discourse units, and the internal nodes correspond to contiguous text spans. Each internal node is marked with a rhetorical relation that holds between its child nodes. Figure 1 provides an example of an RST tree taken from the RST corpus (Carlson et al., 2001). One of the notable differences of RST with other similar theories is that it is structured on the intentions of the writers to use those relations (Taboada, 2006). This distinctive feature can make it even more difficult to build models for automatic identification of rhetorical relations in the context of RST.

Rhetorical relations can be either explicit or implicit. Explicit relations are the ones that are signaled by cues, such as lexical cues, mood, modality, and intonation (Taboada, 2006), while no cue is present in implicit relations. In this study, we are focused on explicit relations in written text that are signaled by the presence of lexical cues. Lexical cues are defined as linguistic expressions that function as explicit indicators of a discourse relation (Hirschberg and Litman, 1993). For example, in the sentence provided in Figure 1, *but* and *because* can be considered lexical cues signaling the existence of the CONCESSION relation and the EXPLANATION-ARGUMENTATIVE relation, respectively.

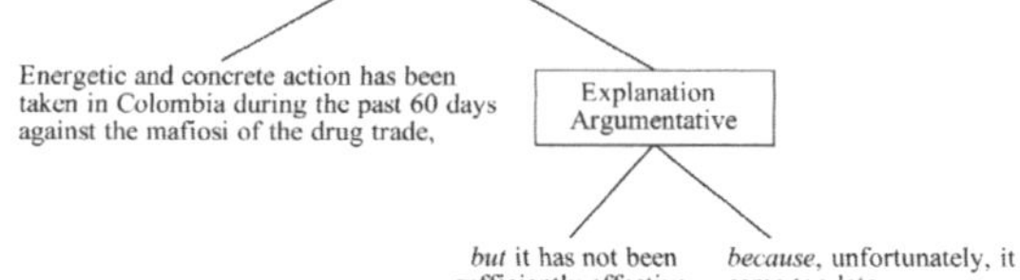

Figure 1: An example sentence parsed in the form of RST

Proceedings of the EMNLP 2015 Workshop on Linking Models of Lexical, Sentential and Discourse-level Semantics, pages 54–63, Lisboa, Portugal, 18 September 2015.

Since this study is part of a larger project to identify rationales in written discourse, we focus on the three relations of CIRCUMSTANCE, EVALUATION, and ELABORATION that are commonly present in rationales (Xiao, 2013a). With the aim of proposing a cue-based approach to extract rhetorical relations, we have carried out some corpus-based experiments on RST annotated corpora. As a result of these experiments, we have generated a list of key n-grams as potential lexical cues for each relation. Such a corpus-based method may result in the discovery of underexplored lexical cues.

Even though lexical cues can be exploited to label rhetorical relations, they are not always unambiguous (Pitler and Nenkova, 2009). Some linguistic expressions may or may not function as a lexical cue, or they may signal different types of relations in different sentences. Hence, here, we propose a graph-based probabilistic model that takes into account the syntactic features of sentences. These models are intended to determine in what syntactic context a lexical cue is indeed signaling the presence of a particular relation. The models are then applied and tested on two corpora that belong to different text genres: news articles and online reviews.

The evaluation results of the approach are presented and discussed for the CIRCUMSTANCE relation. The CIRCUMSTANCE relation exists when a context of time or situation is presented, wherein the main events and ideas provided in the sentence can be interpreted in. CIRCUMSTANCE is chosen as the relation of focus since (Khazaei and Xiao, 2015) revealed that the cue-based approaches can be well-suited for the detection of CIRCUMSTANCE across different genres, while the ELABORATION relation is not normally signaled. In addition, the features of the underlying text genre can significantly influence how EVALUATION is signaled (Khazaei and Xiao, 2015).

The remainder of this paper is organized as follows: An overview of the previous research on lexical cue disambiguation is provided in Section 2. In Section 3, an explanation of the underlying corpora and the methods used to extract and disambiguate the cues is provided. The evaluation results are presented in Section 4. A discussion of the findings is given in Section 5, followed by a conclusion of the study in Section 6.

2 Related Work

The majority of studies focusing on discourse parsing and discourse relation classification report results achieved from both explicit and implicit relations (Soricut and Marcu, 2003; Wellner et al., 2006; Versley, 2013). Among the works that are particularly focused on lexical cue disambiguation, a large proportion are conducted on the Penn Discourse TreeBank (PDTB) (Prasad et al., 2008), while fewer studies have been conducted to study other discourse theories and frameworks.

PDTB annotation is lexically-grounded, and it is theory-neutral with respect to higher-level discourse structure (Rashmi et al., 2014). In the course of the annotation, the annotators were asked to seek lexical items that can signal relations and then annotate their corresponding arguments and relations (Rashmi et al., 2014). Even for implicit relations, annotators were asked to look for adjacent sentences that lacked one of these signals. When a relation could be inferred, they were asked to first label the relation with a lexical item that could serve as a signal and then annotate the relation sense. Such a lexically oriented approach to annotate relations has motivated a lot of work on disambiguation of lexical cues in PDTB.

For example, Miltsakaki et al. (Miltsakaki et al., 2005) have utilized a set of syntactic features along with a supervised model to disambiguate three discourse cues of *while*, *since*, and *when*. Their feature set includes form of the auxiliary *have*, form of the auxiliary *be*, form of the head, and presence of a modal. They obtained an accuracy of 75.5% to classify *since*, 71.8% for *while*, and 61.6% for *when*.

Pitler and Nenkova (Pitler and Nenkova, 2009) used a set of syntactic features to disambiguate cues regarding their discourse and non-discourse usage and sense disambiguation. Their features consist of the syntactic category of the marker, its parent, and its siblings. Two binary features are also taken into account to indicate whether the right sibling contains a VP and/or a trace. Their best feature set also included pairwise interaction features between the cues and syntactic features, and between the syntactic features themselves. Their learning algorithm resulted in an F-score of 92.28% for discourse versus non-discourse usage and an accuracy of 94.15% for sense classification. These results were later improved in (Ibn Faiz and Mercer, 2013), where a set of surface-level and syntactic features are introduced and are combined with the feature set presented in (Pitler and Nenkova, 2009). The results of a classifier trained on this feature set resulted in an F-score of 96.22%.

Within a broader context of building an end-to-end discourse parser for PDTB, Lin et al. (Lin et al., 2014) built a cue classifier to identify whether a lexical item functions as a discourse cue or not. In addition to the features used in (Pitler and Nenkova, 2009), they also included part-of-speech features as well as features related to the syntactic parse path from the cue to the root of the tree. Using their set of lexico-syntactic and path features resulted in an F-score of 95.36%.

Meyer et al. (Meyer et al., 2011) used their own annotation schema developed based on parallel corpora and translation spotting to annotate three cues, two in English and one in French. Their annotation roughly follows a PDTB-like annotation and is likewise lexically-grounded. The annotated corpora was then used to train a learning model based on a set of features deemed valuable, including POS-tagged and parsed sentences, to disambiguate the lexical cues. As their best result, they achieved an accuracy of 85.7%.

Even though RST is one of the most widely accepted frameworks for discourse analysis, relatively little attention has been paid to RST annotated corpora in regards to lexical cue analysis and disambiguation. Unlike PDTB, annotations following RST are not lexically-grounded, and every relation is defined in terms of intentions that lead authors to use those specific relations (Taboada, 2006). Therefore, an RST diagram represents some of the authors' purposes or intentions for including each part of the text (Taboada, 2006). Such attributes of RST annotations make it a challenging task to study the role of lexical items in relation classification and to disambiguate them.

Marcu (Marcu, 2000) attempted to create a rhetorical parsing algorithm. A corpus study was conducted to understand how cues can be used to identify elementary discourse units and hypothesize their corresponding relation. By utilizing prior studies on discourse analysis, he created a list of 450 discourse cues to start with. An average of 17 text spans associated with each cue was then collected from the Brown corpus. All of the sentences were then annotated with two sets of metadata: discourse-related information and algorithmic features. Using these annotations, which mostly capture the orthographic environments of the cues, a set of regular expressions was created manually to recognize potential cues. If a cue had different discourse functions in different orthographic environments, a separate regular expression was made for each case. The algorithm resulted in an 84.9% F-score for the sub-task of cue identification. For the sub-task of relation classification, they achieved an F-score of 58.76%.

HILDA (Hernault et al., 2010) is a discourse parser developed to automatically construct the RST tree by performing the two core tasks of text segmentation and relation labeling. The relation labeling model takes into account the textual organization, structural organization, and lexical information of text as the underlying feature set. The performance results of a supervised model built on this feature set varies widely across different relations, ranging from 95% to 3.9% in F-score. The results are only reported for a subset of relations, within which the CIRCUMSTANCE relation is not present. On average, they achieved an F-score of 47.7% for labeling rhetorical relations.

In (da Cunha, 2013), a set of cues is first extracted from the database of Spanish discourse cues. The context of each cue is then extracted from the RST Spanish Treebank and is given to a syntactic parser. The syntactic features of the context of each cue are then manually analyzed to identify potential linguistic regularities and patterns. By using the results of the analysis, linguistic rules are developed to disambiguate the lexical cues. Their rules achieved an accuracy of 60.65%.

More recent studies on relation labeling in the context of RST have improved these results. For example, (Joty et al., 2013) has obtained an F-score of roughly 55% for their relation detection task. They made use of various organization features, textual features, lexio-syntactic features, lexical chains, as well as a lexical n-gram dictionary. These results are slightly improved by Ji and Eisenstein (Ji and Eisenstein, 2014), as they achieved an F-score of roughly 61% to detect rhetorical relations. They proposed a feature representation learning method in a shift-reduce discourse parser.

Many of the prior works on RST relation annotation are semi-automated and include manual steps. The few approaches that provide fully-automated cue-based techniques (Ji and Eisenstein, 2014; Joty et al., 2013; Hernault et al., 2010) have focused both their training and test process on a similar text genre. Even when focused on a single genre, to the best of our knowledge, the previous state-of-the art in relation labeling have resulted in an F-score of 61.75% (Ji and Eisenstein, 2014). Our work is intended to provide an automated approach to detect potential lexical cues that can indicate rhetorical relations, and to analyze whether their syntactic context can be of value for cue disambiguation across two different text genres.

3 Approach

In this section, we first describe the two RST annotated corpora that are used in the present work: RST corpus (Carlson et al., 2001) and Simon Fraser University (SFU) review dataset (Taboada et al., 2006). Then, an explanation of the approach used to extract a set of key n-grams as potential lexical cues is presented, which is followed by a description of our graph-based approach to disambiguate lexical cues.

3.1 Corpora

We used two human-annotated corpora as our underlying datasets for the experiments: the RST corpus (Carlson et al., 2001) and the SFU review dataset (Taboada et al., 2006). Both corpora are annotated in the RST framework and are constructed using the RSTTool[1].

The RST corpus, which has been made available by the Linguistic Data Consortium over the years, includes 385 *Wall Street Journal* articles and covers more than 178,000 words. Among the relation instances in the RST corpus, there exist around 700 instances of CIRCUMSTANCE, which constitutes almost 3% of the total number of relation instances.

The SFU review corpus is a collection of 400 review documents from movie, book, and consumer products. This dataset contains over 303,000 words and was collected in 2004 from the Epinions Web site[2]. There exist around 1300 CIRCUMSTANCE instances, constituting almost 7% of the annotated instances in the corpus.

[1] http://www.wagsoft.com/RSTTool

[2] http://www.epinions.com/

3.2 Lexical Cue Selection

The news text has a well-structured formal writing style, whereas the online reviews are relatively less structured and informal, written by users with a wide range of writing abilities. Therefore, to extract lexical cues associated with a given relation, we used the RST corpus.

First, all the relation instances are extracted from the RST corpus and are collected in a relation document named after the corresponding relation. Then, following the approach proposed in (Biran and Rambow, 2011), all the n-grams (up to trigrams) are extracted from the composed relation document. For each n-gram, an altered version of TF-IDF metric is then calculated. The IDF measure is still calculated based on the number of documents that contain the n-gram and the total number of documents in the corpus. However, since each line corresponds to one instance of the relation, the TF metric is calculated based on the number of lines that contain at least one instance of the n-gram. This altered metric allows us to offset the potential bias that may be caused by the TF metric for the words appearing more than once in a relation instance.

The list of the extracted n-grams (i.e., lexical cues) is then filtered to only include the n-grams with their TF-IDF above 0.5. To filter any corpus-specific n-grams that may appear in the list, the n-grams extracted from the RST corpus are applied to the SFU review dataset to identify the corresponding relation. The F-score of each n-gram is then calculated independently. Finally, the n-grams with an F-score of above 0.1 are selected as potential lexical cues. The aforementioned procedure resulted in the selection of seven lexical cues for the CIRCUMSTANCE relation: *When*, *after*, *on*, *before*, *with*, *out*, *as*.

3.3 Lexical Cue Disambiguation

Our cue disambiguation approach is mainly inspired by the work of (Hassan et al., 2010) on the detection of sentences with attitudes. In their study, the text fragment that includes a second pronoun is first extracted as the most relevant part of a sentence. These fragments are then represented using different patterns, capturing their syntactic features and semantic orientation. For every kind of pattern, graph models are built based on sentences with and without attitude. Finally, the likelihood of a new sentence being generated from these models is used to predict the existence of an attitude. We adopted their approach for lexical cue disambiguation. Our graph models are built on the RST corpus and evaluated on the SFU review corpus and vice versa. Therefore, the graph building procedure explained below is conducted on both underlying corpora.

3.3.1 Data Collection

For every extracted cue, we first create two corresponding documents from the annotated corpora. One document consists of all of the relation instances that contain the cue and are annotated with the relation of focus (e.g., all of the CIRCUMSTANCE instances that are signaled by *when*). From now on, such instances will be referred to as positive instances. The other document consists of all the relation instances that contain the cue and are annotated as any relation except for the relation of focus (e.g., all of the non-circumstance instances that contain *when*). In the rest of this manuscript, we will refer to these instances as negative instances.

RST postulates a hierarchal structure on text, where a relation instance can be embedded in other instances. Therefore, during the extraction of the instances, we ensured not to collect negative instances that include any positive or negative sub-instance. We also ensured not to collect any positive instances that include negative sub-instances. The inclusion of such embedded instances would have resulted in redundant and incorrect data points. For example, consider the following positive instance from the RST corpus:

[*When* Mr. Gandhi came to power,]

[he ushered in new rules for business]$_{\text{circumstance}}$
When collecting negative instances, it was revealed that this instance was embedded in ten negative instances. However, since *when* is in fact functioning as a circumstance cue in all of them, those ten instances could not qualify as negative instances and so were excluded.

3.3.2 Syntactic Representations

After creation of the documents, each instance is processed and transformed into two different representations, capturing the syntactic features of the instance. To create the first syntactic representation, words in instances are replaced with their corresponding Part-Of-Speech (POS) tags, while the cue itself is kept as is. The second representation includes the shortest path from the root element to the cue in the dependency parse tree. The following is an example of the CIRCUMSTANCE relation, along with its two corresponding syntactic representations:

- Positive instance with *when* as the cue:
  When Mr. Gandhi came to power, he ushered in new rules for business

- POS-based representation:
  When NNP NNP VBD TO NN PRP VBD IN JJ NNS IN NN

- Shortest path representation:
  root advmod

We used the OpenNLP[3] toolkit to tokenize and POS tag the instances and the Stanford dependency parser to generate the parse trees (Klein and Manning, 2003).

3.3.3 Graph Modeling

We encoded the syntactic information of the instances in graph models. We build the directed weighted graph $G = (V, E), w$, where:

- V is the set of all possible tokens that may appear in the representations. For example, for the POS representations, V is the union of the set of all POS tags and the cue set.

- $E = V \times V$ is the set of all possible ordered transitions between any two tokens.

- $w \rightarrow [0 - 1]$ is a weighting function that assigns a probability value to an edge (i, j), which represents the probability of a transition from token i to token j.

Given a set of syntactic representations, the probability of a transition from token i to token j is calculated following a maximum likelihood estimation. Thus, the probability is calculated by dividing the number of times that token i is immediately followed by token j by the number of times that token i itself appears in the set.

This method of building the graphs is similar to language modeling but is conducted over a set of syntactic representations (Hassan et al., 2010). For every kind of representation, we build one graph based on the set of positive instances, and one based on the set of negative instances. As a result, given a cue (e.g., *when*) and its corresponding relation (e.g., CIRCUMSTANCE), we build four graph

[3]https://opennlp.apache.org/

models based on the following sets: POS representations of positive instances, POS representations of negative instances, dependency parsed representations of positive instances, and dependency parsed representations of negative sentences.

3.3.4 Cue Disambiguation Model

Finally, for our final cue disambiguation model, we utilize the probability values obtained from our graph models as the feature set for a standard machine-learning model. Given an instance and a graph, we calculate the likelihood of its syntactic representations to be generated from the corresponding syntactic graphs. The probability of a syntactic representation R that consists of a sequence of tokens $T_1, T_2, ..., T_n$ being generated from graph G is estimated using the following formula. Note that W is the weighting or probability transition function.

$$P_G(R) = \prod_{i=2}^{n} P(T_i|T_1, ..., T_{i-1})$$
$$= \prod_{i=2}^{n} W(T_{i-1}, T_i)$$

Given that we have four graph models, we can generate four probability values as our feature set. These features are further used in a standard supervised learning algorithm to disambiguate the cue and to classify the relation of a given instance. Figure 2 provides a high-level description of the entire process of cue extraction and disambiguation.

4 Evaluation

Given that our ultimate goal is to detect rationales from written discourse, our approach is evaluated for the CIRCUMSTANCE relation as it is the only cue-based relation that is known to be frequently present in rationales (Khazaei and Xiao, 2015; Xiao, 2013a). We carried out experiments using different forms of POS representations based on the number of POS tags surrounding the cue and the granularity of the tags. We conducted experiments using the entire POS tagged instance, using two POS tags before and two tags after the cue, and using one before and one after the cue. We also used three levels of POS tag granularity, including the finest, that is, the Penn English Treebank[4] tagset used by OpenNLP. We also used a medium and a coarse granularity that are created by gathering together similar tags into one high-level tag. Table 1 shows the tags that are grouped in each of these two granularity levels. Note that the tags not mentioned in the granularity levels are used as is.

Label	Medium Granularity	Coarse Granularity
JJ	JJ, JJR, JJS	JJ, JJR, JJS, DT, WDT
NN	NN, NNS, NNP, NNPS	NN, NNS, NNP, NNPS
PRP	PRP, PRP$	PRP, PRP$, WP, WP$
RB	RB, RBR, RBS	RB, RBR, RBS, WRB
WP	WP, WP$	-
VB	VB, VBD, VBN, VBP, VBZ	VB, VBD, VBN, VBP, VBZ, MD, VBG

Table 1: In addition to the POS tags in the Penn English Treebank tag set, experiments are conducted using tags grouped according to different levels of granularity.

Using these three variations of the two POS tag attributes resulted in nine different experimental settings. We achieved our best results on both corpora using one tag before and one tag after the cue and the medium granularity level. In this section, we report results for experiments using this particular POS setting.

The final algorithm built on probability values is evaluated using the Weka workbench[5]. It classifies instances via regression[6], and a stratified ten-fold cross validation is followed to evaluate the model. To gain insight into the effectiveness of the model in the disambiguation of different cues, results are reported for each of the seven cues independently. The SMOTE filter was used when significant class imbalance was encountered.

Table 2 demonstrates the results when the RST corpus was used to build the graphs, and the SFU corpus was used to build and test the final model. Table 3 shows the results of the evaluation, where graphs are built on the SFU corpus and used on the RST dataset. As can be seen, the measures of precision, recall, and F-score are reported, along with their average value. The weighted average of F-score is also provided, taking into account the distribution of relation instances that contain the cues in the test set. This metric is provided while bearing in mind that the test set may not be an accurate representative of the general distribution of relations. According to the results, on average, we were able to classify CIRCUMSTANCE with an F-

[4]http://www.cis.upenn.edu/ treebank/

[5]http://www.cs.waikato.ac.nz/ml/weka/

[6]ClassificationViaRegression algorithm is used with default parameters

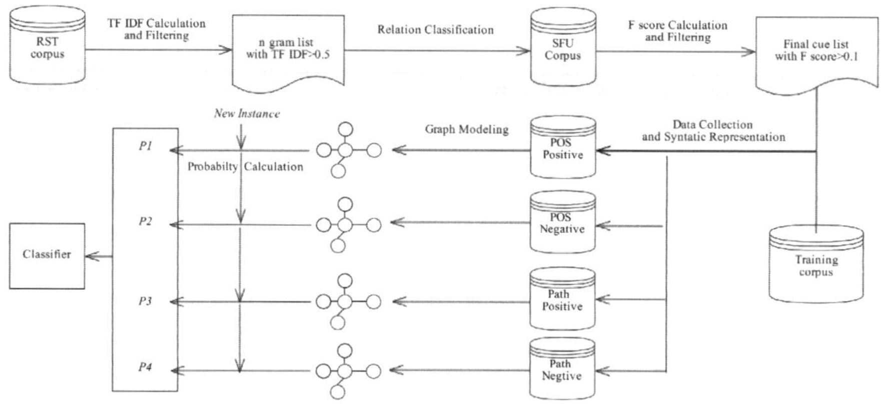

Figure 2: A high-level overview of the cue extraction and disambiguation approach

Cue	Precision	Recall	F-score
When	0.55	0.79	0.65
After	0.46	0.56	0.51
On	0.73	0.75	0.74
Before	0.62	0.60	0.61
With	0.76	0.80	0.78
Out	0.60	0.54	0.57
As	0.71	0.82	0.76
Average	0.63	0.69	0.66
Weighted Average			0.71

Table 2: Classification results of a ten-fold cross validation on the SFU corpus. Probability values used as the underlying feature set are inferred from the graph models built on the RST corpus.

Cue	Precision	Recall	F-score
When	0.62	0.69	0.65
After	0.61	0.57	0.59
On	0.77	0.81	0.79
Before	0.70	0.40	0.51
With	0.77	0.81	0.79
Out	0.75	0.70	0.73
As	0.73	0.67	0.70
Average	0.71	0.67	0.68
Weighted Average			0.69

Table 3: Classification results of a ten-fold cross validation on the RST dataset. Probability values used as the underlying feature set are inferred from the graph models built on the SFU corpus.

score of 0.66% in the SFU review dataset, while the weighted average of F-score is 0.71%. In addition, an average F-score of 0.68% and a weighted average of 0.69% are achieved for the RST corpus.

5 Discussion

The use of syntactic context to disambiguate lexical cues has been shown to be useful to disambiguate cues in lexically oriented relations (e.g., PDTB relations). In this study, we have focused our efforts on RST annotated corpora and explored the potential of syntactic context for cue disambiguation in the RST framework. We have demonstrated that syntactic features can be of great value in the classification of explicit rhetorical relations. In addition, unlike the majority of prior studies on cue disambiguation, we encoded the syntactic context of cues in the form of graphs. This graph-based approach was expected to provide a more generalizable and effective approach.

Earlier studies on the detection of relations in the context of RST are focused on a single text genre for their training phase as well as their test process; hence, their results are not directly comparable with our approach. In addition, they have not reported results for the CIRCUMSTANCE relation separately. Even though our average results for the detection of CIRCUMSTANCE (66% for the SFU corpus and 68% for the RST corpus) are higher than the state-of-the-art (61.75% (Ji and Eisenstein, 2014)), further experiments are required with other RST relations and different genres to make a sound comparison with such earlier works. To highlight the contribution of our work, we conducted experiments to compare the graph-based model with the direct usage of syntactic features. A logistic model was first trained on the RST corpus and tested on the SFU dataset (see Table 4), and then trained on the SFU corpus and tested on the RST corpus (see Table 5). The results are consistently lower for all of the three measures, confirming the superiority of our approach.

Based on the results of our proposed approach, it can be seen that the three lexical cues of *when*, *after*, and *before* have the lowest performance in the RST corpus (see Table 3). They are also

Cue	Precision	Recall	F-score
When	0.50	0.41	0.45
After	0.39	0.15	0.22
On	0.65	0.28	0.39
Before	0.52	0.49	0.51
With	0.53	0.34	0.41
Out	0.51	0.19	0.28
As	0.49	0.24	0.32
Average	0.51	0.30	0.37

Table 4: Classification results on the SFU corpus when the syntactic features are used directly to train a model on the RST corpus

Cue	Precision	Recall	F-score
When	0.53	0.65	0.58
After	0.31	0.14	0.20
On	0.36	0.17	0.23
Before	0.33	0.22	0.26
With	0.62	0.20	0.30
Out	0.57	0.53	0.55
As	0.52	0.25	0.34
Average	0.52	0.25	0.35

Table 5: Classification results on the RST corpus when the syntactic features are used directly to train a model on the SFU corpus

among the four cues with lowest F-score in the SFU dataset (see Table 2). This finding could be attributed to the fact that, for these three cues, the corresponding datasets were among the smallest cue sets. Possibly more importantly, these three cues can function as temporal indicators, which may make it particularly difficult to disambiguate them. For example, consider the following instances extracted from the SFU corpus:

- Positive instance:
  When I have time to kill between flights, I like to wander through and browse
- Negative instance:
  I was surprised *when* he told me that all the equipment was standard even on the base model

The first sentence is an instance of the CIRCUMSTANCE relation signaled by *when*, while in the second one, *when* implies the temporal aspect of the sentence and is not signaling CIRCUMSTANCE. We expect that certain linguistic and contextual features associated with the text, such as verb tense, might be useful in the disambiguation of such lexical cues. Further studies are required to explore these features.

Since RST places an emphasis on the writer's intentions and the effect of the relation on the reader (Taboada, 2006), RST annotations are inherently subjective and are based on the readers' understanding of the text (Taboada, 2006). Hence, there can be differences across the two corpora due to the different knowledge possessed by each set of annotators (Taboada, 2006). Despite the genre disparity and annotation issues, we obtained encouraging results using the proposed model. However, the results are expected to improve when the models are built on corpora from similar genres and are annotated using ground truth rules.

6 Conclusion

The study and analysis of rhetorical relations, as the building blocks of coherence in discourse, can contribute toward the development of sophisticated applications and algorithms. With the aim of facilitating automatic discovery of explicit rhetorical relations in text, we developed an algorithm to first detect potential lexical cues and to later disambiguate them by predicting the relation.

An altered version of TF-IDF was used to extract the cues, and a graph-based model built on syntactic features was used to address the cue disambiguation task. Overall, the evaluation results indicate the effectiveness of syntactic features in the disambiguation of cues and prediction of explicit rhetorical relations across different genres. Our experiments revealed the superiority of encoding such syntactic features in a probabilistic graph compared to their direct usage.

This study is our first attempt toward the identification of rationales in text. A rationale is an explanation of the reasons underlying decisions, conclusions, and interpretations. Prior studies on rationale articulation and sharing suggest that it contributes to quality control, knowledge management, and knowledge reuse (Xiao, 2014; Xiao, 2013b). However, there exists only a few automated methods to identify rationales from ill-structured text (Ghosh et al., 2014; Boltužić and Šnajder, 2014). Our future research efforts are focused on the development of algorithms to extract lightly-signaled and implicit relations and to further explore the potential and limitations of using rhetorical relations in the detection of rationales.

Acknowledgments

This project is funded through the Discovery program of Natural Sciences and Engineering Research Council of Canada (NSERC).

References

Or Biran and Owen Rambow. 2011. Identifying justifications in written dialogs. In *Proceedings of the IEEE International Conference on Semantic Computing*, pages 162–168.

Filip Boltužić and Jan Šnajder. 2014. Back up your stance: Recognizing arguments in online discussions. In *Proceedings of the First Workshop on Argumentation Mining*, pages 49–58.

Lynn Carlson, Daniel Marcu, and Mary Ellen Okurowski. 2001. Building a discourse tagged corpus in the framework of Rhetorical Structure Theory. In *Proceedings of the SIGdial Workshop on Discourse and Dialogue*, pages 1–10.

Iria da Cunha. 2013. A symbolic corpus-based approach to detect and solve the ambiguity of discourse markers. *Research in Computing Science*, 70:93–104.

Debanjan Ghosh, Smaranda Muresan, Nina Wacholder, Mark Aakhus, and Matthew Mitsui. 2014. Analyzing argumentative discourse units in online interactions. In *Proceedings of the First Workshop on Argumentation Mining*, pages 39–48.

Ahmed Hassan, Vahed Qazvinian, and Dragomir Radev. 2010. What's with the attitude? Identifying sentences with attitude in online discussions. In *Proceedings of the Conference on Empirical Methods in Natural Language Processing*, pages 1245–1255.

Hugo Hernault, Helmut Prendinger, David Duverle, Mitsuru Ishizuka, and Tim Paek. 2010. HILDA: A discourse parser using support vector machine classification. *Dialogue and Discourse*, 3(1):1–33.

Julia Hirschberg and Diane Litman. 1993. Empirical studies on the disambiguation of cue phrases. *Computational Linguistics*, 19(3):501–530.

J.R. Hobbs. 1990. *Literature and Cognition*. Center for the Study of Language and Information - Lecture Notes. Cambridge University Press.

Eduard H. Hovy. 1993. Automated discourse generation using discourse structure relations. *Artificial Intelligence*, 63(1-2):341–385.

Syeed Ibn Faiz and Robert Mercer. 2013. Identifying explicit discourse connectives in text. In *Advances in Artificial Intelligence*, pages 64–76.

Yangfeng Ji and Jacob Eisenstein. 2014. Representation learning for text-level discourse parsing. In *Proceedings of the Annual Meeting of the Association for Computational Linguistics*, pages 13–24.

Shafiq Joty, Giuseppe Carenini, Raymond Ng, and Yashar Mehdad. 2013. Combining intra- and multi-sentential rhetorical parsing for document-level discourse analysis. In *Proceedings of the Annual Meeting of the Association for Computational Linguistics*, pages 486–496.

Taraneh Khazaei and Lu Xiao. 2015. Corpus-based analysis of rhetorical relations: A study of lexical cues. In *Proceedings of the IEEE Conference on Semantic Computing*, pages 417–423.

Dan Klein and Christopher D. Manning. 2003. Accurate unlexicalized parsing. In *Proceedings of the Annual Meeting on Association for Computational Linguistics*, pages 423–430.

Alistair Knott and Ted Sanders. 1998. The classification of coherence relations and their linguistic markers: An exploration of two languages. *Journal of Pragmatics*, 30(2):135 – 175.

Alex Lascarides and Nicholas Asher. 1993. Temporal interpretation, discourse relations and commonsense entailment. *Linguistics and Philosophy*, 16(5):437–493.

Ziheng Lin, Hwee Tou Ng, and Min-Yen Kan. 2014. A PDTB-styled end-to-end discourse parser. *Natural Language Engineering*, 20:151–184.

William C. Mann and Sandra A. Thompson. 1988. Rhetorical Structure Theory: Toward a functional theory of text organization. *Text*, 8(3):243–281.

Daniel Marcu. 2000. The rhetorical parsing of unrestricted texts: A surface-based approach. *Computational Linguistics*, 26(3):395–448.

Thomas Meyer, Andrei Popescu-Belis, Sandrine Zufferey, and Bruno Cartoni. 2011. Multilingual annotation and disambiguation of discourse connectives for machine translation. In *SIGdial Meeting on Discourse and Dialogue*, pages 194–203.

Eleni Miltsakaki, Nikhil Dinesh, Rashmi Prasad, Aravind Joshi, and Bonnie Webber. 2005. Experiments on sense annotations and sense disambiguation of discourse connectives. In *Proceedings of the Workshop on Treebanks and Linguistic Theories*.

Emily Pitler and Ani Nenkova. 2009. Using syntax to disambiguate explicit discourse connectives in text. In *Proceedings of the ACL-IJCNLP Conference (Short Papers)*, pages 13–16.

Rashmi Prasad, Nikhil Dinesh, Alan Lee, Eleni Miltsakaki, Livio Robaldo, Aravind Joshi, and Bonnie Webber. 2008. The Penn Discourse TreeBank 2.0. In *Proceedings of the Conference on Language Resources and Evaluation*, pages 2961–2968.

Prasad Rashmi, Bonnie Webber, and Aravind Joshi. 2014. Reflections on the Penn Discourse TreeBank, comparable corpora, and complementary annotation. *Computational Linguistics*, 40(4):921–950.

Radu Soricut and Daniel Marcu. 2003. Sentence level discourse parsing using syntactic and lexical information. In *Proceedings of the Conference of the North American Chapter of the Association for Computational Linguistics on Human Language Technology*, pages 149–156.

Maite Taboada, Caroline Anthony, and Kimberly Voll. 2006. Methods for creating semantic orientation dictionaries. In *Proceedings of the Conference on Language Resources and Evaluation*, pages 427–432.

Maite Taboada. 2006. Discourse markers as signals (or not) of rhetorical relations. *Journal of Pragmatics*, 38(4):567 – 592.

Yannick Versley. 2013. Subgraph-based classification of explicit and implicit discourse relations. In *Proceedings of the International Conference on Computational Semantics*, pages 264–275.

Ben Wellner, James Pustejovsky, Catherine Havasi, Anna Rumshisky, and Roser Saurí. 2006. Classification of discourse coherence relations: An exploratory study using multiple knowledge sources. In *Proceedings of the SIGdial Workshop on Discourse and Dialogue*, pages 117–125.

Lu Xiao. 2013a. Do members converge to similar reasoning styles in teamwork? A study of shared rationales in small team activities. In *Proceedings of the iConference*, pages 524–530.

Lu Xiao. 2013b. The effects of a shared free form rationale space in collaborative learning activities. *Journal of Systems and Software*, 86(7):1727 – 1737.

Lu Xiao. 2014. Effects of rationale awareness in online ideation crowdsourcing tasks. *Journal of the Association for Information Science and Technology*, 65(8):1707–1720.

Bridging Sentential and Discourse-level Semantics through Clausal Adjuncts

Rashmi Prasad[1], **Bonnie Webber**[2], **Alan Lee**[3], **Sameer Pradhan**[4], **Aravind Joshi**[3]
[1]Department of Health Informatics and Administration, University of Wisconsin-Milwaukee
prasadr@uwm.edu
[2]School of Informatics, University of Edinburgh
Bonnie.Webber@ed.ac.uk
[3]Institute for Research in Cognitive Science, University of Pennsylvania
{aleewk, joshi}@seas.upenn.edu
[4]Boulder Language Technologies
pradhan@bltek.com

Abstract

It is in PropBank's ARGM annotation of clausal adjuncts that sentential semantics meets discourse relation annotation in the Penn Discourse TreeBank. This paper discusses complementarities between the two annotation systems: How PropBank ARGM annotation can be used to seed annotation of additional discourse relations in the PDTB, and how PDTB annotation can be used to refine or enrich PropBank ARGM annotation.

1 Introduction

Discourse relations between *abstract objects*, such as facts, events, propositions, etc. (Asher, 1993), can hold either across sentences (i.e., *inter-sententially*), or within a single sentence (i.e., *intra-sententially*), as in Ex. 1–4. (Italics and boldface highlight the two related abstract objects, respectively, and relation signals, when present, are underlined.)

(1) *The federal government suspended sales of U.S. savings bonds* because **Congress hasn't lifted the ceiling on government debt.**

(2) *The House has voted to raise the ceiling to $3.1 trillion,* but **the Senate isn't expected to act until next week at the earliest.**

(3) *Now, we regard this as a largely phony issue,* **but the "long term" is** nonetheless **a big salon topic all around the Beltway**.

(4) *The U.S. wants the removal of ...barriers to investment*; **Japan denies there are real barriers**.

Researchers working on discourse parsing have commented that intra-sentential (intra-S) discourse relations are, in general, easier to recognize than ones whose arguments are found in separate sentences (Joty et al., 2012; Lin et al., 2012; Feng, 2014). They are also quite useful in Language Technology applications that exploit sentence-level relations. Thus, there is particular value in improving the quality of recognizers capable of determining what, if any, discourse relations hold between intra-S units.

Taking abstract objects to be expressed (arguably) typically as clauses headed by verbs or other predicates, the Penn Discourse Treebank (PDTB) (Prasad et al., 2008) includes annotations of intra-S discourse relations but, as noted by Prasad et al. (2014), they are significantly under-annotated in the corpus. At the same time, Prasad et al. (2014) point to possible overlaps between intra-S discourse relations in the PDTB and a subset of verb-argument annotations in PropBank (Palmer et al., 2005). The PropBank annotations of particular interest here are those in which the arguments are clausal adjuncts, labeled ARGM, and further assigned a semantic role. For example, the PropBank annotation of the verb *suspend* in Ex. 1 is shown in (5), with the adjunct clause annotated as ARGM and assigned the role CAU (causal). The PDTB annotation for the same example, shown in (6), marks *because* as the connective, 'Contingency.Cause.Reason' as the sense, the adjunct clause as Arg2 (defined as the argument attached to the connective), and the matrix clause as Arg1 (defined as the non-Arg2 argument).

(5) **PropBank:** Verb = *suspend*
Arg0 = *The federal government*
Arg1 = *sales of U.S. savings bonds*
ARGM-CAU = *because Congress hasn't lifted the ceiling on government debt*

(6) **PDTB:** Connective = *because*
Arg1 = *The federal government suspended sales of U.S. savings bonds*
Arg2 = *Congress hasn't lifted the ceiling on government debt*
Sense = Contingency.Cause.Reason

Proceedings of the EMNLP 2015 Workshop on Linking Models of Lexical, Sentential and Discourse-level Semantics, pages 64–69, Lisboa, Portugal, 18 September 2015.

	TEMPORAL	CONTINGENCY	COMPARISON	EXPANSION	TOTAL
ARGM-ADV (2235)	222	1067	907	157	2353
ARGM-CAU (657)	14	650	0	0	664
ARGM-TMP (2503)	2258	523	73	23	2877
ARGM-PNC (66)	0	65	1	0	66
ARGM-MNR (13)	0	5	1	7	13
TOTAL (5475)	2494	2310	982	187	5973

Table 1: Correspondences between PropBank ARGM- roles and PDTB senses

Given possible overlaps between the PDTB and PropBank, this paper addresses the following questions: (1) To what extent can the PropBank clausal ARGM annotations be taken as conveying information relevant for intra-S discourse relations (Section 2), and can they be useful for increasing the number of intra-S discourse relations annotated in the PDTB (Section 3)?; and (2) Can PDTB annotations be useful for enriching PropBank in any way (Section 4)? Section 5 concludes the paper.

2 PropBank ARGM Roles and Discourse Relations

The PDTB 2.0 (the current version of the corpus) lacks extensive annotation of intra-S relations. Annotations of intra-S relations are provided primarily for relations that are signaled by explicit connectives (subordinating conjunctions (Ex. 1), coordinating conjunctions (Ex. 2), and adverbials (Ex. 3)). The only implicit relations currently annotated are those between clauses connected by a punctuation such as the semi-colon or colon (Ex. 4). Among the relations that are missing are implicit relations linking adjunct clauses that are not subordinated by any explicit form, as in Ex. 7, and adjunct clauses introduced by prepositional subordinators like *by*, *for*, *with*, *without*, *to*, as in Ex. 8-9.

(7) *Second, they channel monthly mortgage payments into semiannual payments,* **reducing the administrative burden on investors.**

(8) To **avoid this deficit**, *Mr. Lawson inflated the pound in order to prevent its rise.*

(9) Critics say *South Carolina is paying a price* by **stressing improved test scores so much.**

These types of unannotated relations involving adjunct clauses in the PDTB have, on the other hand, been annotated in PropBank, as described in Section 1. Hence, a natural question to ask is whether the semantic roles of such adjunct clauses in PropBank can be used to fill in the gap when annotations of intra-S discourse relations are not present in the PDTB for these clauses, thus avoiding duplicate annotation efforts. To explore this possibility, we considered a parallel case: the annotation of adjunct clauses introduced by *explicit* connectives in the PDTB, such as those in Ex. 1, which have been annotated in the corpus. We investigated the extent of the overlap between PropBank and PDTB annotations in such cases. Using the underlying syntactic annotations of the Penn Treebank (PTB) (Marcus et al., 1993), 11534 clausal adjuncts with either of the following six roles were extracted from PropBank:[1] ARGM-ADV (adverbial), ARGM-CAU (causal), ARGM-MNR (manner), ARGM-PNC (purpose), ARGM-PRD (secondary predication), and ARGM-TMP (temporal). Other roles (ARGM-MOD/DIR/EXT/DIS/LOC) were excluded because we did not see them as representing discourse relations. The 11534 ARGMs were then aligned with the PDTB and 48% (5475) were found to contain an explicit subordinating form annotated as a discourse connective in the PDTB. Except for ARGM-PRD, all the discourse-relevant ARGM roles were observed in this set (Table 1). We then looked at the correspondence between the roles assigned to these ARGMs in PropBank and the senses annotated for the connectives in the PDTB. Because the PDTB sense classification is hierarchical and contains many fine-grained relations, we simplified the comparison by considering only the four top level classes of the PDTB – Temporal (TEMP), Contingency (CONT), Comparison (COMP), and Expansion (EXP). The correspondences are shown in Table 1. The numbers in parentheses in the first column represent the total number of ARGM instances annotated with the role shown.

There are several observations to make from Table 1. First, based on the definitions of the ARGM roles in PropBank and those of the senses

[1]For this part of the work, we used PropBank-I.

in the PDTB, we would expect PropBank ARGM-CAU to align with PDTB Contingency, and PropBank ARGM-TMP to align with PDTB Temporal. This is largely borne out for ARGM-CAU, with 99% of the instances labeled as Contingency in PDTB. ARGM-TMP, while showing a greater association with non-Temporal PDTB senses, nevertheless corresponds to PDTB Temporal 90% of the time. While the current PDTB sense classification does not include Purpose and Manner relations, PDTB guidelines followed a convention to label Purpose connectives such as *so that* as 'Contingency.Cause.Result', so we would expect to see ARGM-PNC aligned with Contingency. This is largely borne out as well, with only one instance labeled otherwise. Manner relations, on the other hand, are not addressed in the existing PDTB guidelines at all, which may explain the variable sense annotation of the ARGM-MNR cases in the PDTB. In contrast to the previous four ARGM roles, however, the ARGM-ADV role, which constitutes 41% of all the roles, fails to provide semantically meaningful alignment with the PDTB senses. According to the PropBank guidelines (Bonial et al., 2010), ARGM-ADV is used for syntactic elements which clearly modify the event structure of the verb in question, but which cannot be classified as any of the other roles. As the table shows, this role is ambiguous among all four sense classes in the PDTB, although we see a much higher proportion of Contingency and Comparison than Temporal and Expansion.

The second observation from Table 1 is that the total number of PDTB senses associated with an ARGM role (last column) is in some cases more than the total number of instances for that ARGM role (first column). Altogether, the table shows a total of 5973 PDTB senses associated with a total of 5475 PropBank ARGM roles. This is due to the fact that the PDTB allows multiple relations to be inferred between abstract objects, whereas PropBank only allows a single role to be assigned to any given ARGM. Notably, however, multiple PDTB senses do not appear at all for ARGM-PNC and ARGM-MNR, and appear in only seven instances for ARGM-CAU. ARGM-TMP had the most instances (374) with multiple senses, while ARGM-ADV had 118.

What these observations suggest is that while the correspondence between PropBank clausal ARGM roles and PDTB senses is not exact, they can still be leveraged to some extent. On the one hand, relations with the ARGM-ADV role would need to be manually annotated for the PDTB sense. But on the other hand, the high degree of correspondences seen for other roles suggest the possibility of their straightforward mapping from PropBank to PDTB. The possibility of multiple senses in the PDTB would require further annotation, but this may be needed for only the Temporal sense. And here too, there may be less effort required since the annotator would not need to reason about the Temporal sense but only consider the possibility of inferring a second sense.

We must note that the semantics of the relation is not the only kind of correspondence to consider between PropBank and the PDTB. Mismatches in alignment can also arise between PDTB arguments and PropBanks semantic role structure, in large part because the PropBank annotation is tied directly to the syntactic trees in the PTB. Ex. 10 shows a sentence containing a *when*-clause annotated as ARGM-TMP in PropBank and with a Temporal sense in the PDTB. But the relation between the *when*-clause and its other argument is different between the two corpora. In the PDTB, where annotation is done over the raw text spans, the Arg1 of the connective excludes *he says*, and the temporal relation is annotated between the *winning* and *awarding* events. In contrast, in PropBank, the when-clause is taken to modiy the verb *say*. Hence, we cannot use PropBank's projected clause to automatically annotate the Arg1 of the corresponding PDTB relation as this would be inconsistent with the PDTB guidelines.

(10) **When Mr. Green** *won* **a $240,000 verdict in a land condemnation case against the state in June 1983**, he *says* Judge O'Kicki unexpectedly *awarded* him an additional $100,000.

Given the difference in annotation practice, the extent of such mismatches between the PDTB and PropBank is expected to be the same as that between the PDTB and the PTB (Dinesh et al., 2005). Nevertheless, since the majority of semantic conflicts are due to attribution verbs, one can reduce the annotation effort by automatically highlighting instances with attribution verbs, in contexts that may lead to inconsistent semantics.

3 Using PropBank to Seed New PDTB Annotations

Despite the partial correspondence described above, PropBank is richly annotated with clausal adjunct tokens that in PDTB would be Arg2 of a discourse relation. Therefore, in preparing the next version of the PDTB, we have used these PropBank tokens to seed the corpus with new annotations of intra-S relations. Our search for new tokens uses the latest version of the PropBank layer of the OntoNotes v5.0. corpus, since this PropBank version contains additional tokens for copular verbs and their argument structure, as well as modifications to tokens from PropBank-I. However, since only about 75% of the PTB is included in OntoNotes, the remaining 25% was taken from PropBank-I. Clausal adjuncts identified from these two versions of PropBank were then divided (using the syntactic trees in the PTB) into those that had an explicit subordinating form and those that did not. The former set was filtered to retain tokens not already annotated in PDTB 2.0. Most of these contain subordinators as the connecting elements (as in Ex. 8-9) that we will consider as signals of explicit intra-sentential discourse relations. The latter set yielded free adjuncts (Ex. 7), both present participles and past participles.

Altogether, over 5000 tokens signaling potential intra-sentential relations have been seeded in this way for further annotation, semi-automatically or manually. In the set comprising free adjuncts, approximately 75% were found to be assigned the ARGM-ADV role in Propbank while approximately 19% are assigned the similarly underspecified ARGM-PRD role. This leaves only 6% assigned to the Purpose, Causal, Manner and Temporal roles which, as discussed above, have strong correspondences with PDTB senses. Because of this, the annotation of free adjuncts is being done manually. The annotation guidelines extend directly from those used in annotating PDTB 2.0 while some new senses and refinements have also been introduced, including the addition of Purpose and Manner senses.

Unlike the free adjuncts, we see less underspecification with adjuncts that are subordinated by some explicit form. Adjuncts with the Purpose role are the most frequent, at 50%, followed by ARGM-MNR (26%). ARGM-ADV continues to appear in this set, although less frequently (18%). All other roles account for the remaining 6% of the tokens. We expect that these tokens can be annotated semi-automatically. As noted earlier, because the PDTB senses are in some cases more refined than Propbank roles (for example the Temporal sense, is further distinguished between Temporal.Synchrony and Temporal.Asynchrony) and because the argument spans needs to be consistent with PDTB guidelines, each token will need to be looked at manually. But the overall time and effort spent on annotation will be reduced while consistency with an existing complementary annotation layer is enhanced.

ARGM-ADV	58.11
ARGM-CAU	60.67
ARGM-TMP	76.42
ARGM-PRP[2]	52.40
ARGM-MNR	62.10
Overall	77.44

Table 2: Performance of ASSERT on ARGMs in OntoNotes v5.0.

4 On Enrichment of ARGM Roles in PropBank

The focus in PropBank is on the predicate argument structure of verbs, and while some of the clausal adjunct arguments such as ARGM-ADV, ARGM-CAU, ARGM-MNR, ARGM-PNC and ARGM-TMP can signal intra-sentential discourse relations, distinguishing subtle discourse-specific nuances for such adjuncts was not its primary goal. It is therefore not surprising to find as a semantic role, ARGM-ADV, which was devised to capture adverbials that could not clearly be labeled with one of the more specific adjunct roles. However, many semantic role labeling methods that utilize PropBank-style annotations do try to differentiate between the various ARGM roles. Of interest then are the performance results of semantic role labelers on the task of predicting ARGM roles. As shown in Table 2, although the overall F_1-score of a semantic role labeler ASSERT (Pradhan et al., 2004) on PropBank is in the high 70s (across a diverse set of genres annotated in the OntoNotes v5.0 test set (Pradhan et al., 2013)), the F_1-scores for all ARGM roles, except for ARGM-TMP, is in the low 60s or below 60.

As discussed in Section 2, both ARGM-ADV and ARGM-TMP exhibit the most variability in PDTB senses, the former in terms of the number of PDTB senses associated with it in significant proportions, and both in terms of how often they

[2]ARGM-PRP is the label to which ARGM-PNC was changed, over the course of the OntoNotes project.

are associated with multiple PDTB senses. Therefore, it might be worth enriching these ARGM roles, and possibly others such as ARGM-CAU, in PropBank with the sense distinctions found for them in the PDTB. Not only would this allow semantic role labelers to learn the finer distinctions that are currently lumped into a coarse-grained category, it would also make for a better integrated resource. We can compare this overloading, primarily of ARGM-ADV, with similar overloading of numbered arguments Arg2..Arg5 in PropBank. A study by Yi et al. (2007) demonstrated that refining these numbered arguments with a more fine-grained set of thematic roles, using a mapping from VerbNet (Schuler, 2005), improves classifier performance. In the case of Arg2 (the largest of these numbered argument classes), the F_1-score improved by an absolute 10% points. We feel optimistic that through the proposed PDTB-informed refinement, we can get a significant performance boost in the prediction of ARGMs currently labeled as ARGM-ADV and possibly for other ARGM types as well. We plan to explore this in our future work. The finer distinctions could potentially also allow for prediction of multiple equally plausible labels, thus allowing more accurate evaluation of semantic role labelers that might, for example, learn to annotate some instances as ARGM-CAU rather than ARGM-TMP but are currently being needlessly penalized.

5 Conclusion and Future Work

A complete and well-defined annotation of intra-sentential discourse relations can have far-reaching benefits for Language Technology applications. We have explored the possibility of leveraging the sentential semantics represented in PropBank for closing the gap in the PDTB annotations of such relations. We have also suggested the converse benefit of the PDTB discourse-level semantics for enriching Propbank semantic roles, with beneficial consequences for the semantic role labeling methods that utilize PropBank.

In future work, we plan to examine another PropBank annotated element (ARGM-DIS) as a further source for seeding the PDTB. ARGM-DIS is meant to be used to annotate words or phrases that "connect a sentence to a preceding sentence" (Bonial et al., 2010). While many of these are either irrelevant to the PDTB, such as *vocatives* ("Guys"), *interjections* ("Well", "of course"), *parentheticals* ("not to be crass"), and *attitudinal phrases* ("Clearly", "Maybe"), or already systematically annotated in the PDTB (*coordinating conjunctions*, *discourse adverbials* and *attributive phrases* ("he said")), among the over 6500 tokens of ARGM-DIS annotated in PropBank, some may be *alternative lexicalizations* of the discourse relations annotated in the PDTB (Prasad et al., 2010), including "after all", "at the very least", and "in effect". Those we will examine as possible seeds for inter-sentential and intra-sentential relations.

The current study was limited to arguments of verb predicates. However, we plan to also consider arguments of eventive noun predicates as annotated in NomBank (Meyers et al., 2004). We also plan to explore the use of PDTB–Propbank overlaps to identify annotation inconsistencies in one or the other corpus, following recent work on annotation consistency control (Frank et al., 2012).

Acknowledgments

This work was partially supported by NSF grants IIS-1422186 and IIS-1421067.

References

Asher, N. 1993. *Reference to Abstract Objects in Discourse.* Kluwer, Boston MA.

Bonial, C., Babko-Malaya, O., Choi, J., Hwang, J., and Palmer, M. 2010. PropBank annotation guidelines (version 3.0). Technical Report, Center for Computational Language and Education Research, University of Colorado at Boulder.

Dinesh, N., Lee, A., Miltsakaki, E., Prasad, R., Joshi, A., and Webber, B. 2005. Attribution and the (non)-alignment of syntactic and discourse arguments of connectives In *Proceedings of the ACL Workshop on Frontiers in Corpus Annotation II: Pie in the Sky*, pages 29–36.

Feng, V. W. 2014. *RST-style discourse parsing and its applications in discourse analysis.* PhD thesis, Department of Computer Science, University of Toronto.

Frank, A., Bögel, T., Hellwig, O., and Reiter, N. 2012. Semantic annotation for the digital humanities: Using Markov Logic Networks for annotation consistency control. In *Linguistic Issues in Language Technology*, 7(1), pages 1–21.

Joty, S., Carenini, G., and Ng, R. 2012. A novel discriminative framework for sentence-level discourse analysis. In *Proceedings of the Joint Conference on Empirical Methods in Natural Language Processing and Computational Natural Language Learning (EMNLP/CoNLL)*, pages 904–915.

Lin, Z., Ng, H. T., and Kan, M.-Y. 2012. A PDTB-styled end-to-end discourse parser. *Natural Language Engineering*, 20(02), pages 151–184.

Marcus, M., Santorini, B., and Marcinkiewicz, M. A. 1993. Building a large scale annotated corpus of English: The Penn TreeBank. *Computational Linguistics*, 19(2), pages 313–330.

Meyers, A., Reeves, R., Macleod, C., Szekely, R., Zielinska, V., Young, B., and Grishman, R. 2004. The NomBank project: An interim report. *Proceedings of the HLT/NAACL Workshop: Frontiers in corpus annotation*, pages 24–31.

Palmer, M., Gildea, D., and Kingbury, P. 2005. The Proposition Bank: An annotated corpus of semantic roles. *Computational Linguistics*, 31(1), pages 71–105.

Pradhan, S., Ward, W., Hacioglu, K., Martin, J., and Jurafsky, D. 2004. Shallow semantic parsing using Support Vector Machines. In *Proceedings of the Human Language Technology Conference/North American chapter of the Association of Computational Linguistics (HLT/NAACL)*, pages 233–240.

Pradhan, S., Moschitti, A., Xue, N., Ng, H. T., Björkelund, A., Uryupina, O., Zhang, Y., and Zhong Z. 2013. Towards robust linguistic analysis using OntoNotes. In *Proceedings of the 17th Conference on Computational Natural Language Learning (CoNLL)*, pages 143–152.

Prasad, R., Dinesh, N., Lee, A., Miltsakaki, E., Robaldo, L., Joshi, A., and Webber, B. 2008. The Penn Discourse TreeBank 2.0. In *Proceedings of the 6th International Conference on Language Resources and Evaluation (LREC)*, pages 2961–2968.

Prasad, R., Joshi, A,, & Webber, B. 2010. Realization of discourse relations by other means: Alternative Lexicalizations. In *Proceedings of the 23rd International Conference on Computational Linguistics (COLING): Posters*, pages 1023–1031.

Prasad, R., Webber, B., and Joshi, A. 2014. Reflections on the Penn Discourse Treebank, comparable corpora and complementary annotation. *Computational Linguistics*, 40(4), pages 921–950.

Schuler, K. K. 2005. VerbNet: A broad-coverage, comprehensive verb lexicon. *Ph.D. Thesis*, University of Pennsylvania.

Yi, S. T., Loper, E., and Palmer, M. 2007. Can semantic roles generalize across genres? *Proceedings of HLT/NAACL 2007*, pages 548–555.

Weischedel, R., Palmer, M., Marcus, M., Hovy, E., Pradhan, S., Ramshaw, L., Xue, N., Taylor, A., Kaufman, J., Franchini, M., El-Bachouti, M., Belvin, R., and Houston, A. 2013. OntoNotes release 5.0. Technical report. Linguistic Data Consortium, https://catalog.ldc.upenn.edu/LDC2013T19.

Lexical Level Distribution of Metadiscourse in Spoken Language

Rui Correia
L^2F, INESC-ID
Técnico Lisboa
Portugal
Rui.Correia@inesc-id.pt

Maxine Eskenazi
LTI
Carnegie Mellon University
USA
max@cs.cmu.edu

Nuno Mamede
L^2F, INESC-ID
Técnico Lisboa
Portugal
Nuno.Mamede@inesc-id.pt

Abstract

This paper targets an understanding of how metadiscourse functions in spoken language. Starting from a metadiscourse taxonomy, a set of TED talks is annotated via crowdsourcing and then a lexical grade level predictor is used to map the distribution of the distinct discourse functions of the taxonomy across levels. The paper concludes showing how speakers use these functions in presentational settings.

1 Introduction

Often referred to as discourse about discourse, metadiscourse is the linguistic material intended to help the listener organize and evaluate the information in a presentation (Crismore et al., 1993). Examples include introducing (*I'm going to talk about ...*), concluding (*In sum, ...*), or emphasizing (*The take home message is ...*).

This paper explores how this phenomenon is used in spoken language, in particular how it occurs across presentations with different vocabulary levels. Are these acts used independently of vocabulary complexity? Which ones are used more frequently in more lexically demanding talks?

Finding out the answer to these questions has not only direct applications in language learning, but can also give insight on features that can be used for automatically classifying metadiscourse.

Such classification establishes a link between discourse and lexical semantics, i.e., understanding the speaker's explicit intention can be of help in tasks such as word sense disambiguation. For instance, the word *means*, in most contexts used to signal a definition, can also be used to show entailment, such as in: *[...] these drugs [...] will reduce the number of complications, which* ***means*** *pneumonia and which* ***means*** *death.*

This paper is organized as follows. Section 2 presents related work on metadiscourse with focus to how it relates with grade level. Section 3 explains the choice of taxonomy of metadiscourse, describes the data and its annotation. Section 4 addresses the measure of vocabulary complexity used in this study, and the distribution of the data across different levels. Section 5 shows the results of mapping the metadiscourse functions according to vocabulary level. Finally, Section 6 has a discussion of the results and conclusions.

2 Related Work

The way discourse is used and organized in different grade levels started receiving attention in the early 80's. Crismore (1980) focused on the use of a set of logical connectives at different levels and disciplines (high school through university), showing difficulty of mastery. McClure and Steffensen (1985) examined how linguistic complexity, developmental, and ethnic differences conditioned the use of conjunctions in children (3rd to 9th grade), finding a correlation between correct use of conjunctions and reading comprehension.

The first systematic approaches to metadiscourse were proposed by Williams (1981) and Meyer et al. (1980) and were further adapted and refined by Crismore (1983;1984) in a taxonomy that is still broadly used today. Crismore's taxonomy is divided in two main categories: `Informational` and `Attitudinal` metadiscourse. The former deals with discourse organization, being divided in `pre-plans` (preliminary statements about content and structure), `post-plans` (global review statements), `goals` (both preliminary and review global goal statements), and `topicalizers` (local topic shifts). `Attitudinal` metadiscourse, as the name states, is used to show the speaker's at-

This work was supported through Fundação para a Ciência e a Tecnologia (FCT) with reference UID/CEC/50021/2013 and the PhD Fellowship by FCT with reference SFRH/BD/51156/2010.

Proceedings of the EMNLP 2015 Workshop on Linking Models of Lexical, Sentential and Discourse-level Semantics, pages 70–75,
Lisboa, Portugal, 18 September 2015.

titude towards the discourse, and encompasses saliency (importance), emphatics (certainty degree), hedges (uncertainty degree), and evaluative (speaker attitude towards a fact).

Interestingly, it is in this early approach that we find the only attempt (to our knowledge) at understanding how metadiscourse occurs across grade levels. Crismore's decisions while building the taxonomy are supported with examples extracted from nine social studies textbooks (elementary through college). After an annotation process, Crismore discusses the statistics and occurrence patterns of the various categories of metadiscourse across grade levels and audience. Goals were used very rarely in all text books. Pre-plans increased as students got into middle school and junior high and then declined. Post-plans were used when Pre-plans were used, about half as often. There was no clear trend toward increased use of Post-plans in upper grade texts. Topicalizers were used only at college level. Finally, for Attitudinal metadiscourse the author shows that it occurred more in texts which also contained more Informational metadiscourse, and that there was a tendency for it to increase in higher grade levels.

Intaraprawat and Steffensen (1995) also touched on the topic of metadiscourse and its relations to level, analyzing how 12 English as second language students used organizational language in their essays. When dividing them in *good* and *poor*, the authors observed that good essays contained proportionally more metadiscourse.

Regarding annotation of metadiscourse, and discourse in general, two distinct data-driven projects are broadly referred to and used. One is the Penn Discourse TreeBank (PDTB) (Webber and Joshi, 1998), built directly on top of Penn TreeBank (Marcus et al., 1993), composed of extracts from the *Wall Street Journal*. PDTB enriched the Penn TreeBank with discourse connectives annotation (conjunctions and adverbials), and organized them according to meaning (Miltsakaki et al., 2008). Given its goal to reach out to the NLP community and serve as training data, the resulting senses taxonomy is composed of low-level and fine-grained concepts.

In another approach, Marcu (2000) developed the RST Discourse Treebank, a semantics-free theoretical framework of discourse relations, intended to be "general enough to be applicable to naturally occurring texts and concise enough to facilitate an algorithmic approach to discourse analysis". Similarly to PDTB, the RST Discourse Treebank is a discourse-annotated corpus intended to be used by the NLP community, based on *Wall Street Journal* articles extracted from the Penn Treebank. The difference between PDTB and the RST Discourse Treebank is the discourse organization framework, which in the case of the RST Discourse Treebank is the Rhetorical Structure Theory (Mann and Thompson, 1988).

All these approaches however, focus exclusively on written language. This was the motivation behind building our own corpora of metadiscourse in spoken language (see Section 3).

3 Metadiscourse Annotation

For this experiment we look at how metadiscourse is used in spoken English. We chose TED[1], a source of self-contained presentations widely known for its speakers' quality, and for targeting a general audience. A random sample of 180 talks was used, spanning several years and topics.

Our examination of theoretical underpinnings dealing with spoken language revealed that most approaches focus on the number of stakeholders involved, and never discuss function (Luukka, 1992; Mauranen, 2001; Auria, 2006). However, Ädel (2010) merges previous approaches in a taxonomy built upon MICUSP and MICASE (Römer and Swales, 2009; Simpson et al., 2002), corpora of academic papers and lectures, respectively.

Consequently, Ädel's taxonomy was adapted according to the categories that appeared in the TED talks. More precisely, we consider 16 acts:

- COM – *Commenting on Linguistic Form/Meaning*
- CLAR – *Clarifying*
- DEF – *Definitions* (originally *Manage Terminology*)
- INTRO – *Introducing Topic*
- DELIM – *Delimiting Topic*
- CONC – *Concluding*
- ENUM – *Enumerating*
- POST – *Postponing Topic* (originally *Previewing*)
- ARG – *Arguing*
- ANT – *Anticipating Response*
- EMPH – *Emphasizing* (originally *Managing Message*)
- R&R – collapse of *Repairing* with *Reformulating*
- ADD – collapse of *Adding to Topic* with *Asides*
- EXMPL – collapse of *Exemplifying* with *Imagining Scenarios*
- RECAP – *Recapitulating* (subdivision of the original *Reviewing*)
- REFER – *Refer to Previous Idea* (subdivision of the original *Reviewing*)

[1] https://www.ted.com/talks

Category	occur	conf	α
ADD	93	3.88	0.15
ANT	312	3.61	0.24
ARG	283	3.51	0.32
CLAR	265	3.82	0.15
COM	203	3.10	0.33
CONC	45	4.36	0.44
DEF	169	4.04	0.29
DELIM	26	4.21	0.31
EMPH	330	3.31	0.18
ENUM	343	3.74	0.49
EXMPL	179	3.62	0.38
INTRO	220	3.40	0.40
POST	20	4.17	0.32
RECAP	29	3.33	0.18
REFER	76	3.93	0.32
R&R	224	3.57	0.16

Table 1: Annotation results in terms of occurrence (**occur**), confidence (**conf**) and agreement (α).

Crowdsourcing was used to annotate metadiscourse (Amazon Mechanical Turk[2]). There was one task per metadiscursive category. This decreased the workers' cognitive load per task. Each of the 180 talks was divided into segments of 500 words (truncated to the closest end of sentence). This configuration generated 742 Human Intelligent Tasks (HITs) for each category (not counting gold standard HITs). To annotate a given category, workers had to first pass a training session. Upon successful completion, they were asked to read each segment and select the words that signal the existence of the metadiscursive function in question. For agreement calculation and quality control purposes, each segment was annotated by 3 different workers.

Table 1 presents the annotation results, in terms of number of occurrences found (by majority vote), the average self-reported confidence on a 5-point Likert scale (1 equals to *not confident at all* and 5 equals to *completely confident*)[3], and inter-annotator agreement. Herein, two workers are in agreement when the intersection of the words they select is not empty. We used Krippendorff's alpha since it adjusts itself better to small sample sizes than Cohen's Kappa, for example (Krippendorff, 2007). A value of zero indicates complete disagreement, and $\alpha = 1$ shows perfect agreement.

[2]https://www.mturk.com/mturk/welcome

[3]Confidence measured on a sample of 100 segments

Results show that non-experts have trouble identifying some metadiscourse acts. Metadiscourse is a sparse phenomenon, even more so when dealt with one category at a time. It follows that the probability of two workers selecting the same passage by chance is very low. This quantity is taken into account when calculating agreement, and consequently, the case where one worker selects a word and others do not is severely penalized. Previous annotation attempts on similar phenomena, such as Wilson's (2012) work on metalanguage, also show low agreement for sparser acts (0.09; 0.39), even when annotated by experts and considering only four categories.

Confidence results show all categories scoring above the middle of the scale (3). Workers showed less confidence for *Commenting on Linguistic Form/Meaning* (COM), which corresponds to the speaker commenting on their choice of words (confidence score of 3.1). On the other hand, workers showed the highest confidence for *Concluding Topic* (CONC), *Delimiting Topic* (DELIM) and *Postponing Topic* (POST), interestingly three categories that mark the change of topic in a talk.

4 Lexical Complexity

Evaluating linguistic complexity involves many aspects of language, such as lexis, syntax, semantics (Pilán et al., 2014; Dascalu, 2014). This paper, however, is concerned with the lexical complexity component only. Comparing the occurrences of metadiscourse across different vocabulary levels allows one to analyze its use independently of the syntactic structures that the speaker uses.

Although there is no commonly accepted measure of lexical complexity (Thériault, 2015), strategies typically rely on word unigrams to assure that only lexical clues are captured, since already capture grammatical properties (Vermeer, 2000; Heilman et al., 2007; Yasseri et al., 2011; Vajjala and Meurers, 2012). A drawback of such solutions is their inability of representing multi-word expressions, like fixed phrases or idioms.

This study uses the predictor described in Collins-Thompson and Callan (2004), which is available online[4]. This approach is a specialized Naive Bayes classifier with lexical unigram features only (for the previously mentioned reasons), which creates a model of the lexicon for each grade level – between 1st and 12th.

[4]http://reap.cs.cmu.edu/demo/readability2012/

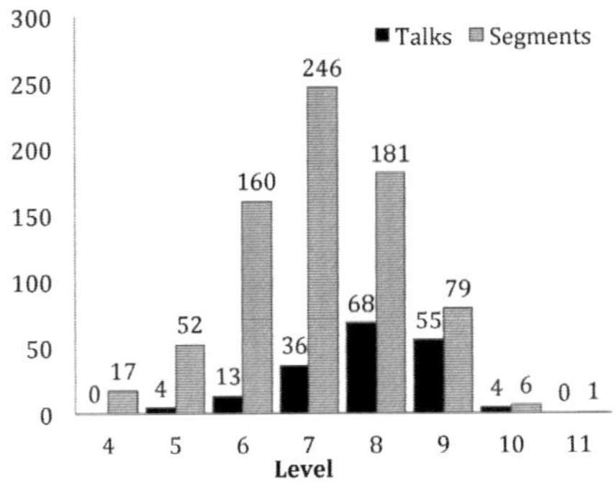

Figure 1: Level distribution of the TED talks.

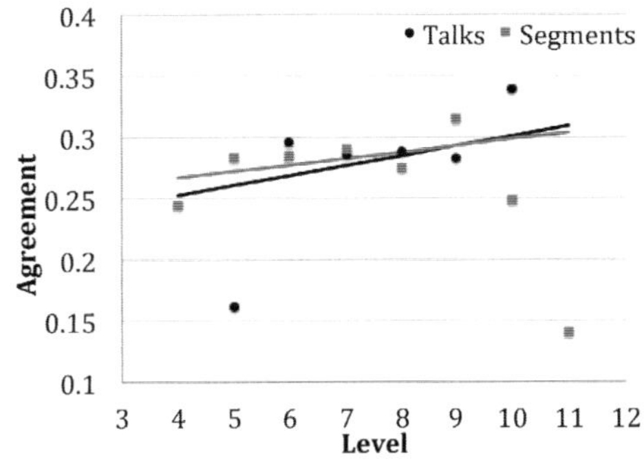

Figure 2: Agreement distribution and correlation.

The training data is composed of 550 English documents evenly distributed across the 12 American grade levels, containing a total of 448,715 tokens and 17,928 types. The documents were drawn from a wide variety of subject areas such as fiction, non-fiction, history, science, etc.

All documents, comprised of both readings and student work, were collected online. Their level classification was directly extracted from the information contained in the web page that hosted them (for instance, a document extracted from a specific classroom page).

The system developed by Collins-Thompson and Callan (2004) first performs morphological stemming and stopword removal. Then, for a given passage P, the classifier computes the likelihood that the words of P were generated from the representative language models of each level. The level where the likelihood is higher is the level that is attributed to P. The classifier performed at a correlation of 0.79 between the real and predicted levels (in a 10-fold cross validation setting).

It is important to note that this level prediction is used herein to distinguish between easier and more complex talks, more than to assign a specific grade level. In other words, one focuses at finding out which metadiscursive functions are used more often in talks with less demanding vocabulary with comparison to more complex ones (or vice-versa), never discussing occurrence at a specific level.

For the remainder of this study, the analysis takes place on two levels: *whole talk* and *segment*. The level predictor will be used on the 180 talks as a whole and on the 742 segments that compose them. The second strategy is a finer-grained local decision, since not all parts in a talk identified as high level are necessarily also complex.

Figure 1 shows level distribution: in black, the predictions when submitting the full talks to the classifier, and in light-gray, the segments prediction. In both cases we observe a normal distribution. It is interesting to notice the difference in the mode of the two cases. Most talks were assigned to a level corresponding to 8th grade when submitted as a whole. However, when partitioned in segments, the most frequent level is the 7th.

To exclude the hypothesis that annotators' performance was impacted by the complexity of the vocabulary, we examined how the vocabulary level of the talks relates with agreement.

Figure 2 shows how inter-annotator agreement is distributed. The correlation of the two variables is $\rho = 0.39$ for the talks and $\rho = 0.30$ for the segments, showing that vocabulary complexity does not negatively affect the capacity of two workers to agree on the annotation. In fact, the opposite trend was observed: workers agree more on segments with higher level vocabulary. This may be due to a higher degree of attention when facing more challenging content.

These results confirm that metadiscourse is independent of the content itself, and its structures can be detected independently of the propositional content in which they are inserted and for which they are used.

5 Results

With a set of 180 talks and 742 segments, annotated with 16 categories of metadisocurse, and automatically assigned to a level according to the lexical predictor described previously, one can now map the occurrences of the different acts across levels and conclude on how its use varies with lexical level of the content.

Category	Occur avg. (%)	Correlation by talk	Correlation by segment
ADD	0.60	**0.95**	**0.50**
ANT	1.20	(0.48)	**(0.85)**
ARG	1.13	**0.63**	**0.68**
CLAR	1.47	**0.58**	(0.16)
COM	1.54	**0.78**	**0.70**
CONC	0.37	(0.07)	**(0.73)**
DEF	1.13	**0.63**	**0.85**
DELIM	0.18	**0.54**	0.12
EMPH	1.90	0.47	(0.27)
ENUM	3.15	0.09	0.23
EXMPL	1.47	0.43	**0.50**
INTRO	1.61	0.37	0.22
POST	0.21	(0.21)	(0.01)
RECAP	0.16	0.15	**(0.50)**
REFER	0.54	**0.94**	(0.33)
R&R	1.23	**0.85**	**0.68**

Table 2: Average occurrence and level correlation.

Table 2 shows the probability of a sentence containing a given metadiscursive act (*Occur avg. (%)*) and how each category correlates with level at both the talk and segment levels. Correlations are weighted for the amount of sentences in each level to decrease the impact of outliers in levels with few cases. Negative correlations are shown between brackets, significant correlations in bold, and high correlations are bold and underlined.

Adding Information (ADD) correlated at both talk and segment level, registering the highest correlation of all at talk level (0.95). Higher frequencies of ADD seem to be associated to talks with higher level vocabulary. This same pattern was also observed for R&R, which tends to occur in talks/segments assigned to higher grade levels.

Commenting on Linguistic Form/Meaning (COM), and *Definitions* (DEF) also showed significant correlation at both levels. However, these categories have strong correlations at segment level, i.e., they do not only occur more frequently in higher level talks, but also in segments that contain words typically found in higher levels.

Anticipating Response (ANT) registered the strongest negative correlation both at sentence and talk levels (-0.85;-0.48). As talks are assigned to higher lexical levels, less instances addressing the audience's previous knowledge are found. As one would expect, the more complex the vocabulary and topic of a talk is, the less assumptions are made about what the audience knows.

Arguing (ARG) shows moderate correlation at both levels. The more complex the vocabulary of a talk/segment is, the more the speaker feels the need to defend a point or prove his position.

Clarifications (CLAR) correlate moderately with the level of the talk but show a negative correlation trend with the segment. This shows that while talks with more demanding vocabulary have more clarifications, they are not necessarily located in lexically complex segments. This pattern is also observed for *Conclusions* (CONC), *Recapitulations* (RECAP), and *References to Previous Ideas* (REFER), all with negative segment correlations. Interestingly, the four categories are related to paraphrasing (whether summarization or simplification). The high correlation for CONC in particular (0.73) shows that a segment that contains a conclusion tends to have simpler vocabulary.

Results for *Delimiting Topic* (DELIM) and *Exemplify* (EXMPL) are at the frontier of low and moderate agreement. The remaining categories (*Emphasizing*, *Enumerating*, *Introducing* and *Postponing Topic*) did not correlate with level ($\rho < 0.5$) and seem to occur independently of the level of the vocabulary of the talk or segment.

6 Conclusions

This study used an empirical approach to understand how metadiscourse is used across different levels in spoken language. It employs a set of TED talks and a functional theory of metadiscourse. Crowdsourcing was used to annotate 16 metadiscourse functions. Comparing annotations with a vocabulary classifier showed that some but not all categories correlate with vocabulary level.

Strategies of topic management (delimiting, introducing, postponing) and broadly used functions (examples, emphasis, enumerations) occur at the same rate in all levels, not correlating with level.

Results also show that functions related to paraphrasing are more frequent in higher level talks, but not necessarily in segments containing the highest level vocabulary. In fact, the occurrence of a strategy that aims at language simplification contributes itself for lower level classification. This shift in correlation polarity from talk to segment level suggests that these strategies do not occur in close context with the ideas they are simplifying.

Contrastingly, functions that manage vocabulary (commentaries and definitions) seem to appear in the context of the vocabulary they address.

Future work includes using the annotation to build metadiscourse classifiers. As observed, the vocabulary level of the talk/segment can be a valuable feature for classification.

References

Annelie Ädel. 2010. Just to give you kind of a map of where we are going: A taxonomy of metadiscourse in spoken and written academic English. *Nordic Journal of English Studies*, 9(2):69–97.

Carmen PL Auria. 2006. Signaling speaker's intentions: towards a phraseology of textual metadiscourse in academic lecturing. *English as a GloCalization Phenomenon. Observations from a Linguistic Microcosm*, 3:59.

Kevyn Collins-Thompson and James P Callan. 2004. A language modeling approach to predicting reading difficulty. In *HLT-NAACL*, pages 193–200.

Avon Crismore, Raija Markkanen, and Margaret S Steffensen. 1993. Metadiscourse in persuasive writing a study of texts written by american and finnish university students. *Written communication*, 10(1):39–71.

Avon Crismore. 1980. Student use of selected formal logical connectors across school level and class type.

Mihai Dascalu. 2014. Analyzing discourse and text complexity for learning and collaborating. *Studies in computational intelligence*, 534.

Michael J Heilman, Kevyn Collins-Thompson, Jamie Callan, and Maxine Eskenazi. 2007. Combining lexical and grammatical features to improve readability measures for first and second language texts. In *Proceedings of NAACL HLT*, pages 460–467.

Puangpen Intaraprawat and Margaret S Steffensen. 1995. The use of metadiscourse in good and poor ESL essays. *Journal of Second Language Writing*, 4(3):253–272.

Klaus Krippendorff. 2007. Computing Krippendorff's alpha reliability. *Departmental Papers (ASC)*, page 43.

Minna-Riitta Luukka. 1992. Metadiscourse in academic texts. In *Text and Talk in Professional Contexts. International Conference on Discourse and the Professions, Uppsala, 26-29 August*, pages 77–88.

William C. Mann and Sandra A. Thompson. 1988. Rhetorical structure theory: Toward a functional theory of text organization. *Text*, 8(3):243–281.

Daniel Marcu. 2000. *The Theory and Practice of Discourse Parsing and Summarization*. The MIT press.

Mitchell P Marcus, Mary Ann Marcinkiewicz, and Beatrice Santorini. 1993. Building a large annotated corpus of english: The penn treebank. *Computational linguistics*, 19(2):313–330.

Anna Mauranen. 2001. *Reflexive academic talk: Observations from MICASE*.

Erica F McClure and Margaret S Steffensen. 1985. A study of the use of conjunctions across grades and ethnic groups. *Research in the Teaching of English*, pages 217–236.

Bonnie JF Meyer, David M Brandt, and George J Bluth. 1980. Use of top-level structure in text: Key for reading comprehension of ninth-grade students. *Reading research quarterly*, pages 72–103.

Eleni Miltsakaki, Livio Robaldo, Alan Lee, and Aravind Joshi. 2008. Sense annotation in the penn discourse treebank. In *Computational Linguistics and Intelligent Text Processing*, pages 275–286. Springer.

Ildikó Pilán, Elena Volodina, and Richard Johansson. 2014. Rule-based and machine learning approaches for second language sentence-level readability. In *Proceedings of the Ninth Workshop on Innovative Use of NLP for Building Educational Applications*, pages 174–184.

Ute Römer and John M. Swales. 2009. The michigan corpus of upper-level student papers (MICUSP). *Journal of English for Academic Purposes*, April.

Rita C Simpson, Sarah L Briggs, Janine Ovens, and John M Swales. 2002. The michigan corpus of academic spoken english. *Ann Arbor, MI: The Regents of the University of Michigan*.

Mélissa Thériault. 2015. The development of lexical complexity in sixth-grade intensive english students.

Sowmya Vajjala and Detmar Meurers. 2012. On improving the accuracy of readability classification using insights from second language acquisition. In *Proceedings of the Seventh Workshop on Building Educational Applications Using NLP*, pages 163–173. Association for Computational Linguistics.

Anne Vermeer. 2000. Coming to grips with lexical richness in spontaneous speech data. *Language testing*, 17(1):65–83.

Bonnie Webber and Aravind Joshi. 1998. Anchoring a lexicalized tree-adjoining grammar for discourse. In *Coling/ACL workshop on discourse relations and discourse markers*, pages 86–92.

Joseph M Williams. 1981. Ten lessons in clarity and grace. *University of Chicago Press, Chicago*.

T Yasseri, A Kornai, and J Kertész. 2011. A practical approach to language complexity: a Wikipedia case study. *PloS one*, 7(11):e48386–e48386.

Idiom Paraphrases: Seventh Heaven vs Cloud Nine

Maria Pershina **Yifan He** **Ralph Grishman**
Computer Science Department
New York University
New York, NY 10003, USA
{pershina,yhe,grishman}@cs.nyu.edu

Abstract

The goal of paraphrase identification is to decide whether two given text fragments have the same meaning. Of particular interest in this area is the identification of paraphrases among short texts, such as SMS and Twitter. In this paper, we present idiomatic expressions as a new domain for short-text paraphrase identification. We propose a technique, utilizing idiom definitions and continuous space word representations that performs competitively on a dataset of 1.4K annotated idiom paraphrase pairs, which we make publicly available for the research community.

1 Introduction

The task of paraphrase identification, i.e. finding alternative linguistic expressions of the same or similar meaning, attracted a great deal of attention in the research community in recent years (Bannard and Callison-Burch, 2005; Sekine, 2005; Socher et al., 2011; Guo et al., 2013; Xu et al., 2013; Wang et al., 2013; Zhang and Weld, 2013; Xu et al., 2015).

This task was extensively studied in Twitter data, where millions of user-generated tweets talk about the same topics and thus present a natural challenge to resolve redundancy in tweets for many applications, such as textual entailment (Zhao et al., 2014), text summarization (Lloret et al., 2008), first story detection (Petrovich, 2012), search (Zanzotto et al., 2011), question answering (Celikyilmaz, 2010), etc.

In this paper we explore a new domain for the task of paraphrase identification - idiomatic expressions, in which the goal is to determine whether two idioms convey the same idea.

This task is related to previous short-text paraphrase tasks, but it does not have access to many of the information sources that can be exploited in Twitter/short text paraphrasing: unlike tweets, idioms do not have hashtags, which are very strong topic indictors; unlike SMS, idioms do not have timestamp or geographical metadata; and unlike news headlines, there are no real world events that can serve as anchors to cluster similar expressions. In addition, an idea, or a moral of the idiom is often expressed in an indirect way, e.g. the idioms

(1) make a mountain out of a molehill
(2) tempest in a teapot

convey similar ideas[1]:

(1) If somebody makes a mountain out of a molehill they exaggerate the importance or seriousness of a problem.
(2) If people exaggerate the seriousness of a situation or problem they are making a tempest in a teapot.

There is a line of research focused on extracting idioms from the text or identifying whether a particular expression is idiomatic (or a non-compositional multi-word expression) (Muzny and Zettlemoyer, 2013; Shutova et al., 2010; Li and Sporleder, 2009; Gedigian et al., 2006; Katz and Giesbrecht, 2006). Without linguistic sources such as Wiktionary, usingenglish.com, etc, it is often hard to understand what the meaning of a particular idiom is. It is even harder to determine whether two idioms convey the same idea or find alternative idiomatic expressions. Using idiom definitions, given by linguistic resources, one can view this problem as identifying paraphrases between definitions and thus deciding on paraphrases between corresponding idioms. Efficient techniques for identifying idiom paraphrases would complement any paraphrase identification system, and thus improve the downstream applications, such as question answering, summariza-

[1]Definitions of these idioms are taken from http://www.usingenglish.com

Proceedings of the EMNLP 2015 Workshop on Linking Models of Lexical, Sentential and Discourse-level Semantics, pages 76–82,
Lisboa, Portugal, 18 September 2015.

tion, opinion mining, information extraction, and machine translation.

To the best of our knowledge we are the first to address the problem of determining whether two idioms convey the same idea, and to propose a new scheme that utilizes idiom definitions and continuous space word representation (word embedding) to solve it. By linking word- and sentence-level semantics our technique outperforms state-of-the-art paraphrasing approaches on a dataset of 1.4K annotated idiom pairs that we make publicly available.

2 Related Work

There is no strict definition of a paraphrase (Bhagat and Hovy, 2013) and in linguistic literature paraphrases are most often characterized by an approximate equivalence of meanings across sentences or phrases.

A growing body of research investigates ways of paraphrase detection in both supervised (Qiu et al., 2006; Wan et al., 2006; Das and Smith, 2009; Socher et al., 2011; Blacoe and Lapata, 2012; Madnani and Tetreault, 2012; Ji and Eisenstein, 2013) and unsupervised settings (Bannard and Callison-Burch, 2005; Mihalcea et al., 2006; Rus et al., 2008; Fernando and Stevenson, 2008; Islam and Inkpen, 2007; Hassan and Mihalcea, 2011). These methods mainly work on large scale news data. News data is very different from ours in two aspects: most news text can be interpreted literally and similar news events (passing a legislation, death of a person, elections) happen repeatedly. Therefore, lexical anchors or event anchors can work well on news text, but not necessarily on our task.

Millions of tweets generated by Twitter users every day provide plenty of paraphrase data for NLP research. An increasing interest in this problem led to the **P**araphrase and Semantic Similarity **I**n **T**witter (PIT) task in SemEval-2015 competition (Xu et al., 2015). Existing bias towards Twitter paraphrases results in sophisticated systems that exploit character level similarity or metadata. But models relying on these insights are not necessarily applicable to other domains where misspellings are rare, or metadata is not available.

Idiomatic expressions constitute an essential part of modern English. They often behave idiosyncratically and are therefore a significant challenge for natural language processing systems. Recognizing when two idiomatic expressions convey similar ideas is crucial to recognizing the sentiment of the author, identifying correct triggers for events, and to translating the idiom properly. However, although there are several existing models to identify paraphrases in short text, idioms have very different characteristics from the data that those models are built on. In this paper, we experiment with two state-of-the-art paraphrasing models that are outperformed on our dataset of idiomatic expressions by a simple technique, raising a question on how well existing paraphrase models generalize to new data.

3 The Challenge

Identifying idiom paraphrases is an interesting and challenging problem. Lexical similarity is not a reliable clue to find similar idioms. Some idioms look very similar, differ in only one or two words, and convey the same idea. For example, "like two peas in a pod" vs "like peas in a pod" ("if people or things are like peas in a pod they look identical"), but other idioms that look similar can have very different meaning, e.g. "well oiled" vs "well oiled machine" ("if someone is well oiled they have drunk a lot" vs "something that functions very well is a well oiled machine").

Finally, there are idioms that do not have any words in common at all and may seem quite different for a person not familiar with idiomatic expressions, but still have similar meaning. For example, "cross swords" vs "lock horns" ("when people cross swords they argue or dispute" vs "when people lock horns they argue or fight about something"). Thus, a natural way to identify idiom paraphrases is to focus on idiom definitions that explain meaning of an idiom in a clear and concise way.

4 Lexical vs Semantic Similarities

Our dataset consists of pairs $\langle idiom, definition\rangle$.

We use two types of similarity measures to compute how similar definitions of different idioms are: the $lexical$ similarity is based on a lexical (word) overlap between two definitions, and the $semantic$ similarity captures the overall semantic meaning of the whole sentence.

Lexical similarity. We compute cosine similarity between vectors $\overrightarrow{v}_{d_1}$ and $\overrightarrow{v}_{d_2}$, representing idiom descriptions d_1 and d_2 and weight each word in these vectors by its tf-idf score:

$$lexSim(d_1, d_2) = cosine(\overrightarrow{v}_{d_1}, \overrightarrow{v}_{d_2}), \quad (1)$$

where $\overrightarrow{v}_d$ is a $|V|$-dimensional vector with V being the vocabulary of all definition words.

Semantic similarity. To capture the overall meaning of the definitions d we combine word embeddings (Collobert et al., 2011; Turian et al., 2010) for all words in d using two combination schemes:

- Averaged sum:

$$\overrightarrow{averaged_d} = \frac{1}{|d|} \sum_{word \in d} \overrightarrow{emb(word)} \quad (2)$$

- Weighted sum:

$$\overrightarrow{weighted_d} = \quad (3)$$

$$\frac{1}{\sum_{word \in d} \text{tfidf}_{word}} \sum_{word \in d} \text{tfidf}_{word} \cdot \overrightarrow{emb(word)}$$

Then semantic similarity is measured as

$$semSim(d_1,d_2) = cosine(comb_{d_1},comb_{d_2}) \quad (4)$$

where $\overrightarrow{comb_d}$ is a 100-dimensional vector combined from word embeddings $\overrightarrow{emb(word)}$ (Turian et al., 2010) for words in description d using either averaged (2) or weighted (3) combination schemes. [2]

4.1 IdiomSim

There is a tradeoff between the two similarity measures $lexSim$ and $semSim$ (Section 4): while the first one captures the actual lexical overlap, the second one can better capture the closeness in semantic meaning. To find an optimal balance between the two we consider their weighted sum

$$IdiomSim(d_1, d_2) = \quad (5)$$

$$(1 - \alpha) \cdot lexSim(d_1, d_2) + \alpha \cdot semSim(d_1, d_2)$$

and decide on an α by optimizing for a maximal F-score on a development dataset.

5 Experiments

Data. We collected 2,432 idioms from http://www.usingenglish.com, a site for English learners, where every idiom has a unique description giving a clear explanation of the idiom's meaning. As opposed to tweets there are no hashtags, no topics or trends, no timestamps, or any other default evidence, that two idioms may convey similar ideas. Thus it becomes a challenging task itself to construct a dataset of pairs that is guaranteed to have a certain fraction of true paraphrases.

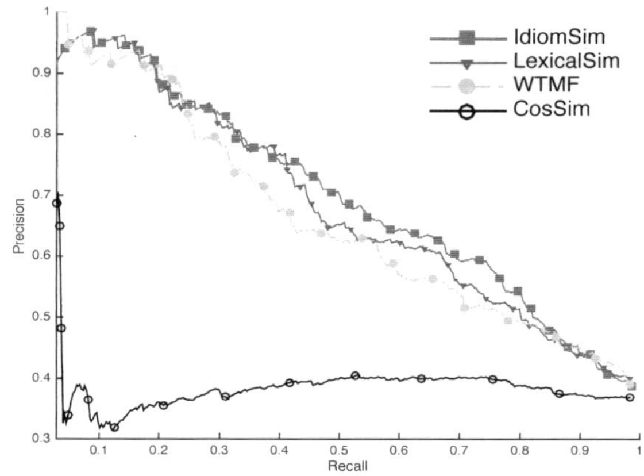

Model	F1	P	R
CosSim	53.7	37.1	97.2
ASOBEK	55.1	59.4	51.4
WTMF	61.4	51.4	76.3
LexicalSim	63.7	60.8	67.0
$\text{IdiomSim}^{\text{ave}}$	64.4	56.2	75.5
IdiomSim	65.9	59.2	74.4
IdiomSim+	66.6	62.2	71.9

Figure 1: Comparison of IdiomSim with baselines CosSim, LexicalSim, and state-of-the-art paraphrasing models: ASOBEK, WTMF.

We used a simple cosine similarity between all possible idiom definitions pairs to have a ranked list and labeled the top 1.5K pairs. Three annotators were asked to label each pair of idiom definitions as "similar" (score 2), "have something in common" (score 1), "not similar" (score 0). 0.1K pairs received a total score of 4 (either 2+2+0, or 2+1+1), and were further removed as debatable. The rest of the labeled pairs were randomly split into 1K for test data and 0.4K for development. Only pairs that received a total score of 5 or higher were considered as positive examples. There are 364 and 96 true paraphrases in our test and development sets respectively. [3]

Baselines. Our baselines are simple and tf-idf weighted cosine similarity between idiom description sentences: CosSim and LexicalSim.

We compare our method with the deterministic state-of-the-art ASOBEK model (Eyecioglu and

[2]We use 100-dimensional Turian word embeddings available at http://metaoptimize.com/projects/wordreprs/

[3]https://github.com/masha-p/Idiom_Paraphrases

Idioms	Descriptions
seventh heaven cloud nine	if you are in seventh heaven you are extremely happy if you are on cloud nine you are extremely happy
face only a mother could love stop a clock	when someone has a face only a mother could love they are ugly a face that could stop a clock is very ugly indeed
take your medicine face the music	if you take your medicine you accept the consequences of something you have done wrong if you have to face the music you have to accept the negative consequences of something you have done wrong
well oiled drunk as a lord	if someone is well oiled they have drunk a lot someone who is very drunk is as drunk as a lord
cheap as chips to be dog cheap	if something is very inexpensive it is as cheap as chips if something is dog cheap it is very cheap indeed
great minds think alike on the same wavelength	if two people have the same thought at the same time if people are on the same wavelength they have the same ideas and opinions about something
could eat a horse hungry as a bear	if you are very hungry you could eat a horse if you are hungry as a bear it means that you are really hungry
cross swords lock horns	when people cross swords they argue or dispute when people lock horns they argue or fight about something
talk the hind legs off a donkey talk the legs off an iron pot	a person who is excessively or extremely talkative can talk the hind legs off a donkey somebody who is excessively talkative or is especially convincing is said to talk the legs off an iron pot

Table 1: Examples of extracted idiom paraphrases.

Keller, 2015) that was ranked first among 19 teams in the Paraphrase in Twitter (PIT) track on the SemEval 2015 shared task (Xu et al., 2015). This model extracts eight simple and elegant character and word features from two sentences to train an SVM with linear kernel. It achieves an F-score of 55.1% on our test set.[4]

We also compare our method with the state-of-the-art Weighted Textual Matrix Factorization model (WTMF) (Guo et al., 2013),[5] which is specifically developed for short sentences by modeling the semantic space of words, that can be either present or absent from the sentences (Guo and Diab, 2012). This model achieves a maximal F-score of 61.4% on the test set.

The state-of-the-art model for lexically divergent paraphrases on Twitter (Xu et al., 2015) is tailored for tweets and requires topic and anchor words to be present in the sentence, which is not applicable to idiom definitions.

Evaluation and Results. To evaluate models we plot precision-recall curves for CosSim, WTMF, LexicalSim, and IdiomSim (for clarity we omit curves for other models). We also compare maximal F-score for all models. We observe that simple cosine similarity (CosSim) achieves a maximal F-score of 53.7%, LexicalSim is a high baseline and achieves an F-score of 63.75%. When we add averaged word embeddings the maximal F-score is 64.4% (IdiomSim^{ave}). With tfidf weighted word embeddings we achieve F-score of 65.9% (IdiomSim). By filtering out uninformative words such as "a", "the", etc (12 words total) we improve the F-score to 66.6% (IdiomSim+), outperforming state-of-the-art paraphrase models by more than 5% absolute (Figure 1). Both IdiomSim and IdiomSim+ outperform WTMF significantly according to a paired t-test with p less than 0.05.

Examples and Discussion. We use threshold, corresponding to a maximal F-score obtained on the development dataset, and explore paraphrases from test dataset scored higher and lower than this threshold. Examples of extracted idiom paraphrases are in Table 1. Examples of false positives and false negatives are in Table 2.

Simple word overlap is not a reliable clue to de-

[4]We thank Asli Eyecioglu for running her ASOBEK model on our test data.

[5]The source code for WTMF is available at http://www.cs.columbia.edu/~weiwei/code

Idioms	Descriptions
False positives	
healthy as a horse an apple a day keeps the doctor away	if you are as healthy as a horse you are very healthy eating healthy food keeps you healthy
jersey justice justice is blind	jersey justice is a very severe justice justice is blind means that justice is impartial and objective
heart of steel heart of glass	when someone has a heart of steel they do not show emotion or are not affected emotionally when someone has a heart of glass they are easily affected emotionally
False negatives	
like a kid in a candy store bee in your bonnet	if someone is like a kid in a candy store they are very excited about something if someone is very excited about something they have a bee in their bonnet
easy as falling off a log no sweat	something very easy or simple to do is as easy as falling off a log no sweat means something is easy
hopping mad off on one	if you are hopping mad you are extremely angry if someone goes off on one they get extremely angry indeed

Table 2: Examples of false positive and false negative paraphrases.

cide on a paraphrase between two idiom descriptions. Since words are main units in the computation (5) our metric is biased towards lexical similarity. Thus we get a false positive paraphrase between "healthy as a horse" and "an apple a day". The first one is rather a statement about someone's health while the second one is an advice on how to be healthy. Moreover, idioms "heart of steel" vs "heart of glass" convey opposite ideas of being "not affected emotionally" vs being "easily affected emotionally". Having "heart" and "affected emotionally" in both idiom descriptions leads to a high cosine similarity between them and results in a false positive decision. For the same reason lexically divergent idiom descriptions get a lower rank while convey similar ideas, e.g. "hopping mad" vs "off on one".

Combining lexical and sentence similarity via (5) performs better than lexical similarity alone (Figure 1) but still does not capture all aspects of a true paraphrase.

6 Conclusion and Future Work

In this paper we present a new domain for the paraphrase identification task: to find paraphrases among idiomatic expressions. We propose a simple scheme to compute the similarity of two idiom definitions that outperforms state-of-the-art paraphrasing models on the dataset of idiom paraphrases that we make publicly available.

Our future work will be focused on exploring different strategies to compute semantic similarity between sentences, developing a comprehensive idiom similarity measure that will utilize both idioms and their definitions, and on comparing text with an idiom and a general text as a realistic scenario for paraphrase identification. It is a new and a challenging task and thus opens up many opportunities for further research in paraphrase identification and all its downstream applications.

Acknowledgments

We thank Thien Huu Nguyen of New York University and Asli Eyecioglu of University of Sussex for their help and advice.

References

Eneko Agirre, Mona Diab, Daniel Cer, and Aitor Gonzalez-Agirre. (2012). Semeval-2012 task 6: A pilot on semantic textual similarity. In *Proceedings of the First Joint Conference on Lexical and Computational Semantics (*SEM)*.

Eneko Agirre, Carmen Banea, Claire Cardie, Daniel Cer, Mona Diab, Aitor Gonzalez-Agirre, Weiwei Guo, Inigo Lopez-Gazpio, Montse Maritxalar, Rada Mihalcea, German Rigau, Larraitz Uria, and Janyce Wiebe. (2015). Semeval-2015 task 2: Semantic textual similarity, English, Spanish and Pilot on Interpretability. In *Proceedings of the 9th International Workshop on Semantic Evaluation (SemEval)*.

Colin Bannard and Chris Callison-Burch. (2005). Paraphrasing with Bilingual Parallel Corpora. In *Proceedings of the 43th Annual Meeting of the Association for Computational Linguistics (ACL).*

Marco Baroni, Georgiana Dinu, and German Kruszewski. (2014). Don't count, predict! A systematic comparison of context-counting vs. context-predicting semantic vectors. In *Proceedings of the 52th Annual Meeting of the Association for Computational Linguistics (ACL).*

Rahul Bhagat and Eduard Hovy. (2013). What is a paraphrase? In *Proceedings of the International Conference on Computational Linguistics (COLING).*

Julia Birke and Anoop Sarkar. (2006). A clustering approach for nearly unsupervised recognition of nonliteral language. In *Proceedings of the Conference of the European Chapter of the Association for Computational Linguistics (EACL).*

William Blacoe and Mirella Lapata. (2012). A comparison of vector-based representations for semantic composition. In *Proceedings of EMNLP-CoLNN.*

Asli Celikyilmaz, Dilek Hakkani-Tur, and Gokhan Tur. (2010). LDA based similarity modeing for question answering. In *Proceedings of the NAACL HLT 2010 Workshop on Semantic Search.*

Ronan Collobert, Jason Weston, Leon Bottou, Michael Karlen, Koray Kavukcuoglu, and Pavel Kuksa (2011). Natural Language Processing (Almost) from Scratch. In *Journal of Machine Learning Research (JMLR).*

Dipanjan Das and Noah A. Smith. (2009). Paraphrase identification as probabilistic quasi-synchronous recognition. In *Proceedings of the Joint Conference of the 47th Annual Meeting of the ACL and the 4th International Joint Conference on Natural Language (ACL-IJCNLP).*

Asli Eyecioglu and Bill Keller. (2015). ASOBEK: Twitter Paraphrase Identification with Simple Overlap Features and SVMs In *Proceedings of 9th International Workshop on Semantic Evaluation (SemEval).*

Samuel Fernando and Mark Stevenson (2008). A semantic similarity approach to paraphrase detection. *Computational Linguistics UK (CLUK) 11th Annual Research Colloquium.*

Matt Gedigian, John Bryant, Srini Narayanan, and Branimir Ciric. (2006). Catching metaphors. In *Proceedings of the Third Workshop on Scalable Natural Language Understanding (ScaNaLU).*

Weiwei Guo and Mona Diab. (2013). Modeling Sentences in the Latent Space. In *Proceedings of the 50th Annual Meeting of the Association for Computational Linguistics (ACL).*

Weiwei Guo, Hao Li, Heng Ji, and Mona Diab. (2013). Linking Tweets to News: A Framework to Enrich Short Text Data in Social Media. In *Proceedings of the 51th Annual Meeting of the Association for Computational Linguistics (ACL).*

Samer Hassan and Rada Mihalcea. (2011). Semantic relatedness using salient semantic analysis. In *Proceedings of the twenty-fifth Association for the Advancement of Artificial Intelligence Conference (AAAI).*

Aminul Islam and Diana Inkpen. (2007). Semantic similarity of short texts. In *Proceedings of Conference on Recent Advances in Natural Language Processing (RANLP).*

Yangfeng Ji and Jacob Eisenstein. (2013). Discriminative improvements to distributional sentence similarity. In *Proceedings of the Conference on Empirical Methods in Natural Language Processing (EMNLP).*

Graham Katz and Eugenie Giesbrecht. (2006). Automatic identification of non-compositional multiword expressions using latent semantic analysis. In *Proceedings of the Workshop on Multiword Expressions: Identifying and Exploiting Underlying Properties (MWE).*

Linlin Li and Caroline Sporleder. (2009). Classifier combination for contextual idiom detection without labeled data. In *Proceedings of the Conference on Empirical Methods in Natural Language Processing (EMNLP).*

Elena Lloret, Oscar Ferrandez, Rafael Munoz, and Manuel Palomar. (2008). A text summarization approach under the influence of textual entailment. In *Proceedings of the 5th International Workshop on Natural Language Processing and Cognitive Science (NLPCS).*

Nitin Madnani and Joel Tetreault. (2012). Reexamining machine translation metrics for paraphrase identification. In *Proceedings of the North American Chapter of the Association for Computational Linguistics - Human Language Technologies (NAACL-HLT).*

Rada Mihalcea, Courtney Corley, and Strapparava. (2006). Corpus-based and knowledge-based measures of text semantic similarity. In *Proceedings of the Association for the Advancement of Artificial Intelligence Conference (AAAI).*

Tomas Mikolov, Kai Chen, Greg Corrado, and Jeffrey Dean. (2013). Efficient estimation of word representations in vector space. In *Proceedings of Workshop at the International Conference on Learning Representations (ICLR).*

Grace Muzny and Luke Zettlemoyer. (2013). Automatic Idiom Identification in Wiktionary. In *Proceedings of the Conference on Empirical Methods on Natural Language Processing (EMNLP).*

Sasa Petrovic, Miles Osborne, and Victor Lavrenko (2012). Using paraphrases for improving first story detection in news and Twitter. In *Proceedings of the North American Chapter of the Association for Computational Linguistics - Human Language Technologies (NAACL-HLT)*.

Long Qiu, Min-Yen Kan, and Tat-Seng Chua. (2006). Paraphrase recognition via dissimilarity significance classification. In *Proceedings of the Conference on Empirical Methods on Natural Language Processing (EMNLP)*.

Vasile Rus, Philip M. McCarthy, Mihai C. Lintean, Danielle S. McNamara, and Arthur C. Graesser (2008). Paraphrase identification with lexico-syntactic graph subsumption. In *Proceedings of the Twenty-First International FLAIRS Conference*.

Satoshi Sekine, (2005). Automatic paraphrase discovery based on context and keywords between NE pairs. In *Proceedings of the 3rd International Workshop on Paraphrasing*.

Yusuke Shinyama, Satoshi Sekine, and Kiyoshi Sudo. (2002). Automatic paraphrase acquisition from news articles. In *Proceedings of the 2nd International Conference on Human Language Technology Research (HLT)*.

Ekaterina Shutova, Lin Sun, and Anna Korhonen. (2010). Metaphor identification using verb and noun clustering. In *Proceedings of the International Conference on Computational Linguistics (COLING)*.

Richard Socher, Eric H Huang, Jeffrey Pennington, Andrew Y Ng, and Christopher D Manning. (2011). Dynamic pooling and unfolding recursive autoencoders for paraphrase detection. In *Proceedings of Advances in Neural Information Processing Systems (NIPS)*.

Joseph Turian, Lev Ratinov, and Yoshua Bengio. (2010). Word representations: A simple and general method for semi-supervised learning. In *Proceedings of the 48th Annual Meeting of the Association for Computational Linguistics (ACL)*.

Stephen Wan, Mark Dras, Robert Dale, and Cecile Paris. (2006). Using dependency-based features to take the parafarce out of paraphrase. In *Proceedings of the Australasian Language Technology Workshop*.

Ling Wang, Chris Dyer, Alan W Black, and Isabel Trancoso. (2013). Paraphrasing 4 microblog normalization. In *Proceedings of the Conference on Empirical Methods on Natural Language Processing (EMNLP)*.

Wei Xu, Chris Callison-Burch, and William B. Dolan. (2015). SemEval-2015 Task 1: Paraphrase and Semantic Similarity in Twitter (PIT). In *Proceedings of the 9th International Workshop on Semantic Evaluation (SemEval)*.

Wei Xu, Alan Ritter, Chris Callison-Burch, William B. Dolan, and Yangfeng Ji. (2015). Extracting Lexically Divergent Paraphrases from Twitter. *Transactions of the Association for Computational Linguistics (TACL)*.

Wei Xu, Alan Ritter, and Ralph Grishman. (2013). Gathering and Generating Paraphrases from Twitter with Application to Normalization. In *Proceedings of the Sixth Workshop on Building and Using Comparable Corpora (BUCC)*.

Fabio Massimo Zanzotto, Marco Pennacchiotti, and Kostas Tsioutsiouliklis (2011). Linguistic redundancy in Twitter. In *Proceedings of the Conference on Empirical Methods on Natural Language Processing (EMNLP)*.

Congle Zhang and Daniel S. Weld (2013). Harvesting parallel news streams to generate paraphrases of event relations. In *Proceedings of the Conference on Empirical Methods on Natural Language Processing (EMNLP)*.

Jiang Zhao, Man Lan, Zheng-Yu Niu, and Dong-Hong Ji. (2014). Recognizing cross-lingual textual entailment with co-training using similarity and difference views. In *Proceedings of International Joint Conference on Neural Networks (IJCNN)*.

Jiang Zhao, Man Lan, and Jun Feng Tian. (2015). ECNU: Using Traditional Similarity Measurements and Word Embedding for Semantic Textual Similarity Estimation. In *Proceedings of the 9th International Workshop on Semantic Evaluation (SemEval)*.

Where Was Alexander the Great in 325 BC?
Toward Understanding History Text with a World Model

Yuki Murakami and Yoshimasa Tsuruoka
The University of Tokyo, 3-7-1 Hongo, Bunkyo-ku, Tokyo, Japan
{murakami,tsuruoka}@logos.t.u-tokyo.ac.jp

Abstract

We present a toy world model for interpreting textual descriptions of the movement record of a historical figure such as Genghis Khan or Napoleon. We cast the problem of document understanding as the task of finding episodes that do not violate the soft constraint conditions derived from the document. The model thus allows us to infer his or her locations by finding multiple solutions of an optimization problem. Our experimental results using Wikipedia text on Alexander the Great demonstrate that such inference can indeed be performed with reasonable accuracy. We also show that the information obtained from such inference is useful in solving a hard coreference resolution problem.

1 Introduction

Recent decades have witnessed great strides in data-driven language processing technology, yet there are still many unsolved problems when the machine has to deal with the meaning of a document. Let us consider the following simple question-answering problem.

- Document:
  David left Paris on the 20th of July, driving his favorite Peugeot. He arrived in Athens on the 22nd.
- Question:
  Where was David on the 21st?
  A. London B. Budapest C. Berlin D. New York

A possible answer to this question would be "He was probably in Budapest, although there is a small chance that he was in Berlin". Putting aside the problem of natural language generation, the machine would have to have geographical knowledge and perform some kind of inference about his movement if it is to give a sensible answer to this question.

This paper presents a toy world model that allows us to perform such inference. We test this approach as a first step toward building a computer system that can "understand" documents on world history and answer various questions about historical figures and events. Our aim is to go beyond traditional question-answering frameworks in which the system can only answer the questions about the facts that are explicitly written in the document. We aim to build a system that can simulate what could have happened in the world history using an internal model and give a reasonable answer to any question as long as the answer can be inferred from other pieces of information available in the document.

In this paper, we focus on the much simpler subproblem of modeling the movement record of a historical figure. Our world model is simply an undirected graph with an agent moving on it, and his potential movement histories are obtained as possible solutions to an optimization problem. In experiments, we show that our system can perform inference about his locations with reasonable accuracy and the information obtained from such inference is useful in solving a hard coreference resolution problem.

2 Related Work

There is an increasing body of research on using world knowledge and inference in high-level text processing tasks such as textual entailment, coreference resolution and question answering (Tatu and Moldovan, 2005; Fowler et al., 2005; Rahman and Ng, 2011; Peng et al., 2015; Berant et al., 2015). However, most of the existing approaches use "static" knowledge that is typically expressed as a collection of n-ary relations between entities, and there is little work that attempts to model the dynamics of a world.

Proceedings of the EMNLP 2015 Workshop on Linking Models of Lexical, Sentential and Discourse-level Semantics, pages 83–88,
Lisboa, Portugal, 18 September 2015.

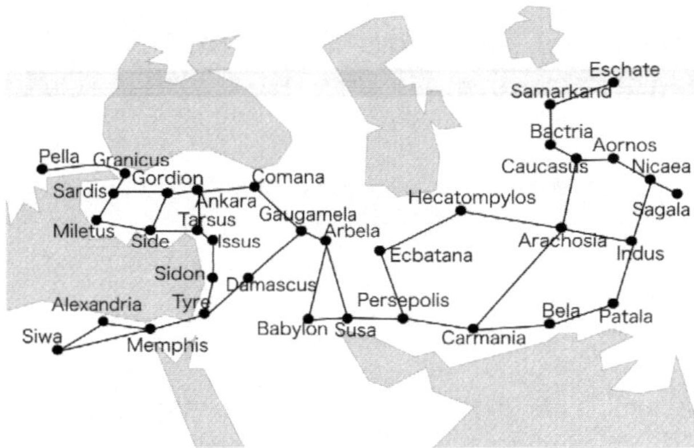

Figure 1: The graph overlayed on the map

Our work is much closer in spirit to SHRDLU (Winograd, 1971), where natural language queries were processed using a world model for toy blocks. More recent research efforts for connecting language with physical world include Logical Semantics with Perception (Krishnamurthy and Kollar, 2013), referential grounding (Liu et al., 2014), 3D scene generation from text (Chang et al., 2014) and generation of QA tasks by simulation (Weston et al., 2015). Our work can be seen as an attempt of grounding textual descriptions in history text to a simulation model for world history.

Our work is also related to previous work on representing structured sequences of actions and events using *scripts* (Schank and Abelson, 1977). Chambers and Jurafsky (2008) proposed a narrative chain model based on scripts. They focused on a particular character, extracted chains of events on his behavior using verbs and their arguments, and sorted them by learning.

3 Model and Inference

3.1 Toy World Model

Our toy world model consists of an agent and an undirected graph $G = (V, E)$, where V is the set of its nodes and E is the set of its edges. Let $h_t \in V$ denote the location of the agent at some discrete time t. The agent starts from the initial node h_0 and, at each time step, either stays at the same node or moves from the current node to its adjacent node. The entire history of his movement, which we hereafter call an *episode*, is thus defined as $< h_0, h_1, ..., h_T >$.

Here, we formulate the problem of understanding a document about an agent as the task of finding an episode that does not contradict the textual descriptions about the agent's locations. In other words, the descriptions in the documents serve as the constraints in finding a possible episode. Note that, in general, there are many episodes that satisfy the constraints, because documents rarely provide the full detail of the movement history of an agent. Once we obtain those episodes, we can use them to resolve questions about the location of the agent at any particular time.

3.2 Alexander's Expeditions

In this work, we create a world model for interpreting documents on *Alexander the Great*, who was a famous king of ancient Macedonia. Figure 1 shows the graph that we have manually created from a map using frequent location names in Wikipedia. It shows the 35 locations names used in our experiments. Note that this graph is a very crude approximation to the real geographical cost and constraints in those days. Ideally, we should incorporate more detailed information such as distance, terrain, and environment into the model, but we leave it for future work.

Constraint conditions are generated from a document. For example, the sentence "Alexander the Great won a battle near Granicus river in May 334 BC." would produce the constraint that his location in May 334 BC is Granicus, which translates into something like h_2 = Granicus in our model. Although sophisticated information extraction techniques could be used to do this, we simply use the co-occurrence of the term "Alexander the Great", time and location expressions within a sentence to generate the constraints. Note

Algorithm 1 Finding feasible episodes

```
function FINDFEASIBLEEPISODES(maxR, maxIter, α)
  feasibleEpisodes ← {}
  for round = 1 to maxR do
    currentE ← GETRANDOMEPISODE()
    bestE ← currentE
    for iter = 1 to maxIter do
      nextE ← GETNEIGHBOREPISODE(currentE)
      if Val(currentE) < Val(nextE) then
        currentE ← nextE
        if Val(nextE) > Val(bestE) then
          bestE ← nextE
        end if
      else
        temperature ← (1/30) α^(iter/maxIter)
                                  ▷ 0 < α < 1 : α is constant
        if rand(0, 1) ≤ e^((Val(nextE) − Val(currentE)) / temperature) then
          currentE ← nextE
        end if
      end if
    end for
    feasibleEpisodes.insert(bestE)
  end for
  return feasibleEpisodes
```

Algorithm 2 Computing a neighbor episode

```
function GETNEIGHBOREPISODE(currentEpisode)
  e ← currentEpisode
  if rand(0, 1) < 0.5 then
    p1, p2 ← GETCONSECUTIVESAMESTATES(e)
    e.remove(p2)
    p3 ← GETRANDOMSTATE(e)
    e.insert(p3)                          ▷ at next p3
  end if
  if rand(0, 1) < 0.5 then
    p1 ← GETRANDOMSTATE(e)
    p2 ← GETADJACENTSTATE(p1)
    e.insert(p2, p1)                      ▷ at next p1
  end if
  if rand(0, 1) < 0.5 then
    p1, p2, p3 ← GETDETOUR(e)             ▷ p1 = p3
    e.remove(p2, p3)
  end if
  if rand(0, 1) < 0.5 then
    loop ← GETRANDOMLOOP(G)               ▷ G is the graph
    if loop contains some state in e then
      e.reverseInLoop(loop)
    end if
  end if
  return e                                ▷ as a neighbor episode
```

that this simplistic method can generate erroneous constraints as well, but we will later show that reasonable inference can be performed even with these noisy constraints.

3.3 Calculation of Feasible Episodes

We use simulated annealing (Kirkpatrick et al., 1983) to find the episodes that satisfy the (soft) constraint conditions. Other approaches to optimization such as integer linear programming can be used for this purpose, but we chose simulated annealing due to its generality and easiness of implementation.

Algorithm 1 shows how we calculate feasible episodes. The score of an episode, $Val(e)$, is computed as the proportion of the constraint conditions satisfied by the episode. In this algorithm, we start with a random episode and attempt to find the episode that has the best score. More specifically, at each iteration, we generate a new episode by making a small modification to the current episode. Finally, we add the episode having the best score to the list of the feasible episodes. We repeat this whole process $maxR$ times to obtain multiple episodes.

Algorithm 2 describes the four operations to compute a neighbor episode in Algorithm 1. The first operation changes the time when the agent stays at the same place. For example, $< Ankara \rightarrow Ankara \rightarrow Tarsus \rightarrow Issus >$ is changed to $< Ankara \rightarrow Tarsus \rightarrow Tarsus \rightarrow Issus >$. The second operation adds a detour to the episode. For example, $< Ankara \rightarrow Tarsus >$ is changed to $< Ankara \rightarrow Gordion \rightarrow Ankara \rightarrow Tarsus >$. The third operation removes a detour from the episode. For example, $< Ankara \rightarrow Gordion \rightarrow Ankara \rightarrow Tarsus >$ is changed to $< Ankara \rightarrow Tarsus >$. The fourth operation alters the path from one location to another. For example, $< Caucasus \rightarrow Aornos \rightarrow Nicaea >$ is changed to $< Caucasus \rightarrow Arachosia \rightarrow Indus \rightarrow Nicaea >$. Each of these four operations is performed with 50% probability.

4 Experiments

4.1 Corpus and Settings

We used the English Wikipedia dataset[1] for the experiments. In this data set, there were 482 sentences which include the strings of "Alexander the Great" and "BC". Among them, 87 sentences included a location name in our list, and they were used to generate (noisy) constraint conditions. The constraints which had the same time and location conditions were treated as one constraint, so we did not take into account the frequency of appearance. As a result, 39 (noisy) constraints were generated. We manually checked those 39 constraints and found that 32 of them correctly describe Alexander's location at a particular time.

The simulation setting is as follows:

- The initial place is "Pella", i.e., h_0 = Pella.

[1] downloaded in November 2013.

Time	Place (Ans)
331 BC	Arbela
A century later, the "Men of the Mountain Land," from north of Kabul River, served in the army of Darius III of Persia when he fought against **Alexander the Great** at **Arbela** in **331 BC**.	
330 BC	Persepolis
After invading Persia, **Alexander the Great** sent the main force of his army to **Persepolis** in the year **330 BC** by the Royal Road.	

Table 1: Examples of questions

- One time step corresponds to two months.
- At each time step, the agent (Alexander) either stays at the same node or moves from the current node to one of its adjacent nodes.
- Each episode consists of 72 steps (i.e. $T = 71$), which correspond to Alexander's twelve-year expedition from 334 BC to 323 BC.

The values of α and $maxR$ in Algorithm 1 were set to 0.001 and 1,000 respectively.

4.2 Question Answering

First, we examine how accurately our system can answer questions like "Where was Alexander the Great in 325 BC?", when the answer is not explicitly written in the text. We have created 32 questions from the aforementioned 32 constraints that correctly describe Alexander's locations. Table 1 shows examples of questions with the Wikipedia sentences from which the questions were created.

When the system infers the answer to a question, we make sure that the system has no access to the sentences that convey the information about the correct answer. In other words, we exclude those sentences when generating the constraint conditions for the simulation.

For each question, the system calculates 1,000 episodes by simulated annealing and ranks the places according to how many times they have appeared during the time period specified in the question. The system then returns the top N places as the answer. We consider the answer to be correct if the correct place is included in the top N places.

As a baseline method for comparison, we also calculate the top N places according to their temporal distance to the time specified by the question. For example, we prioritize the mention pair (Tyre, 332 BC) over (Ankara, 333 BC) if the time specified by the question is 331 BC.

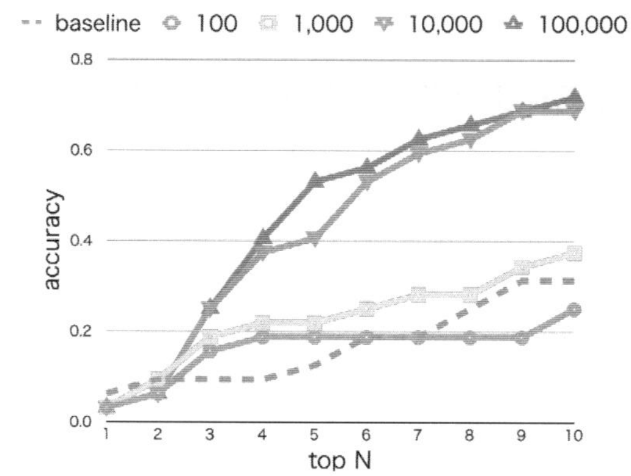

Figure 2: The accuracy of the top-N answers

Figure 2 shows the accuracy of the top-N answers for the 32 questions. The dotted line shows the result of the baseline method and the four solid lines show the results of our inference-based approach when the maximum numbers of iterations (maxIter) in Algorithm 1 are set to 100, 1,000, 10,000 and 100,000. As can be seen, the accuracy rate improves as the number of iterations in simulated annealing increases. The accuracy rates achieved by performing more than 10,000 iterations are significantly higher than those of the baseline. As for the computational cost, it took about half an hour to obtain 1,000 episodes (with maxIter = 100,000) for each question using eight cores of Xeon X5680.

4.3 Coreference Resolution

We show an example of coreference resolution using our world model. Table 2 shows a paragraph created from the Wikipedia text[2], where the phrase "the area" in the last sentence could refer to any of the four difference places mentioned in the sentences. Since there are few syntactic or lexical clues for disambiguation, it is a difficult coreference resolution problem[3].

When performing the inference for this problem, we did not use the constraints derived from the sentences that contain the candidate places,

[2]We have replaced "It" at the beginning of the original sentence with "Bela".

[3]We tested two publicly available coreference resolution systems (Stanford Core NLP and Illinois coreference System). Neither of them could not identify the correct antecedent.

time	325 BC
anaphor	the area
antecedent	Bela
other candidates	Arachosia, Carmania, Babylon

Bela is directly to the south of the ancient provinces of **Arachosia** and Drangiana, to the east of **Carmania** and due west of the Kingdoms of Ancient India. In **325 BC**, **Alexander the Great** crossed **the area** on his way back to **Babylon** after campaigning in the east.

Table 2: Example of coreference resolution

candidates	maxIter		
	1,000	10,000	100,000
Bela (Ans)	**247/1,000**	**547/1,000**	**745/1,000**
Carmania	210/1,000	454/1,000	640/1,000
Arachosia	154/1,000	404/1,000	651/1,000
Babylon	35/1,000	8/1,000	1/1,000

Table 3: Coreference resolution by inference

since we are interested in the situation where no explicit information is available in the document.

The inference results are shown in Table 4.3. The values in the table show how many times the places appeared in the 1,000 episodes at the times corresponding to 325 BC. The correct antecedent, Bela, has the highest values, and the infeasible antecedent, Babylon, has very low values, which demonstrate the usefulness of the inference in coreference resolution.

4.4 Error Analysis

We discuss the constraint conditions which could never be satisfied by any resulting episodes. Two examples are shown below.

- Constraint: 334 BC, Alexandria
- Sentence: The port of **Alexandria**, founded by **Alexander the Great** in **334 BC**, was a hub for Mediterranean trade for centuries.

- Constraint: 323 BC, Memphis
- Sentence: Arrhidaeus, one of **Alexander the Great**'s generals, was entrusted with the conduct of Alexander's funeral to **Egypt** in **323 BC**.

The first constraint is problematic because, in actual history, Alexander the Great was not in Egypt in 334 BC. This seemingly erroneous constraint was created by the ambiguity of the word "Alexandria", because it can refer to many other cities having the same name. The sentence of the second constraint does not describe Alexander the Great—it describes Arrhidaeus, who was one of his generals. However, our simplistic co-occurrence-based method wrongly created a constraint from it. These results suggest that our world model could help us to detect and suppress wrong interpretations of text since the constraints derived from wrong interpretations are unlikely to be satisfied in the simulation.

5 Conclusion

We have presented a toy world model that allows us to simulate the movement history of a historical figure and perform inference about his locations. Experimental results using Wikipedia text demonstrate its inference ability and potential usefulness in high-level NLP applications such as question-answering and coreference resolution.

In future work, we plan to develop a more robust environment on which we can quantitatively evaluate the level of document understanding by using a world model. We aim to build an evaluation method for comparing different approaches.

Our future work should also encompass extending the toy world model. Currently, the agent only moves on the graph, and thus the historical events that can be represented by the model is limited. Increasing the variety of actions that the agent can perform and the number of historical figures should be an interesting direction of future work.

Acknowledgments

We thank the anonymous reviewers for their helpful comments and suggestions.

References

Jonathan Berant, Noga Alon, Ido Dagan, and Jacob Goldberger. 2015. Efficient global learning of entailment graphs. *Computational Linguistics*, 41(2):221–264.

Nathanael Chambers and Dan Jurafsky. 2008. Unsupervised learning of narrative event chains. In *Proceedings of ACL-08*, pages 789–797.

Angel X Chang, Manolis Savva, and Christopher D Manning. 2014. Learning spatial knowledge for text to 3D scene generation. In *Proceedings of Empirical Methods in Natural Language Processing, EMNLP*, pages 2028–2038.

Abraham Fowler, Bob Hauser, Daniel Hodges, Ian Niles, Adrian Novischi, and Jens Stephan. 2005. Applying cogex to recognize textual entailment. In *Proceedings of the PASCAL Challenges Workshop on Recognising Textual Entailment*, pages 69–72.

Scott Kirkpatrick, MP Vecchi, et al. 1983. Optimization by simmulated annealing. *Science*, 220(4598):671–680.

Jayant Krishnamurthy and Thomas Kollar. 2013. Jointly learning to parse and perceive: Connecting natural language to the physical world. *Transactions of the Association for Computational Linguistics*, 1:193–206.

Changsong Liu, Lanbo She, Rui Fang, and Joyce Y Chai. 2014. Probabilistic labeling for efficient referential grounding based on collaborative discourse. In *Proceedings of the 52nd Annual Meeting of the Association for Computational Linguistics (Volume 2: Short Papers)*, pages 13–18.

Haoruo Peng, Daniel Khashabi, and Dan Roth. 2015. Solving hard coreference problems. In *Proceedings of the 2015 Conference of the North American Chapter of the Association for Computational Linguistics: Human Language Technologies*, pages 809–819.

Altaf Rahman and Vincent Ng. 2011. Coreference resolution with world knowledge. In *Proceedings of the 49th Annual Meeting of the Association for Computational Linguistics: Human Language Technologies-Volume 1*, pages 814–824.

Roger Schank and Robert P Abelson. 1977. *Scripts, plans, goals and understanding: An inquiry into human knowledge structures*. Lawrence Erlbaum.

Marta Tatu and Dan Moldovan. 2005. A semantic approach to recognizing textual entailment. In *Proceedings of the conference on Human Language Technology and Empirical Methods in Natural Language Processing*, pages 371–378.

Jason Weston, Antoine Bordes, Sumit Chopra, and Tomas Mikolov. 2015. Towards ai-complete question answering: a set of prerequisite toy tasks. *arXiv preprint arXiv:1502.05698*.

Terry Winograd. 1971. *Procedures as a representation for data in a computer program for understanding natural languages*. Ph.D. thesis, Massachusetts Institute of Technology, Project Mac.

Predicting word sense annotation agreement

Héctor Martínez Alonso† **Anders Johannsen**† **Oier Lopez de Lacalle**‡ **Eneko Agirre**‡
†University of Copenhagen
‡University of the Basque Country
{alonso,johannsen}@hum.ku.dk {e.agirre,oier.lopezdelacalle}@ehu.eus

Abstract

High agreement is a common objective when annotating data for word senses. However, a number of factors make perfect agreement impossible, e.g. the limitations of sense inventories, the difficulty of the examples or the interpretation preferences of the annotators. Estimating potential agreement is thus a relevant task to supplement the evaluation of sense annotations. In this article we propose two methods to predict agreement on word-annotation instances. We experiment with a continuous representation and a three-way discretization of observed agreement. In spite of the difficulty of the task, we find that different levels of agreement can be identified—in particular, low-agreement examples are easier to identify.

1 Introduction

Sense-annotation tasks show less-than-perfect agreement scores. However, variation in agreement is not the result of featureless, white noise in the annotations; Krippendorff (2011) defines disagreement as *by chance*—caused by unavoidable inconsistencies in annotator behavior—and *systematic*—caused by properties of the data.

Our goal is to predict the agreement of sense-annotated examples by examining their linguistic properties. If we can identify properties predictive of low or high agreement, then we can claim that some of the agreement variation in the data is indeed systematic.

Artstein and Poesio (2008) provide an interpretation of Kripperdorff's α coefficient to describe the reliability of a whole annotation task and the way that observed agreement (A_o) is calculated for each example. Strictly speaking, the value of α only provides an indication of the replicability of an annotation task, but we propose that the difficulty of annotating a particular example will influence its local observed agreement. Thus, easy examples will have a high A_o, that will be lower for more difficult examples.

Identifying low-agreement examples by their linguistic features would help characterize contexts that make words difficult to annotate. Estimating the agreement of examples has an immediate application for data collection, as a way of estimating the proportion of examples of each difficulty level that one wants to sample. Moreover, a model of (dis)agreement can help interpret the mispredictions of a word-sense disambiguation system without requiring the data to be multiply annotated.

Observed agreement A_o is a continuous-valued variable in the unit interval and we tackle its prediction as a regression task (Section 4.1). We also experiment with a discretized version of observed agreement into low, mid and high agreement, which is predicted using classification (Section 4.2).

2 Related work

In their study, Yarowsky and Florian (2002) examine the relation between agreement variation and predictive power of word-sense disambiguation systems, which is later expanded by Lopez de Lacalle and Agirre (2015a). Our work is different in that we do not study the relation between agreement and performance, but between example properties and agreement. Martínez Alonso (2013) experiments with prediction of agreement for coarse-sense annotation.

Tomuro (2001) uses the disagreement between annotators of two English sense-annotated corpora to provide insights on the relations between synsets, and more recent studies (Jurgens, 2013; Plank et al., 2014; Jurgens, 2014; Lopez de Lacalle and Agirre, 2015b) have empirically tackled

Proceedings of the EMNLP 2015 Workshop on Linking Models of Lexical, Sentential and Discourse-level Semantics, pages 89–94, Lisboa, Portugal, 18 September 2015.

the issue of inter-annotator disagreement as a phenomenon that is potentially informative for natural language processing. Other research efforts advocate for models of annotator behavior (Passonneau et al., 2009; Passonneau et al., 2010; Passonneau and Carpenter, 2014; Cohn and Specia, 2013).

3 Data

We conduct our study on sense-annotated datasets, keeping only the examples with at least two annotations per item. In the datasets with two annotators and one adjudicator, we disregard adjudications given their potentially different bias.

1 MASCC The English crowdsourced lexical-sample word-sense corpus from Passonneau and Carpenter (2014).

2-5 MASCE* The expert annotations for a series of English lexical-sample words from Passonneau et al. (2012), with several annotation rounds. We include the second, third and fourth round of annotation in our experiments. We use on the whole dataset (MASCEW) pooling all the rounds together, as well as on each round independently, namely MASCE2, MASCE3 and MASCE4.

6 FNTW The English Twitter FrameNet data of Søgaard et al. (2015). We treat the frame-name layer as a word-sense layer, and disregard the arguments.

7 ENSST The English supersense-annotated data of Johannsen et al. (2014).

8 EUSC The Basque lexical-sample SemCor of Agirre et al. (2006).

9 DASST The Danish supersense-annotated data of Martínez Alonso et al. (2015).

Table 1 provides the characteristics of the datasets. The annotation task can be lexical-sample (ls) or all-words (aw). The number of instances is different from the number of sentences for all-words annotation. The type of annotators can be expert (ex) or crowdsourced (cs). The α scores can differ from those reported in the datasets' documentation given our example-selection criteria. The last two columns describe the target variables of observed agreement (A_o) and the proportion of low-, mid- and high-agreement instances, cf. 3.2 for details.

3.1 Features

We define an *instance* as a sentence with a target word for annotation. If a sentence has n annotated target words, it yields n instances. For each instance, we obtain features for a word w and its syntactic parent p in a sentence s, organized in feature groups. The word identities of w and p are not included in the features to keep the models more general. Number of features are in parentheses.

Frequency(2) We calculate the frequency of w and p, scaling by $log(rank(x)+1)^{-1}$.

Morphology (5) We consider the part-of-speech tag (POS) of w, of p, and the POS-bigram at the left and at the right of w. In order to incorporate information on inflectional complexity, we calculate which proportion of the frequency of the stem of w is covered by w, e.g. the occurrences of 'jumping' constitute 22% of the occurrences of the stem 'jump'.

Syntax (5) We calculate the number of dependents of w and p, and a bag of words for the labels of the dependents of w and p. We also include the distance from w to the root node, and the linear distance between w and p.

Context (5) We calculate the length of s in tokens, the proportion of w made up of content words, and a bag of words of the context of w, i.e. all the words of s except w. To capture context specificity, we calculate the maximum and the sum of the sentence-wise idf of each stem in s.

Sense inventory (2) We calculate the number of possible senses for w, plus an additional sense when w could be discarded from the annotation—like the tag 'O' for supersenses—or the right synset was not present in WordNet. We also calculate the sense entropy for each word following Yarowsky and Florian (2002).

We use TreeTagger (Schmid, 1994) for POS tagging and TurboParser (Martins et al., 2010) for dependency parsing, both trained on Universal Dependencies v1.1,[1] to allow cross-language feature comparison. We estimate frequencies on a 100M-word corpus for English (Ferraresi et al., 2008) and Danish (Asmussen and Halskov, 2012), and on 13M for Basque (Leturia, 2012), using Snowball stemming.

3.2 Target variable

Regression Instance-wise observed agreement (A_o) is the target variable for the regression experiments. We obtain A_o for each example by counting the pairwise matches in the annotation and dividing over the amount of pairwise combi-

[1] https://lindat.mff.cuni.cz/repository/xmlui/handle/11234/LRT-1478

Dataset	lang	inventory	task	sent	inst	ann	type	α	$A_o \pm \sigma$	L/M/H
MASCC	English	synset	ls	44.6k	44.6k	13-25	cs	.40	$.14 \pm .24$	25/44/31
MASCEW	English	synset	ls	2.6k	2.6k	2-6	ex	.48	$.07 \pm .35$	24/21/55
—MASCE2	English	synset	ls	1.5k	1.5k	5-6	ex	.51	$.41 \pm .30$	21/36/43
—MASCE3	English	synset	ls	500	500	3	ex	.69	$.80 \pm .33$	28/00/72
—MACSE4	English	synset	ls	618	618	2	ex	.63	$.73 \pm .44$	27/00/73
ENSST	English	supersense	aw	39	326	3	ex	.67	$.69 \pm .36$	45/00/55
FNTW	English	frame	aw	236	958	3	ex	.82	$.82 \pm .31$	26/00/74
EUSC	Basque	synset	ls	20.6k	20.6k	2	ex	.76	$.76 \pm .43$	24/00/76
DASST	Danish	supersense	aw	1.2k	9.5k	2	ex	.65	$.67 \pm .47$	33/00/67

Table 1: Dataset characteristics in terms of language, sense inventory, task (al:all-words, ls:lexical sample), no. of sentences, no. of instances, no. of annotators, type of annotators (ex:expert,cs:crowdsourced), α, observed agreement and percentage of LOW/MID/HIGH agreement examples.

nations. Note that α is an aggregate measure that is obtained dataset-wise, and A_o is the only agreement measure available for individual instances.

Classification The target variable for the classification experiments is a discretization of A_o into three agreement-level classes, namely LOW, MID and HIGH. The threshold for LOW is set at $A_o \leq \frac{1}{3}$, and for HIGH at $A_o \geq \frac{2}{3}$. The MID value is only possible for datasets with more than three annotators (cf. Table 1).

4 Experiments

We use the scikit-learn[2] implementation for all learning algorithms, and train and test on 10-fold cross validation.

Regression We use L2-regularized linear regression. The baselines for regression are MEAN, where all instances receive the mean A_o of the dataset, and MEDIAN, that assigns the median A_o.

Classification We use a maximum-entropy classifier. The baselines for classification are MFC, where all instances receive most frequent class, and the two random baselines: STRA, where the assigned values are randomly selected via stratified sampling from the distribution of classes in the dataset, and UNI where values are assigned from the uniform distribution of the three labels.

4.1 Regression

Table 2 shows the results for regression in terms of mean absolute error (MAE). This metric is more suitable than root-mean-square error (RMSE) when evaluating regression in the [0,1] interval.

	REGRESSION	MEAN	MEDIAN
MASCC	**0.19**	0.21	0.21
MASCEW	**0.31**	0.32	0.37
—MASCE2	0.27	0.26	0.25
—MASCE3	0.36	0.29	0.20
—MASCE4	0.46	0.40	0.27
ENSST	0.43	0.35	0.31
FNTW	0.27	0.26	0.18
EUSC	0.35	0.37	0.24
DASST	0.42	0.44	0.33

Table 2: Mean absolute error of prediction for regression and for mean and median baselines. Datasets where the system outperforms the best-performing baseline are marked in bold.

Datasets where the system outperforms both baselines are in bold.

The results for regression show that predicting instance-wise A_o is a hard task. The learnability of the task is limited by the resolution of the target variable; the only two datasets that can beat all baselines (and thus have lower MAE) have many instances, and many annotators (about 50% of the instances in MASCEW have five or more annotators). Also, size of the dataset is a relevant factor for a good estimation of A_o.

We also examine goodness of fit in terms of R^2 (determination coefficient or explained variance). R^2 does not strictly say how much agreement is systematic, but how much of the agreement variation within a dataset can be explained by the features. The only two datasets with positive R^2 are MASCC and EUSC, at .082 and 0.014 respectively. EUSC has only two annotators per instance, but it

[2] http://scikit-learn.org/

	MAXENT	MFC	STRA	UNI
MASCC	**0.45** (0.13)	0.27	0.35	0.37
MASCEW	**0.48** (0.15)	0.39	0.39	0.35
—MASCE2	**0.39** (0.08)	0.25	0.34	0.33
—MASCE3	**0.62** (0.05)	0.60	0.57	0.53
—MASCE4	**0.63** (0.03)	0.62	0.62	0.55
ENSST	0.50 (-0.02)	0.39	0.51	0.49
FNTW	**0.71** (0.22)	0.63	0.61	0.51
EUSC	**0.68** (0.09)	0.65	0.63	0.54
DASST	**0.60** (0.11)	0.53	0.55	0.53

Table 3: Agreement prediction as classification compared against the most-frequent, stratified and uniform baseline. Datasets where the system outperforms the hardest baseline are marked in bold, error reduction in parentheses.

is a large dataset that allows mapping some properties of the features onto the variance of A_o.

The two datasets with a goodness of fit over baseline are the largest ones. This behavior indicates that the regression method suffers from the data bottleneck. Smooth estimation of continuous values might be more sensitive to data volume than estimation of discrete values, therefore we experiment with classification in the next section.

4.2 Classification

Table 3 shows the results for classification in terms of micro-averaged F_1 score. Error reduction over the hardest baseline is given in parentheses.

The ENSST dataset is the only dataset where the system cannot beat both baselines, albeit by a small margin. It is a small, all-words dataset, and the data might be too heterogenous for the model to make sense of it with only 326 instances. The F_1 scores are not very high in absolute terms, but agreement prediction is as least as hard as sense prediction.

MAE and F_1 are not comparable measures; without evaluating both on error reduction over equivalent baselines, we cannot strictly say that classification outperforms regression. Nevertheless, classification seems a promising approach.

4.3 Feature analysis

Figure 1 shows the Spearman correlation with A_o for the numeric features on two English datasets, namely MASCC and FNTW. Even though there is variation in the magnitude across datasets, we observe strong negative correlation of the sense inventory features (*z_senseentropy*, *z_nlabels*), but also for the frequency of the target word (*a_targetfreq*). Notice that these features are also colinear, and in word-sense annotation high-frequency words can be partly more difficult to annotate because they can be more polysemous.

Given these correlations, the feature repertoire we use captures better the low-agreement area of the data, but no feature has a consistently high positive correlation with agreement. That is, the predictors for low-agreement are more reliable than those for high agreement.

A possible candidate for high-agreement prediction could be the proportion of content words over the length of the context, arguably because more lexically rich context are easier to desambiguate by the annotators. This feature has a positive value for most datasets except MASCC. This property has already been noted by Passonneau et al. (2009), who mention that 'greater specificity in the contexts of use leads to higher agreement'.

Syntactic complexity is also an indicator of difficulty. Words with many dependents are often more difficult to annotate (*d_targetdeps* has a consistently negative correlation with A_o), while words with many syntactic siblings are placed in more specific contexts and are easier to annotate, giving *d_headdeps* a slight positive correlation with A_o. This behavior holds for all the English datasets except MASCC, as well as for EUSC.

We have also performed group-wise feature ablation tests on regression and classification, with similar results. Based on the contribution of single feature groups, we find that the sense-inventory group constantly outperforms the other groups, followed by the morphology group. When the sense inventory is ignored from the features, performance almost always decreases, indicating that sense inventory information is very valuable to predict agreement. However, context information is necessary to distinguish between examples of the same word (say, in a one-lemma lexical-sample dataset), where the sense-inventory features would be constant across the whole dataset.

Similarly, in the class-based experiments of Martínez Alonso (2013), certain features like plural or number of dependents are strong predictors for low agreement when annotating between the *container* and the *content* senses of words like *bowl* and *glass*. However, our datasets are ei-

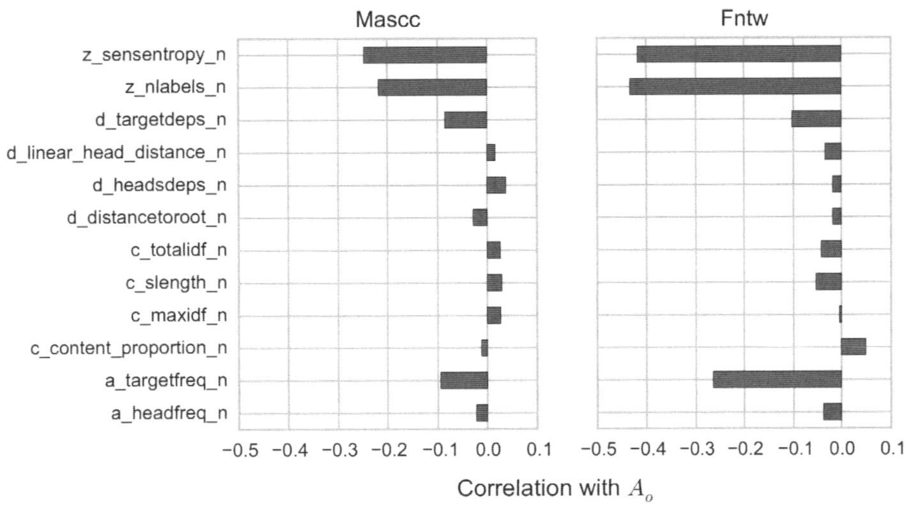

Figure 1: Correlation between the numeric-valued features and A_o for MASCC and FNTW

ther all-words or groupings of lexical-sample annotations for different words (e.g. MASC2 contains examples of *fair-j*, *know-v*, *land-n*, etc.), which means that some of the class- or lemma-dependent features might be swamped by the superposition of features from the other words.

Nevertheless, the systems do not always improve when adding context features, which suggests that there is room for improvement in capturing contextual information for sense-annotated instances.

5 Conclusions and further work

This article addresses the prediction of instance-wise agreement for sense-annotated data. We have described a method to model agreement as a continuous value, and as a set of three discrete values. We use a feature scheme that tries to give account for the lexical, morphologic and syntactic properties of the examples. We have conducted experiments on nine datasets, which comprise three languages, all-words vs. lexical-sample word annotations, and crowdsourced vs. expert annotations.

The overall conclusiveness of the study requires expanding this research to more datasets and languages, as well as further exploring the difference in annotator bias between expert and crowdsourced annotations. Our feature repertoire can be expanded with characteristics of the sense inventory in terms of sense relatedness like autohyponymy, depth in the sense ontology, or qualitative properties of the senses such abstractness. Context features can also be expanded by adding information from word sense induction and distributional models.

Moreover, if we are to examine agreement variation in full-document (as opposed to sentence-by-sentence) annotation, we suggest that document-level frequency would help concretize the meaning of a certain word, following the principle of one sense per discourse (Gale et al., 1992).

If the numeric prediction of agreement is desirable over classification, a metric like annotation entropy (Lopez de Lacalle and Agirre, 2015a) is worth considering as an alternative measure to A_o, since it an information-theoretical measure that also gives account for distribution skewness.

References

Eneko Agirre, Izaskun Aldezabal, Jone Etxeberria, Eli Izagirre, Karmele Mendizabal, Eli Pociello, and Mikel Quintian. 2006. A methodology for the joint development of the Basque WordNet and Semcor. In *LREC*.

Ron Artstein and Massimo Poesio. 2008. Inter-coder agreement for computational linguistics. *Computational Linguistics*, 34(4):555–596.

Jørg Asmussen and Jakob Halskov. 2012. The CLARIN DK Reference Corpus. In *Sprogteknologisk Workshop*.

Trevor Cohn and Lucia Specia. 2013. Modelling annotator bias with multi-task Gaussian processes: An application to machine translation quality estimation. In *ACL*.

Adriano Ferraresi, Eros Zanchetta, Marco Baroni, and Silvia Bernardini. 2008. Introducing and evaluating ukwac, a very large web-derived corpus of english. In *Proceedings of the 4th Web as Corpus Workshop (WAC-4) Can we beat Google*.

William A Gale, Kenneth W Church, and David Yarowsky. 1992. One sense per discourse. In *Proceedings of the workshop on Speech and Natural Language*.

Anders Johannsen, Dirk Hovy, Héctor Martínez Alonso Alonso, Barbara Plank, and Anders Søgaard. 2014. More or less supervised supersense tagging of Twitter. *Lexical and Computational Semantics (* SEM 2014)*.

David Jurgens. 2013. Embracing ambiguity: A comparison of annotation methodologies for crowdsourcing word sense labels. In *HLT-NAACL*.

David Jurgens. 2014. An analysis of ambiguity in word sense annotations. In *LREC*.

Klaus Krippendorff. 2011. Agreement and information in the reliability of coding. *Communication Methods and Measures*, 5(2):93–112.

Igor Leturia. 2012. Evaluating different methods for automatically collecting large general corpora for Basque from the web. In *Proceedings of COLING 2012*, Mumbai, India, December. The COLING 2012 Organizing Committee.

Oier Lopez de Lacalle and Eneko Agirre. 2015a. Crowdsourced word sense annotations and difficult words and examples. *IWCS*.

Oier Lopez de Lacalle and Eneko Agirre. 2015b. A methodology for word sense disambiguation at 90% based on large-scale crowdsourcing. In *Lexical and Computational Semantics (*SEM)*.

Héctor Martínez Alonso, Anders Johannsen, Nimb Sussi, Sussi Olsen, and Bolette Sandford Pedersen. 2015. Supersense tagging for Danish. In *NODALIDA*.

Héctor Martínez Alonso. 2013. *Annotation of regular polysemy: an empirical assessment of the underspecified sense*. Ph.D. thesis, University of Copenhagen.

André FT Martins, Noah A Smith, Eric P Xing, Pedro MQ Aguiar, and Mário AT Figueiredo. 2010. Turbo parsers: Dependency parsing by approximate variational inference. In *EMNLP*. Association for Computational Linguistics.

Rebecca J Passonneau and Bob Carpenter. 2014. The benefits of a model of annotation. *TACL*, 2:311–326.

Rebecca J Passonneau, Ansaf Salleb-Aouissi, and Nancy Ide. 2009. Making sense of word sense variation. In *Proceedings of the Workshop on Semantic Evaluations: Recent Achievements and Future Directions*. Association for Computational Linguistics.

Rebecca J Passonneau, Ansaf Salleb-Aouissi, Vikas Bhardwaj, and Nancy Ide. 2010. Word sense annotation of polysemous words by multiple annotators. In *LREC*.

Rebecca J Passonneau, Collin Baker, Christiane Fellbaum, and Nancy Ide. 2012. The MASC word sense sentence corpus. In *LREC*.

Barbara Plank, Dirk Hovy, and Anders Søgaard. 2014. Linguistically debatable or just plain wrong? In *ACL*.

Helmut Schmid. 1994. Probabilistic part-of-speech tagging using decision trees. In *Proceedings of the International Conference on New Methods in Language Processing*.

Anders Søgaard, Barbara Plank, and Héctor Martínez Alonso Alonso. 2015. Using frame semantics for knowledge extraction from Twitter. In *AAAI*.

Noriko Tomuro. 2001. Systematic polysemy and interannotator disagreement: Empirical examinations. In *First International Workshop on Generative Approaches to Lexicon*.

David Yarowsky and Radu Florian. 2002. Evaluating sense disambiguation across diverse parameter spaces. *Natural Language Engineering*, 8(04):293–310.

Distributional Semantics in Use

Raffaella Bernardi* **Gemma Boleda*** **Raquel Fernández**† **Denis Paperno***
*Center for Mind/Brain Sciences
University of Trento
†Institute for Logic, Language and Computation
University of Amsterdam

Abstract

In this position paper we argue that an adequate semantic model must account for language in use, taking into account how discourse context affects the meaning of words and larger linguistic units. Distributional semantic models are very attractive models of meaning mainly because they capture conceptual aspects and are automatically induced from natural language data. However, they need to be extended in order to account for language use in a discourse or dialogue context. We discuss phenomena that the new generation of distributional semantic models should capture, and propose concrete tasks on which they could be tested.

1 Introduction

Distributional semantics has revolutionised computational semantics by representing the meaning of linguistic expressions as vectors that capture their co-occurrence patterns in large corpora (Turney et al., 2010; Erk, 2012). This strategy has been shown to be very successful for modelling word meaning, and it has recently been expanded to capture the meaning of phrases and even sentences in a compositional fashion (Baroni and Zamparelli, 2010; Mitchell and Lapata, 2010; Grefenstette and Sadrzadeh, 2011; Socher et al., 2012). Distributional semantic models are often presented as a robust alternative to representing meaning, compared to symbolic and logic-based approaches in formal semantics, thanks to their flexible representations and their data-driven nature. However, current models fail to account for aspects of meaning that are central in formal semantics, such as the relation between linguistic expressions and their referents or the truth conditions of sentences. In this position paper we focus on one of the main limitations of current distributional approaches, namely, their unawareness of the unfolding discourse context.

Standardly, distributional models are constructed from large amounts of data in batch mode by aggregating information into a vector that synthesises the general distributional meaning of an expression. Some of the recent distributional models account for contextual effects within the scope of a phrase or a sentence, (e.g., (Baroni and Zamparelli, 2010; Erk et al., 2013)), but they are not intended to capture how the meaning depends on the incrementally built discourse context where an expression is used. Since words and sentences are not used in isolation but are typically part of a discourse, the traditional distributional view is not sufficient. We argue that, to grow into an empirically adequate, full-fledged theory of meaning and interpretation, distributional models must evolve to provide meaning representations for actual language use in discourse and dialogue. Specifically, we discuss how the type of information they encode needs to be extended, and propose a series of tasks to evaluate pragmatically aware distributional models.

2 Meaning in Discourse

As we just pointed out, distributional semantics has been successful at providing data-driven meaning representations that are however limited to capturing generic, conceptual aspects of meaning. To use well established knowledge representation terms, distributional models capture the terminological knowledge (T-Box) of Description Logic, whereas they lack the encoding of assertional knowledge (A-Box), which refers to individuals (Brachman and Levesque, 1982). Proper natural language semantic modelling should capture both kinds of knowledge as well as their relation. Furthermore, distributional models have so far missed the main insights provided by the Dynamic Semantics tradition (Grosz et al., 1983;

Proceedings of the EMNLP 2015 Workshop on Linking Models of Lexical, Sentential and Discourse-level Semantics, pages 95–101,
Lisboa, Portugal, 18 September 2015.

Grosz and Sidner, 1986; Kamp and Reyle, 1993; Asher and Lascarides, 2003; Ginzburg, 2012), namely, that the meaning of an expression consists in its context-change potential, where context is incrementally built up as a discourse proceeds.

We contend that a distributional semantics for language use should account for the *discourse context-dependent*, *dynamic*, and *incremental* nature of language. Generic semantic knowledge won't suffice: one needs to encode somehow the discourse state or common ground, which will enable modeling discourse and dialogue coherence. In this section, we first look into examples that illustrate the dependence of interpretation on discourse and dialogue context and then consider the dynamic meaning of sentences as context-change potential.

2.1 Word and Phrase Meaning

As is well known, standard distributional models provide a single meaning representation for a word, which implicitly encodes all its possible senses and meaning nuances in general. A few recent models do account for some contextual effects within the scope of a sentence: For instance, the different shades of meaning that an adjective like *red* takes depending on the noun it modifies (e.g., *car* vs. *cheek*). However, such models, e.g. Erk and Padó (2008), Dinu and Lapata (2010), and Erk et al. (2013), typically use just a single word or sentence as context. They do not look into how word meaning gets progressively constrained by the common ground of the speakers as the discourse unfolds.

A prominent type of "meaning adjustment" in discourse and dialogue is the interaction with the properties of the referent a particular word is associated to. For example, when we use a word like *box*, which a priori can be used for entities with very different properties, we typically use it to refer to a specific box in a given context, and this constrains its interpretation. The referential effects extend to composition. Consider, for instance, the following example by McNally and Boleda (2015): Adrian and Barbara are sorting objects according to color in different, identical, brown cardboard boxes. Adrian accidentally puts a pair of red socks in the box containing blue objects, and Barbara remarks *'no, no, these belong in the red box'*. Thus, even if *red* when modifying *box* (or indeed any noun denoting a physical object) will typically refer to its colour, it may also refer to other properties of the box referent (such as its contents) if these are prominent in the current discourse context and have become part of the common ground.

Indeed, the emergence of ad hoc meaning conventions in conversation is well attested empirically. In the classic psycholinguistic experiments by Clark and Wilkes-Gibbs (1986), speakers may first refer to a Tangram figure as *the one that looks like an angel* and end up using simply the word *angel* to mean that figure. As Garrod and Anderson (1987) point out, this idiosyncratic use of language "depends as much upon local and transient conventions, set up during the course of the dialogue, as [it does] on the more stable conventions of the larger linguistic community" (cf. Lewis (1969)). Arguably, current distributional models mainly capture the latter stable conventions. The challenge is thus to be able to also capture the former, discourse-dependent meaning.

Moreover, even function words, which are not-referential and are usually considered to have a precise (logical) meaning, are subject to pragmatic effects. For instance, the meaning of the determiner *some* is typically taken to be that of an existential quantifier (i.e., there exists at least one object with certain properties). Yet, its 'at least one' meaning may be refined in particular discourse contexts, as shown in the following examples:

(1) a. If you ate some of the cookies, then I won't have enough for the party.
$\leadsto$ *some and possibly all*
b. A: Did you eat all the cookies?
B: I ate some. $\leadsto$ *some but not all*

Distributional models have so far not been particularly successful in modelling the meaning of function words (but see Baroni et al. (2012); Bernardi et al. (2013); Hermann et al. (2013)). We believe that discourse-aware distributional semantics may fare better in this respect. We elaborate on this idea further in the next subsection since their impact is seen beyond words and phrases level.

2.2 Beyond Words and Phrases

Following formal semantics, so far distributional semantics has modelled sentences as a product of a compositional function (Baroni et al., 2014; Socher et al., 2012; Paperno et al., 2014). The main focus has been on evaluating which compositional operation performs best against tasks such as classifying sentence pairs in an entailment relation, evaluating sentence similarity (Marelli et al., 2014), or predicting the so-called "sentiment" (positive, negative, or neutral orientation) of phrases and sentences (Socher et al., 2013). None of these tasks have considered sentence pairs within a wider discourse or dialogue context.

We propose to take a different look on what the distributional meaning of a sentence is. Sentences are part of larger communicative situations and, as highlighted in the Dynamic Semantic tradition, can be considered relations between the discourse so far and what is to come next. We thus challenge the distributional semantics community to develop dynamic distributional semantic models that are able to encode the "context change potential" that sentences and utterances bring about as well as their coherence within a discourse context, including but not limited to anaphoric accessibility relations.

We believe that in this dynamic view function words will play a prominent role, since they have a large impact on how discourse unfolds. For instance, negation is known to generally block antecedent accessibility, as exemplified in (2a). Another example is presented in (2b) (see Paterson et al. (2011)): Speakers typically continue version (i) by mentioning properties of the reference set (e.g., *They listened carefully and took notes*), and (ii) by talking about the complement set (e.g., *They decided to stay at home instead*).

(2) a. It's not the case that John loves a woman$_i$. *She$_i$ is smart.
b. (i) A few / (ii) Few of the students attended the lecture. They ...

In the context of dialogue, adequate compositional distributional models should aim at capturing how an utterance influences the common ground of the dialogue participants (Stalnaker, 1978; Clark, 1996) and constrains possible follow-ups (Asher and Lascarides, 2003; Ginzburg, 2012). This requires taking into account the dialogue context, as exemplified in (3) from Schlöder and Fernández (2014), where the same utterance form (*Yes it is*) acts as either an acceptance (3a) or a rejection (3b) depending on its local context.

(3) a. A: But it's uh yeah it's an original idea.
B: Yes it is.
b. A: the shape of a banana is not- it's not really handy.
B: Yes it is.

3 Tasks

Developing distributional semantic models that can tackle the phenomena discussed above is certainly challenging. However, we believe that, given the many recent advances in the field, the distributional semantics community is ready to take up this challenge. We have argued that, in order to account for the dynamics of situated common ground and coherence, it is critical to capture the discourse context-dependent and incremental nature of meaning. Here we sketch out a series of tasks related to some of the main phenomena we have discussed, against which new models could be evaluated.

In Section 2.1 we have considered the need to interface conceptual meaning with referential meaning incrementally built up as a discourse unfolds. A good testbed for evaluating these aspects is offered by the recent development of cross-modal distributional semantic frameworks that are able to map between language and vision (Karpathy et al., 2014; Lazaridou et al., 2014; Socher et al., 2014). Current models have shown that images representing a concept can be retrieved by mapping a word vector into a visual space, and more recently image generation systems that create images from word vectors have also been introduced (Lazaridou et al., 2015a; Lazaridou et al., 2015b). These frameworks could be used to test whether an incrementally constructed, discourse-contextualised word vector is able to retrieve and generate different, more contextually appropriate images than its out-of-context vector counterpart. For instance, a vector for a phrase like *red box* in a context where *red* refers to the box' contents should be mapped to different types of images depending on whether it has been constructed by a pragmatically aware model or not. Such a dataset could be constructed by creating images of referents of the same phrase used in different contexts, where the task would be to pick the best image for each context.

A related task would be reference resolution in a situated visual dialogue context (which can be seen as a situated version of image retrieval). This task has recently been tackled by Kennington and Schlangen (2015), who present an incremental account of word and phrase meaning with an approach outside the distributional semantics framework but very close in spirit to the issues we have discussed here. Given a representation of a referring expression and a set of visual candidate referents, the task consists in picking up the intended referent by incrementally processing and composing the words that make up the expression. Such a task (or versions thereof where contextual information beyond the referring expression is used) thus seems a good candidate for evaluating dynamic distributional models.

In Section 2.2, we have highlighted the context update potential of utterances as a feature that should be captured by compositional distributional models beyond the word/phrase level. Recent work has evaluated such models on dialogue act tagging tasks (Kalchbrenner and Blunsom, 2013; Milajevs et al., 2014). However, these approaches consider utterances in isolation and rely on a predefined set of dialogue act types that are to a large extent arbitrary, and in any case of a metalinguistic nature. Similar comments would apply to the task of identifying discourse relations connecting isolated pairs of sentences. Instead, we argue that pragmatically-aware distributional models should help us to induce dialogue acts in an unsupervised way and to model them as context update functions. Thus, we suggest to adopt tasks that target coherence and the evolution of common ground — which is what discourse relations and dialogue acts are meant to convey in the first place — in a more direct way.

One possible task would be to assess whether (or the extent to which) an utterance is a coherent continuation of the preceding discourse. Another one would be to predict the next sentence or utterance. Simple versions of similar tasks have started to be addressed by recent approaches (Hu et al., 2014, among others), see Section 4 for discussion. We propose to adopt these tasks, namely *coherence ranking of possible next sentences* and *next sentence prediction*, to evaluate pragmatically aware compositional distributional semantic models. Given the crucial role that function words, as discussed above, play with respect to how the discourse can unfold, these tasks should include the effects of function words on discourse/dialogue continuation.

For the design of other concrete instances of these tasks, it would be worth to take into account the evaluation frameworks developed in the field of applied dialogue systems research (and thus outside the distributional semantics tradition) by Young et al. (2013), who have proposed probabilistic models that can compute distributions over dialogue contexts, and can thus to some extent predict (or choose) a next utterance.

4 Related Work

In this position paper we have focused on the shortcomings of existing standard distributional models regarding their ability to capture the dynamics of the discourse/dialogue context and their impact on meaning. Some models have aimed at capturing the word meaning of a specific word occurrence in context. These approaches offer a very valuable starting point, but their scope differs from ours. In particular, we can identify the following three main traditions: (1) Word Sense Disambiguation (Navigli, 2009, offers an overview), which aims to assign one of the predefined list of word senses to a given word, depending on the context. These are typically dictionary senses, and so do not capture semantic nuances that depend on the specific use of the word in a given discourse or dialogue context. (2) Word meaning in context as modeled in the lexical substitution task (McCarthy and Navigli, 2007; Erk et al., 2013), which predicts one or more paraphrases for a word in a given sentence. Unlike Word Sense Disambiguation, word meaning in context is specific to a given use of a word, that is, it doesn't assume a pre-defined list of senses and can account for highly specific contextual effects. However, in this tradition context is restricted to one sentence, so the semantic phenomena modeled do not extend to discourse or dialogue. (3) Compositional distributional semantics (Baroni and Zamparelli, 2010; Mitchell and Lapata, 2010; Boleda et al., 2013), which predicts the meaning of a phrase or sentence from the meaning of its component units. For instance, compositional distributional semantics accounts for how the generic distributional representation of, say, *red* makes different contributions when composed with nouns like *army*, *wine*, *cheek*, or *car*, by modeling the resulting phrase. However, these methods are again limited to intrasentential context and only yield one single interpretation per phrase (presumably, the most typical one), thus not accounting for context-dependent interpretations of the *red box* type, discussed in

Section 2.1.

A few existing approaches can be seen as first steps towards a more discourse-aware distributional semantics, like the paper by McNally and Boleda (2015), which sketches a way to integrate compositional distributional semantics into Discourse Representation Theory (Kamp and Reyle, 1993). In addition, Herbelot (2015) has provided contextualized distributional representations for referential entities denoted by proper nouns in literary works. However, her procedure is still non-incremental in nature. Newer distributional models, such as Mikolov's SKIP-GRAM model (Mikolov et al., 2013), could incrementally update the representation of entities, and some work has been done in linking this model to the external world through images (Lazaridou et al., 2015c). However, these models do not yet account for specific, differentiated, discourse context-dependent interpretations of words of the sort discussed above, and they give a simple distributional representation of function words that does not readily account for their role in discourse.

Coherence ranking and sentence prediction, which we propose as the core testing ground, recently started being addressed, even if existing benchmarks have not been developed with the goals we highlighted above. The systems developed in Hu et al. (2014) have been successfully applied, among other things, to the task of choosing the correct response to a tweet, while Vinyals and Le (2015) and Sordoni et al. (2015) use neural models to *generate* responses for online dialogue systems and tweets, respectively (in the latter case taking into account a wider conversational context). These initial approaches are very promising, but they are disconnected from the referential context. Moreover, they have so far been trained specifically to achieve their goals, and it is not clear to what extent they can be integrated with a general semantic theory to serve other purposes.

Finally, the possibility of developing a pragmatically-oriented distributional semantics has been pointed out by Purver and Sadrzadeh (2015), who focus on opportunities for cross-fertilisation between dialogue research and distributional models. We certainly agree that the time is ripe for those and the other proposals made in this paper.

5 Conclusions

Distributional models are an important step towards building computational systems that can mimic human linguistic ability. However, we have argued that, as they stand, they still cannot account for language in use – that is, language within a discourse or a dialogue context, in a situated environment. We have described several linguistic phenomena that a comprehensive semantic model should account for, and proposed some concrete tasks that could serve to evaluate the adequacy of new-generation semantic systems targeting them. One crucial aspect that should be explored, however, is to what extent current distributional models need to be extended, and to what extent they need to be integrated into different frameworks, if the phenomena we have explored in this paper fall outside the distributional scope. We really hope that the community will take on this and the other challenges we have put forth in this paper.

Acknowledgements

This project has received funding from the European Union's Horizon 2020 research and innovation programme under the Marie Sklodowska-Curie grant agreement No 655577 (LOVe), FP7 programme ERC 2011 Starting Independent Research Grant n. 283554 (COMPOSES), and the Netherlands Organization for Scientific Research (NWO). This paper reflects the authors' view only, and the funding agency is not responsible for any use that may be made of the information it contains. Also thanks to the anonymous reviewers and the workshop organizers, as well as Marco Baroni, Aurelie Herbelot, and all the members of the FLOSS reading group, for helpful feedback.

References

Nicholas Asher and Alex Lascarides. 2003. *Logics of Conversation*. Cambridge University Press.

Marco Baroni and Roberto Zamparelli. 2010. Nouns are vectors, adjectives are matrices: Representing adjective-noun constructions in semantic space. In *Proceedings of EMNLP*, pages 1183–1193, Boston, MA.

Marco Baroni, Raffaella Bernardi, Ngoc-Quynh Do, and Chung-chieh Shan. 2012. Entailment above the word level in distributional semantics. In *Proceedings of the 13th Conference of the European Chap-*

ter of the Association for Computational Linguistics, pages 23–32.

Marco Baroni, Raffaella Bernardi, and Roberto Zamparelli. 2014. Frege in space: A program for compositional distributional semantics. *Linguistic Issues in Language Technology*, 9(6):5–110.

Raffaella Bernardi, Georgiana Dinu, Marco Marelli, and Marco Baroni. 2013. A relatedness benchmark to test the role of determiners in compositional distributional semantics. In *Proceedings of ACL 2013 (Volume 2: Short Papers)*, pages 53–57.

Gemma Boleda, Marco Baroni, The Nghia Pham, and Louise McNally. 2013. Intensionality was only alleged: On adjective-noun composition in distributional semantics. In *Proceedings of the 10th International Conference on Computational Semantics (IWCS 2013)*, pages 35–46.

Ronald J. Brachman and Hector J. Levesque. 1982. Competence in knowledge representation. In *Proceedings of AAAI*, pages 189–192.

Herbert H. Clark and Deanna Wilkes-Gibbs. 1986. Referring as a collaborative process. *Cognition*, 22(1):1–39.

Herbert H. Clark. 1996. *Using language*. Cambridge University Press.

Georgiana Dinu and Mirella Lapata. 2010. Measuring distributional similarity in context. In *Proceedings of the 2010 Conference on Empirical Methods in Natural Language Processing*, pages 1162–1172, Cambridge, MA, October. Association for Computational Linguistics.

Katrin Erk and Sebastian Padó. 2008. A structured vector space model for word meaning in context. In *Proceedings of EMNLP*, Honolulu, HI. To appear.

Katrin Erk, Diana McCarthy, and Nicholas Gaylord. 2013. Measuring Word Meaning in Context. *Computational Linguistics*, 39(3):511–554, September.

Katrin Erk. 2012. Vector space models of word meaning and phrase meaning: A survey. *Language and Linguistics Compass*, 6(10):635–653.

Simon Garrod and Anthony Anderson. 1987. Saying what you mean in dialogue: A study in conceptual and semantic co-ordination. *Cognition*, 27(2):181–218.

Jonathan Ginzburg. 2012. *The Interactive Stance*. Oxford University Press.

Edward Grefenstette and Mehrnoosh Sadrzadeh. 2011. Experimental support for a categorical compositional distributional model of meaning. In *Proceedings of EMNLP*, pages 1394–1404.

Barbara J. Grosz and Candace L. Sidner. 1986. Attention, intentions, and the structure of discourse. *Computational linguistics*, 12(3):175–204.

Barbara J. Grosz, Aravind K. Joshi, and Scott Weinstein. 1983. Providing a unified account of definite noun phrases in discourse. In *Proceedings of the 21st annual meeting on Association for Computational Linguistics*, pages 44–50.

Aurélie Herbelot. 2015. Mr Darcy and Mr Toad, gentlemen: distributional names and their kinds. In *Proceedings of the 11th International Conference on Computational Semantics*, pages 151–161. ACL.

Karl Moritz Hermann, Edward Grefenstette, and Phil Blunsom. 2013. "Not not bad" is not "bad": A distributional account of negation. In *Proceedings of the Workshop on Continuous Vector Space Models and their Compositionality*, pages 74–82. ACL.

Baotian Hu, Zhengdong Lu, Hang Li, and Qingcai Chen. 2014. Convolutional neural network architectures for matching natural language sentences. In Z. Ghahramani, M. Welling, C. Cortes, N.D. Lawrence, and K.Q. Weinberger, editors, *Advances in Neural Information Processing Systems 27*, pages 2042–2050. Curran Associates, Inc.

Nal Kalchbrenner and Phil Blunsom. 2013. Recurrent convolutional neural networks for discourse compositionality. In *Proceedings of the 2013 Workshop on Continuous Vector Space Models and their Compositionality*.

Hans Kamp and Uwe Reyle. 1993. *From Discourse to Logic*. Dordrecht: Kluwer.

Andrej Karpathy, Armand Joulin, and Li Fei-Fei. 2014. Deep Fragment Embeddings for Bidirectional Image Sentence Mapping. *Available at arXiv:1406.5679*.

Casey Kennington and David Schlangen. 2015. Simple learning and compositional application of perceptually grounded word meanings for incremental reference resolution. In *Proceedings of the Conference for the Association for Computational Linguistics (ACL)*.

Angeliki Lazaridou, Elia Bruni, and Marco Baroni. 2014. Is this a wampimuk? cross-modal mapping between distributional semantics and the visual world. In East Stroudsburg PA: ACL, editor, *Proceedings of ACL 2014*, pages 1403–1414.

Angeliki Lazaridou, Dat Tien Nguyen, Raffaella Bernardi, and Marco Baroni. 2015a. Unveiling the dreams of word embeddings: Towards language-driven image generation. Technical report, University of Trento. Submitted, available at arXiv:1506.03500.

Angeliki Lazaridou, Nghia Pham, and Marco Baroni. 2015b. Combining language and vision with a multimodal skip-gram model. In East Stroudsburg PA: ACL, editor, *Proceedings of NAACL HLT 2015*, pages 153–163.

Angeliki Lazaridou, Nghia The Pham, and Marco Baroni. 2015c. Combining language and vision with a multimodal skip-gram model. In *Proceedings of NAACL HLT 2015*, pages 153–163.

David Lewis. 1969. *Convention: A philosophical study*. Harvard University Press.

Marco Marelli, Luisa Bentivogli, Marco Baroni, Raffaella Bernardi, Stefano Menini, and Roberto Zamparelli. 2014. Semeval-2014 task 1: Evaluation of compositional distributional semantic models on full sentences through semantic relatedness and textual entailment. In *Proceedings of the 8th International Workshop on Semantic Evaluation (SemEval 2014)*, pages 1–8.

Diana McCarthy and Roberto Navigli. 2007. Semeval-2007 task 10: English lexical substitution task. In *Proceedings of the Fourth International Workshop on Semantic Evaluations (SemEval-2007)*, pages 48–53, Prague, Czech Republic, June. Association for Computational Linguistics.

Louise McNally and Gemma Boleda. 2015. Conceptual vs. referential affordance in concept composition. In Y. Winter and J. Hampton, editors, *Concept Composition and Experimental Semantics/Pragmatics*. Springer. Accepted for publication.

Tomas Mikolov, Kai Chen, Greg Corrado, and Jeffrey Dean. 2013. Efficient estimation of word representations in vector space. *CoRR*, abs/1301.3781.

Dmitrijs Milajevs, Dimitri Kartsaklis, Mehrnoosh Sadrzadeh, and Matthew Purver. 2014. Evaluating neural word representations in tensor-based compositional settings. In *Proceedings of the 2014 Conference on Empirical Methods in Natural Language Processing (EMNLP)*, pages 708–719.

Jeff Mitchell and Mirella Lapata. 2010. Composition in distributional models of semantics. *Cognitive Science*, 34(8):1388–1429.

Roberto Navigli. 2009. Word sense disambiguation: A survey. *ACM Computing Surveys*.

Denis Paperno, Nghia The Pham, and Marco Baroni. 2014. A practical and linguistically-motivated approach to compositional distributional semantics. In *Proceedings of ACL*, pages 90–99, Baltimore, MD.

Kavin Paterson, Ruth Filik, and Linda Moxey. 2011. Quantifiers and discourse processing. *Language and Linguistics Compass*, pages 1–29.

Matthew Purver and Mehrnoosh Sadrzadeh. 2015. From distributional semantics to distributional pragmatics? In *Proceedings of the IWCS 2015 Workshop on Interactive Meaning Construction*, pages 21–22, London, UK.

Julian J. Schlöder and Raquel Fernández. 2014. The role of polarity in inferring acceptance and rejection in dialogue. In *Proceedings of the SIGdial 2014 Conference*.

Richard Socher, Brody Huval, Christopher D Manning, and Andrew Y Ng. 2012. Semantic compositionality through recursive matrix-vector spaces. In *Proceedings of EMNLP-CNLL*, pages 1201–1211.

Richard Socher, Alex Perelygin, Jean Wu, Jason Chuang, Christopher D. Manning, Andrew Ng, and Christopher Potts. 2013. Recursive deep models for semantic compositionality over a sentiment treebank. In *Proceedings of the 2013 Conference on Empirical Methods in Natural Language Processing*, pages 1631–1642.

Richard Socher, Andrej Karpathy, Quoc V. Le, Christopher D. Manning, and Andrew Y. Ng. 2014. Grounded Compositional Semantics for Finding and Describing Images with Sentences. *Transactions of the Association for Computational Linguistics*.

Alessandro Sordoni, Michel Galley, Michael Auli, Chris Brockett, Yangfeng Ji, Meg Mitchell, Jian-Yun Nie, Jianfeng Gao, and Bill Dolan. 2015. A neural network approach to context-sensitive generation of conversational responses. Conference of the North American Chapter of the Association for Computational Linguistics Human Language Technologies (NAACL-HLT 2015), June.

Robert Stalnaker. 1978. Assertion. In P. Cole, editor, *Pragmatics*, volume 9 of *Syntax and Semantics*, pages 315–332. New York Academic Press.

Peter D Turney, Patrick Pantel, et al. 2010. From frequency to meaning: Vector space models of semantics. *Journal of Artificial Intelligence Research*, 37(1):141–188.

Oriol Vinyals and Quoc V. Le. 2015. A neural conversational model. *CoRR*, abs/1506.05869.

Steve Young, Milica Gasic, Blaise Thomson, and Jason Williams. 2013. Pomdp-based statistical spoken dialogue systems: a review. *Proceedings of the IEEE*, PP(99):1–20.

Author Index

Agirre, Eneko, 89

Bernardi, Raffaella, 95
Boleda, Gemma, 95

Clark, Chris, 22
Clark, Stephen, 1
Correia, Rui, 70

Delmonte, Rodolfo, 32
Dickinson, Anna, 22

Eskenazi, Maxine, 70

Fernandez, Raquel, 95
Frank, Anette, 44
Friedrich, Annemarie, 12, 44

Grishman, Ralph, 76

He, Yifan, 76

Johannsen, Anders, 89
Joshi, Aravind, 64

Khazaei, Taraneh, 54

Lee, Alan, 64
Lopez de Lacalle, Oier, 89
Louis, Annie, 22

Mamede, Nuno, 70
Martínez Alonso, Héctor, 89
Mavridou, Kleio-Isidora, 12
Mercer, Robert, 54
Murakami, Yuki, 83

Palmer, Alexis, 12, 44
Paperno, Denis, 95
Peate Sørensen, Melissa, 12
Pershina, Maria, 76
Pinkal, Manfred, 12
Polajnar, Tamara, 1
Pradhan, Sameer, 64
Prasad, Rashmi, 64

Rimell, Laura, 1
Rohde, Hannah, 22

Tripodi, Rocco, 32
Tsuruoka, Yoshimasa, 83

Webber, Bonnie, 22, 64

Xiao, Lu, 54

Zhou, Mengfei, 44